AS LONG AS THE EARTH ENDURES

AS LONG AS THE EARTH ENDURES

The Bible, Creation and the Environment

Edited by Jonathan Moo & Robin Routledge

APOLLOS (an imprint of Inter-Varsity Press)
Norton Street, Nottingham NG7 3HR, England
Website: www.ivpbooks.com
Email: ivp@ivpbooks.com

First published 2014

British Library Cataloguing in Publication Data
A catalogue record for this book is available from the British Library.

ISBN: 978-1-78359-038-4

Set in Monotype Garamond 11/13pt
Typeset in Great Britain by CRB Associates, Potterhanworth, Lincolnshire
Printed and bound in Great Britain by Ashford Colour Press Ltd, Gosport, Hampshire

CONTENTS

CONTRIBUTORS

David Baker is Senior Lecturer in Old Testament and Dean of Students at Trinity Theological College, Perth, Western Australia.

R. J. (Sam) Berry is Emeritus Professor of Genetics at University College London.

David Firth is Lecturer in Old Testament and Director of Research Degrees at St John's College, Nottingham.

Jamie A. Grant is Vice-Principal and Lecturer in Biblical Studies at the Highland Theological College, Dingwall, Scotland.

Sean McDonough is Professor of New Testament at Gordon-Conwell Theological Seminary.

Alister McGrath is Chair in Theology, Ministry and Education, and Head of the Centre for Theology, Religion and Culture at Kings' College London.

I. Howard Marshall is Professor Emeritus of New Testament at Aberdeen University.

Jonathan Moo is Assistant Professor of Biblical Studies at Whitworth University, Spokane, Washington.

David Rainey is Senior Lecturer and Research Fellow in Theology at Nazarene Theological College, Manchester.

Robin Routledge is Senior Lecturer in Old Testament and Academic Dean at Mattersey Hall, England.

Graham Watts is Tutor in Christian Doctrine and Ethics at Spurgeon's College, London.

Paul Williamson is Lecturer in Old Testament, Hebrew and Aramaic at Moore College, Sydney.

ABBREVIATIONS

1QIsa^a	*Isaiah Scroll* (Dead Sea Scrolls)
2 Apol.	*Second Apology* (Justin Martyr)
AB	Anchor Bible
ANE	ancient Near East/Eastern
ANTC	Abingdon New Testament Commentaries
Aug	*Augustinianum*
Autol.	*To Autolycus* (Theophilus)
AV	Authorized (King James) Version
BBR	*Bulletin for Biblical Research*
BCOTWP	Baker Commentary on the Old Testament Wisdom and Psalms
BECNT	Baker Exegetical Commentary on the New Testament
Bib	*Biblica*
BJHS	*British Journal of the History of Science*
BJRL	*Bulletin of the John Rylands University Library of Manchester*
BSac	*Bibliotheca sacra*
BST	The Bible Speaks Today
CBQ	*Catholic Biblical Quarterly*
CNT	Commentaire du Nouveau Testament
COQG	Christian Origins and the Question of God
CSR	*Christian Scholars' Review*
CTM	*Concordia Theological Monthly*

DCH	*Dictionary of Classical Hebrew*, ed. D. J. A. Clines, 6 vols. (Sheffield: Sheffield Phoenix, 1993–2008)
Dial.	*Dialogue with Trypho* (Justin Martyr)
DSS	Dead Sea Scrolls
EBC	*The Expositor's Bible Commentary*, ed. F. E. Gaebelein, 12 vols. (Grand Rapids: Zondervan, 1984)
ECC	Eerdmans Critical Commentary
ECM	*Novum Testamentum Graecum: Editio Critica Maior*, vol. 4: *Catholic Letters*, instalment 2: *Peter*, ed. Barbara Aland, Kurt Aland, Gerd Mink, Holger Strutwolf and Klaus Wachtel (Stuttgart: Deutsche Bibelgesellschaft, 2000)
EKK	Evangelisch-Katholischer Kommentar zum Neuen Testament
ERT	*Evangelical Review of Theology*
ET	English translation
EvQ	*Evangelical Quarterly*
ExpTim	*Expository Times*
Gk.	Greek
GNT	Good News Translation
HALOT	L. Koehler and W. Baumgartner (eds.), *The Hebrew and Aramaic Lexicon of the Old Testament*, tr. and ed. under the supervision of M. E. J. Richardson, 5 vols. (Leiden: Brill, 1994–2000)
Hebr.	Hebrew
IBT	Interpreting Biblical Texts
ICC	International Critical Commentary
IJST	*International Journal of Systematic Theology*
Int	*Interpretation*
JASA	*Journal of the American Scientific Affiliation*
JBQ	*Jewish Bible Quarterly*
JCTR	*Journal for Christian Theological Research*
JETS	*Journal of the Evangelical Theological Society*
JPT	*Journal of Pentecostal Theology*
JSNT	*Journal for the Study of the New Testament*
JSOTSup	Journal for the Study of the Old Testament, Supplement Series
JTS	*Journal of Theological Studies*
JTSA	*Journal of Theology for Southern Africa*
KD	*Kerygma und Dogma*
KEK	Kritisch-exegetischer Kommentar über das Neue Testament
lit.	literally
LNTS	Library of New Testament Studies
LXX	Septuagint

marg.	margin
MT	Masoretic Text
NA27	*Nestle-Aland Novum Testamentum Graece*, ed. Barbara and Kurt Aland, Johannes Karavidopoulos, Carlo M. Martini and Bruce M. Metzger, 27th rev. ed. (Stuttgart: Deutsche Bibelgesellschaft, 1993)
NA28	*Nestle-Aland Novum Testamentum Graece*, ed. Barbara and Kurt Aland, Johannes Karavidopoulos, Carlo M. Martini and Bruce M. Metzger, 28th rev. ed. (Stuttgart: Deutsche Bibelgesellschaft, 2012)
NCB	New Century Bible
NET	New English Translation
NIB	*The New Interpreter's Bible*, ed. L. E. Keck, 12 vols. (Nashville: Abingdon, 1993–2002)
NIBC	New International Biblical Commentary
NICNT	New International Commentary on the New Testament
NICOT	New International Commentary on the Old Testament
NIDOTTE	*New International Dictionary of Old Testament Theology and Exegesis*, ed. W. A. VanGemeren, 5 vols. (Carlisle: Paternoster; Grand Rapids: Zondervan, 1996)
NIGTC	New International Greek Testament Commentary
NIV	New International Version
NJB	New Jerusalem Bible
NJPS	New Jewish Publication Society Tanakh
NLT2	New Living Translation, 2nd ed.
NovT	*Novum Testamentum*
NRSV	New Revised Standard Version
NSBT	New Studies in Biblical Theology
NT	New Testament
NTS	*New Testament Studies*
NZSTh	*Neue Zeitschrift für systematische Theologie und Religionsphilosophie*
OBT	Overtures to Biblical Theology
OT	Old Testament
OTL	Old Testament Library
PNTC	Pillar New Testament Commentary
PSCF	*Perspectives on Science and Christian Faith*
REB	Revised English Bible
RelS	*Religious Studies*
RSV	Revised Standard Version
SCB	*Science and Christian Belief*

SiC	*Science in Context*
Sir.	Sirach
SJT	*Scottish Journal of Theology*
SNTSMS	Society for New Testament Studies Monograph Series
SP	Sacra pagina
STR	*Southeastern Theological Review*
TDNT	*Theological Dictionary of the New Testament*, ed. G. Kittel and G. Friedrich, tr. G. W. Bromiley, 10 vols. (Grand Rapids: Eerdmans, 1964–76)
TDOT	*Theological Dictionary of the Old Testament*, ed. G. J. Botterweck, H. Ringgren and H.-J. Fabry, 15 vols. (Grand Rapids: Eerdmans, 1974–2006)
TOTC	Tyndale Old Testament Commentaries
tr.	translation / translated by
TrinJ	*Trinity Journal*
TS	*Theological Studies*
TynB	*Tyndale Bulletin*
VE	*Verbum et Ecclesia*
VoxEv	*Vox evangelica*
VT	*Vetus Testamentum*
WBC	Word Biblical Commentary
WTJ	*Westminster Theological Journal*
WUNT	Wissenschaftliche Untersuchungen zum Neuen Testament
WW	*Word and World*
ZAW	*Zeitschrift für die alttestamentliche Wissenschaft*

INTRODUCTION

Jonathan Moo and Robin Routledge

> I climbed to the top of the peak. When I looked, I knew I might never again
> see so much of the earth so beautiful, the beautiful being something you know
> added to something you see, in a whole that is different from the sum of its
> parts. What I saw might have been just another winter scene, although an
> impressive one. But what I knew was that the earth underneath was alive and
> that by tomorrow, certainly by the day after, it would all be green again. So what
> I saw because of what I knew was a kind of death with the marvellous promise
> of less than a three-day resurrection.
>
> (Norman Maclean)[1]

Seeing the world

In the opening chapter of this volume, Alister McGrath challenges us to consider
that 'part of our "discipleship of the mind" must be to learn to cultivate theological acuity, so that we see things as God sees them – and act accordingly'.
The aim of this book is to contribute towards the development and sharpening
of this sort of vision, to see the world of God's creation more nearly as he sees
it. Our sight will always be limited, and our conclusions, as Howard Marshall
acknowledges in the 'Afterword', necessarily approximate and tentative. Yet, as
the following chapters amply attest, the light of the gospel of Jesus Christ
illumines much about creation and our responsibilities in and for it that otherwise would remain shadowy and unresolved. This volume brings together a
variety of biblical, theological and scientific perspectives on creation and the

---

1. Norman Maclean, *A River Runs Through It and Other Stories* (Chicago: University of
   Chicago Press, 1976), p. 146.

environment in the hope that we may learn to see the world more clearly, to perceive its beauty and its brokenness when and where we ought, and to reflect God's love and wisdom in how we relate to all he has made.[2]

As I begin to write this introduction, I (Jonathan) am sitting in the shade of a Ponderosa pine in a grassy meadow in rural north-eastern Washington State. The gently-sloping meadow in which I sit was once a forest, probably of ancient white pine, fir, cedar and larch. The timber long since harvested, the hay field that replaced it is now slowly reverting again to forest. At the edge of the meadow is a stand of aspen, and, just beyond, a weaving line of alder and cottonwood marks the path of a stream through a darker forest of pine, larch, fir and the occasional cedar and spruce. Next to me an artist is drawing the stand of aspen, seeking to capture the shimmering leaves, the refracted light, the white trunks stark against the conifers, her own vision transforming the scene even as she preserves it on her sketch pad. She sees things, no doubt, that I do not. Yet for us both it is a beautiful scene, however ordinary it may be in this part of the world. It is a landscape that invites quiet exploration, study, reflection and worship, a testimony, we think, to the glory of God. Even the old clear-cut (as we might also name the meadow) is a reminder of creation's resilience, and this wide, sunlit gap in the forest canopy is, we know, a good place for deer and moose.

But do we see this meadow, these trees, this forest aright? If I invited my friend and next-door neighbour here, he might share my love for this place; yet as a logger he would probably think more than I do about the board feet of lumber that the remaining trees could supply, the homes that could be built and heated, the income that logging the yet-unharvested portions of this parcel could yield. He would also see the potential here for the thrill of off-road exploration by all-terrain vehicle and, in winter, by snowmobile. And if God gave us the earth for our provision and enjoyment, on what basis other than

---

2. Most of the chapters in this volume are revised versions of papers originally delivered at the Tyndale Fellowship Triennial Conference held in Northampton, England, in July 2012. The only exceptions are the two NT essays: Jonathan Moo's essay (chapter 7) is based on his 2009 Tyndale Lecture in Ethics and Social Theology, delivered in Cambridge on 9 July 2009, which previously appeared in a slightly different form in the *Tyndale Bulletin*; and Sean McDonough's essay (chapter 8) was solicited especially for this volume. We are grateful to Peter Williams and the editorial board of the *Tyndale Bulletin* both for the permission to reprint Moo's essay and for waiving the rights to first publication of the plenary lectures included here by Alister McGrath (chapter 1) and Paul Williamson (chapter 6).

personal preference can I argue instead for conserving this land and travelling more lightly?

Perhaps in any case we should instead see here only the life-and-death struggle that underlies the apparently placid scene: the ongoing competition for water and light that shapes which tree grows where and for how long; the aphids and beetles that attack, maim and in places kill these trees, while at the same time providing food for the pileated woodpeckers and other birds that we delight in seeing; the various defences, from thorns to toxins, that some of the grasses, flowers and trees have erected against the herbivores (like the deer and moose) that depend on them for food; the complicated ways in which these same plant communities are affected even by the predators of the herbivores, as they modify their prey's numbers and behaviour; and the fight all creatures face to survive in a climate that one season is dry and hot and the next cold and snowy. The beauty we perceive here may well lead us to worship God and stir in us the desire to conserve and care well for the land; but this beauty is birthed and sustained in blood and death, struggle and decay.

Perhaps our vision of God is such that we are able to accommodate all this, and we are still able to discern his glory here. Or perhaps we attribute all we do not like to the 'fallenness' of this world; or we consider it merely the signs of an incomplete creation that is yet on its way to a greater glory when 'the wolf will live with the lamb' (Isa. 11:6 NIV). We may also find such explanations useful if we look at this landscape through the eyes of a pessimistic environmentalist. The scars of logging that we see may lead us to despair over the loss of the vast old-growth forests that once grew here, seemingly limitless and yet now nearly all vanished. We may lament too the mountain caribou that once grazed the lichen that grew in the shade of this region's ancient forests but which now are extinct, or nearly so, in the entire lower forty-eight states. The invasive grasses and weeds in parts of the meadow, species that in places nearby crowd out the natives and invite wildfire while providing little benefit to browsing animals, reveal yet more about our own species' outsized role. Even the insect infestations that are killing some of these trees now seem to bear a human fingerprint, the scale and severity of such infestations increasing dramatically as the climate warms and as our forest management veers from overuse and abuse to neglect and back again. It is unsurprising, perhaps, that the narrative of a good creation tainted by human sin remains irresistible even in the largely post-Christian context of contemporary environmentalism.

But which of these ways – or a myriad of other ways we could list – of seeing this meadow, these trees and the whole of creation is nearest to how God would have us see it? This matters, not least because our actions – to the extent that they are connected to our beliefs – are shaped by such visions.[3] It matters too for how we present the gospel and for how we engage with science, politics, art and ethics. As Christians, we need to articulate what McGrath calls a 'whole view of reality' and learn to live in the light of it; and that includes the focus of this book – how we understand and relate to the rest of creation.

Readers may be disappointed to discover that, even among the contributors to this volume, there are plenty of differences in how such a vision is articulated. Disagreements persist about how we are to conceive of the goodness of creation; the nature and extent of a cosmic fall; how our role within creation as God's image-bearers is best articulated; and precisely what the relationship is between this world and the world to come – just how long it is that 'the earth endures' (Gen. 8:22 NIV). As we seek to interpret Scripture and to view all of reality in its light, such differences remind us of our ongoing need for charity and humility. We surely must also continue, as Sam Berry reminds us (chapter 11), to cultivate a greater attentiveness to what science reveals to us about the nature of the world and bring it into dialogue with God's revelation in his Word. We must keep listening and learning from the diverse perspectives of our brothers and sisters in the faith, from the insights of the worldwide church both today and throughout the ages. Above all, we must go on praying for discernment and the illumination of the Holy Spirit. As McGrath suggests, theology is best practised in the context of worship and prayer.

In any case, however clouded our vision remains even at the end of all our study and exploration, however necessarily tentative some of our conclusions, the general contours of Scripture's portrayal of the creation stand out clearly enough; and ignorance of, or disagreement over some of the details does not absolve us of our profound responsibilities in and for God's world. In Norman Maclean's story 'A River Runs Through It' the protagonist struggles all the days of his brother's life to understand him, longing to know how best to help him. Yet in the end he recognizes that 'you can love completely without complete understanding'.[4] Such love is demanded of us now, as indeed it always has been.

---

3. Obviously, our actions are shaped by lots of things other than our beliefs. For a recent theological and practical exploration of the significance of the fact that many of our everyday decisions are determined by habituation and 'liturgies', secular and otherwise, see James K. A. Smith, *Imagining the Kingdom: How Worship Works* (Grand Rapids: Baker Academic, 2013); *Desiring the Kingdom: Worship, Worldview, and Cultural Formation* (Grand Rapids: Baker Academic, 2009).

4. Maclean, *River Runs Through*, p. 103.

Responding to the world

Nearly all recent treatments of 'creation and the environment'[5] acknowledge that our contemporary context adds particular urgency to the task of re-envisioning creation and our responsibilities within it. There is not space here to detail all the 'environmental' threats we face, but it is worth being reminded again at least of the scale of human influence on earth in our time and the challenges that such an influence necessarily poses to the flourishing of human and non-human life.[6]

With over seven billion people alive today, human beings are now collectively the greatest biological and geological force on earth. In a time in which we have directly influenced nearly 85 per cent of the global ice-free land surface, in which humanity moves twice as much earth and rock as all natural erosion does and co-opts up to a third of all the primary productivity of the earth's plants, it is unsurprising that scientists have begun to refer to our age as the 'Anthropocene'. The rapid growth in the size of humankind's 'footprint' on earth is so great that there are today a third fewer wild animals on earth than there were just forty years ago. We are headed towards, or in the midst of what some scientists are labelling as the sixth great extinction event in earth's history, with the current rate of extinction anywhere from 100 to 1,000 times higher than the normal background rate. Most of this loss of species is the result of intensive land use; just since 1970, for example, roughly 20 per cent of the forest of the Brazilian Amazon rainforest has been felled or burned, often to make way for cattle.

Increasingly depleted freshwater supplies means that by 2030 nearly half of the world's population will be living in areas with high water stress; even today, only half the world has access to clean water on tap. Our unsustainable agricultural practices means that an area of land the equivalent of the size of China

---

5. We have retained here and in the title of the book the potentially redundant phrase 'creation and the environment', both because this was the official theme of the Tyndale Conference that inspired this volume and also because the conventional language of 'environment' is useful for indicating that the themes treated in this book have more to do with how we understand the present creation in the light of its origin and its future than simply with how we understand creation's origins. Lamentably, use of the term 'creation' on its own often signifies only the latter.

6. For a more extensive summary of the present state of the planet and for the sources of the data that follow, see Jonathan A. Moo and Robert S. White, *Hope in an Age of Despair: The Gospel and the Future of Life on Earth* (Nottingham: Inter-Varsity Press, 2013), pp. 22–88.

and the USA combined has been degraded. As a result, nearly a third of the arable lands worldwide had to be taken out of production just in the latter half of the twentieth century. The intensive use of nitrogen fertilizers, often with locally devastating consequences for both soil and water, has, according to some scientists, put us over a 'planetary boundary'. Beyond such planetary boundaries, we risk potentially catastrophic changes in how the earth functions and supports human civilization.

The consequences of the dramatic human-caused increase in greenhouse gases in the atmosphere are summarized briefly in chapter 7, but it is worth observing here that the accompanying warming of the climate and increase in weather extremes exacerbates nearly all of the challenges summarized above. Among other things, it makes agriculture in the short to medium term more challenging by forcing sometimes radical adaption in how and where we grow food. In the longer term, a warming climate may simply make it impossible to grow even as much food as we do now. Climate change threatens water supplies in many parts of the world and will make many areas essentially uninhabitable. It also is putting our already-stressed oceans at risk, as their increasing acidification (already 30% higher than in pre-industrial times as a result of their uptake of carbon dioxide) threatens all those organisms with calcium carbonate shells that form the bottom of the oceanic food chain. Meanwhile, rising sea levels as a result of the expansion of warming water and the release of meltwater from previously frozen ice sheets threaten coastal regions and low-lying islands around the world.

Such challenges understandably and rightly frame the context for contemporary discussions of creation and environment. Yet, even in the absence of these challenges, the theological and practical task would remain. Christian books on creation and the environment are usually pitched as responses either to the 'environmental crisis' itself or to the indictment of Christianity as responsible for the crisis – the indictment made famous by the short, over-cited essay by historian Lynn White, Jr.[7] But Christianity has always offered its own compelling visions of the nature of creation and our place within it, and in our desire to respond to our own context we ought not to let our horizon be limited by today's agendas. Perhaps we should more often begin by citing not Lynn White but a biblical scholar like C. F. D. Moule, who, a few years before Lynn White's paper, reflected on the significance of what the NT has to say about 'man and nature' and perceived already the challenges and opportunities

---

7. And now cited yet again: Lynn White, Jr., 'The Historical Roots of Our Ecologic Crisis', *Science* 155 (1967), pp. 1203–1207.

of its vision for contemporary Christian ethics.[8] Better yet, we could go way back to the church fathers and mothers. We might consider, for example, Basil of Caesarea's radical vision of a God who is saviour both of human beings and our 'brothers' the animals. Or perhaps Irenaeus, whose rich theology of creation still stimulates creative theological reflection today (as it did for Colin Gunton; see chapter 10). As biblical scholars, we (the editors) might of course want to suggest that Scripture itself should more often set the agenda for our discussions of creation and the environment. The point is that, while we must not neglect our contemporary context and the particular questions it raises for us, we also need to seek to hear Scripture afresh, in dialogue with its interpreters ancient and modern, and in the end to let our vision be shaped by its 'comprehensive vision of reality'. It is only then that we can hope to develop a response to our own situation that is both adequate to the task and rooted deeply in the whole story of what God has done and is doing in Christ through the Holy Spirit.

Biblical and theological visions

The chapters that follow provide resources for exploring and articulating the significance of this vision held out to us in Scripture. In chapter 1, 'The Doctrine of Creation: Some Theological Reflections', Alister McGrath sets the context by reminding us, as we have already observed, that theology is about seeing things as they really are – and, more than this, about being *captivated* by the big picture of reality given to us in the gospel. The doctrine of creation, McGrath suggests, is but one point of entry into this picture; and we shall find in any case that we cannot consider any one doctrine in isolation, and so exploring the doctrine of creation will lead us eventually to consider all the other themes to which it is linked. McGrath goes on to explain how a comprehensive Christian vision of reality provides a lens through which we can see nature properly and learn our responsibilities as its stewards. It also provides an apologetic framework in which 'natural theology' can play its appropriate role, not as a means of 'proving God's existence without resorting to special revelation' but as *a posteriori* confirmation of the consonance of a Christian world view with the beauty and order that we observe in the natural world.

---

8. C. F. D. Moule, *Man and Nature in the New Testament: Some Reflections on Biblical Theology*, The Ethel M. Wood Lecture, University of London, 9 Mar. 1964 (London: Athlone, 1964).

McGrath raises other pertinent issues that recur in later chapters. For example, the question of whether we are to understand creation as an event or a process or, as McGrath argues, as both, is a theme that is taken up in David Firth's exploration of the Spirit's role in creation (chapter 5) and appears again in David Rainey's interaction with Jürgen Moltmann (chapter 9) and Graham Watts's analysis of Colin Gunton's theology (chapter 10). McGrath's argument that greater attentiveness to the history of biblical interpretation might help alleviate evangelicals' concerns about the compatibility of biological evolution (and scientific cosmology) with the biblical doctrine of creation is a theme developed at greater length in Sam Berry's essay (chapter 11). The place of humanity within creation, which McGrath observes is a necessary focus in any attempt to construct a Christian environmental ethos, is a theme that is explored in different ways throughout the rest of volume. McGrath also provides an appreciative but cautious assessment of the recent attention given to trinitarian approaches to the doctrine of creation. He expresses his concern that, in so far as is possible, our use of such language ought to remain biblically rooted. McGrath concludes his chapter by suggesting a few reasons why the doctrine of creation has recently gained a rather higher profile within evangelicalism, and he encourages readers to go on exploring the richness of this doctrine as well as the larger picture of reality into which it invites us.

In chapter 2, '"In the Beginning It Was Very Good": Genesis 1 – 2 and the Environment', David Baker reflects on creation as it was meant to be, from the perspective of the first two chapters of Genesis. He groups the material on creation and the environment in those chapters under four key headings: biodiversity, dominion – which, in line with the fairly widespread view, particularly among evangelicals, he takes to refer to responsible stewardship – food and agriculture. He discusses each of these in relation to the biblical text, which is taken to set out God's intention for creation, and the role and responsibility of human beings, who, as God's representatives, should marvel at, celebrate and seek to maintain what God has initiated.

Baker notes, though, that all too often human beings have not acted responsibly towards creation and the environment. Thus, in place of biodiversity, because of human carelessness (and worse), many species have become endangered or extinct; in place of responsible stewardship towards the environment there is exploitation. Baker notes particular issues in today's world in relation to agriculture and food, where the fruits of new research that could be beneficial to humankind in general are selfishly controlled by large corporations, which are driven by profit and the interest of shareholders rather than any wider concern for people or the environment. Baker sees human pride and greed as significant factors in this, and he points out that God will ultimately judge these things. However, he also argues that that does not absolve human beings from the need to challenge questionable practices and to be involved in 'caring for God's good creation'. By setting out what the first chapters of Genesis understand as God's purpose for creation and the environment, Baker has given a model that helps to inform and challenge our commitment to creation care.

In chapter 3, 'Cursing and Chaos: The Impact of Human Sin on Creation and the Environment in the Old Testament', Robin Routledge continues the focus on the early chapters of Genesis. A popular view in Christian theology is that when human beings sinned, not only did they fall, but the created order fell too. As a result creation is subjected to 'futility' and 'decay' (Rom. 8:20–21 NRSV). And this 'cosmic fall' accounts for the presence of natural disasters within the created order. Recently that view has been questioned – partly because it raises serious scientific issues, but also because the OT writers make no direct reference to it. In this chapter Routledge argues that while the idea of a cosmic fall has limitations, the OT writers do point to a significant change in the created order as a result of human sin. The result is that the natural world is not as it should be, nor as God intended it to be, and that God's good purpose for human beings in relation to creation has been disrupted. This disjunction is explained by the cursing of the ground (Gen. 3:17), which represents a frustration of the divine purpose in creation and that, Routledge argues, is closely associated with, and opens the possibility of, a 'return to chaos' – where human sin undermines the order of creation and allows disorder to re-emerge. This is seen particularly in the flood – and Routledge discusses the close link in Genesis 8:21 between the cursing of the ground and the devastation associated with the flood – but also in the description of other disasters, such as the exile, which Jeremiah views as a kind of 'uncreation' (Jer. 4:23).

This link between cursing and chaos has implications for the way human beings respond to the environment and environmental issues. The curse on the ground is evident in everyday life, and linking this with the return to chaos suggests that this too may be evident in the more general disjunction in the created order, including natural disasters and what is sometimes termed 'natural evil'. One significant outcome of this is that the current disorder in creation may be viewed not just as a result of divine judgment (which, some might argue, we should not try to resist) but also as a frustration of God's purpose. Our responsibility, as God's representatives, made in his image and called to exercise responsible stewardship over his world, is to resist disruption in God's purpose in creation, and to seek, with him, to bring order into the present chaos. And this is done in the confident hope that in the end, as at the beginning, God will defeat all that threatens his good creation and establish new heavens and a new earth.

In chapter 4, 'Creation and Kingship: Environment and Witness in the *Yhwh mālāk* Psalms', Jamie Grant looks at Psalms 93 – 100 and, within those psalms, 'the voice of creation and the created order that testifies both to Yahweh's universal rule and also calls all peoples to worship him as a result'. Grant gives some context to these psalms, suggesting that, while their theology goes back to Israel's earliest understanding of God and of their relationship with him, they have been recontextualized as a response to the crisis of exile – and emphasize God's reign over the whole earth. This in turn requires a faithful response from the worshipping community, which can no longer be limited to ethnic Israel. The king of the whole earth must receive worship from the whole earth! Thus these psalms have a missional focus: they invite all peoples to recognize Yahweh's universal rule and to join in worshipping him.

Grant then explores the means by which the nations are made aware of Yahweh's rule. He first notes Israel's responsibility to make this message known. He then asks why the nations would be willing to respond to such a message, and, taking Psalm 97:6 (NIV) – 'the heavens proclaim his righteousness, and all peoples see his glory' – as a hermeneutical key, he asserts the crucial role played by creation and the environment, noting three key factors evident in this group of psalms. First, God is King because he is Creator: his worthiness to rule is evident in that he established the world and asserted victory over the primeval waters. Secondly, the created order longs for the institution of divine justice and the restoration that it brings. Thirdly, the creation itself declares and bears witness to God's glory.

If creation has this apologetic role, then we should resist anything that damages the created order and so diminishes its witness. Grant points out that there are many other good reasons for creation care (as we see in other chapters of this volume); this is one that is less obvious, but should not be overlooked. He notes, further, that as part of this apologetic role, contemplation of the created order can provide the beginnings of a 'bridge' between a sceptical world and faith in the God of creation. And, finally, Grant argues for the importance of the worshipping community, which, like the natural order, is called to express its wonder at what God has done.

The OT focus continues in Chapter 5, 'The Spirit and the Renewal of Creation: An Old Testament Perspective'. David Firth begins by asserting that the *rûaḥ 'ĕlōhîm* in Genesis 1:2 is a reference to God's Spirit, and thus that the Spirit has a significant role in creation. This provides the basis for the continued work of the Spirit in sustaining creation, and ultimately in its renewal within the OT. Firth then looks at three texts that appear to allude to Genesis 1 and point to the sustaining work of God's Spirit – Psalms 33:6, 147:18 and 104:29–30. The view of creation in these psalms is not always positive: creation may at times be threatening. However, recognizing and praising God for his ongoing creative activity gives hope in challenging circumstances. In these passages divine activity is closely associated with the divine *rûaḥ*, and *rûaḥ* in such contexts could be translated 'breath'. However, in the light of references to creation and allusions to Genesis 1, Firth suggests that it is appropriate to consider the wider semantic range of the term and to link *rûaḥ* here with the 'Spirit' of God, who is active in creation in Genesis 1:2. Thus God's continuing involvement in creation is linked with divine *rûaḥ*, who was present in the beginning and who continues to sustain what has been made.

Firth goes on to consider the Spirit's role in the renewal of creation, with particular focus on two passages in the book of Isaiah (32:15–20 and 34:9–17). In Isaiah 32:15–20, in stark contrast to the desolation that is the result of judgment, the outpouring of the Spirit is associated with blessings, fruitfulness and divine justice that will extend to all creation. Isaiah 34:9–17 also contains the threat of judgment. Here, though, the land remains desolate for those humans who resist God, though the activity of the Spirit ensures continuing provision for animals – thus emphasizing divine commitment to the wider creation. These passages indicate that, in the OT, creation is not viewed as something that has been concluded; rather, it 'is a continued sphere of Yahweh's work'. And that continuing divine activity, which results in renewal and justice, is effected through the Spirit. It seems reasonable to expect that the work of the Spirit today includes a similar focus on creation, evoking in us a greater environmental awareness that results in praise and an increased sense of responsibility, together with the hope of justice and the ultimate renewal of all that God has made.

In chapter 6, 'Destruction or Transformation? Earth's Future in Biblical Perspective', Paul Williamson looks at the future of our planet from the perspective of biblical theology. He notes the diversity of opinion in this area, with various views claiming support from a particular set of biblical texts, and he asks if there is one, or several, biblical views. To answer that question he discusses the place of the earth within the biblical metanarrative and goes on to analyse relevant texts, with a view to giving a balanced reading of the biblical data, rather than one weighted on one side or other of the ecological debate. Williamson notes that the earth is prominent in the original creation and in the eschatological new creation. Between those key events, the environment, though tainted by human sin, shares the hope of eventual redemption. This raises the question of what form the redeemed earth will take. Will it be a transformed version of the old, or will the old order be replaced by something radically new?

After considering texts that include references to the permanence, or otherwise, of the earth and heavens, across the main sections of the Old and

New Testaments, Williamson notes two contrasting emphases: 'one that stresses
stability, permanence and continuity; another that emphasizes vulnerability,
transience and discontinuity'. One text, Genesis 8:22, which provides the title
for this volume, typifies this ambiguity. The expression 'as long as' (lit. 'all the
days of') usually refers to a limited period of time – frequently an individual's
lifespan (e.g. Gen. 3:17; 5:5; 8:11; 9:29; Deut. 4:9; Josh. 1:5; 1 Kgs 5:1) – and thus
implies that the earth will not last for ever. In this context, though, the emphasis
is on permanence and stability. Williamson notes, further, that both of these
emphases are evident across the biblical witness, suggesting that for the Bible
writers these things are not necessarily mutually exclusive. That, in turn, indicates
that we should interpret references to the permanence or transience of the
cosmos in a qualified rather than an absolute sense. Williamson concludes that
while there is a sense in which the present order will pass away, there is also a
'significant material continuity between the present cosmos and the new
creation'. The extent of that continuity is unclear. However, the fact that, at
least to some degree, the world we now inhabit will also be our home in the
eschatological future gives us an incentive to ensure its present well-being.

In chapter 7, 'New Testament Hope and a Christian Environmental Ethos',
Jonathan Moo continues the concentration on eschatology, narrowing the focus
to three NT texts that may be said to represent something of the diversity of
the biblical perspectives explored more broadly in Williamson's chapter. Focusing
on the interpretation of Romans 8:18–25, 2 Peter 3:10–13 and Revelation
21 – 22, Moo attempts to ground a distinctively Christian ethic of creation care
on what these texts reveal about the future of the earth and the role that human
beings are seen to have in the light of this future. Like Williamson, Moo notes
that all these texts envision both continuity and discontinuity between this
creation and the new creation to come. Moo especially emphasizes that the
fundamental material continuity (and corresponding hope for the future of this
creation) that is evident in Romans 8 remains even in the more radically discon-
tinuous vision of 2 Peter 3 and in the expansive picture of Revelation 21 – 22.
Along the way Moo argues that the primary background for the 'groaning' of
creation in Romans 8 is to be found in the prophets, above all in Isaiah 24; that
if we are to live as God's children, our relationship with the earth must even
now reflect God's ultimate purpose to liberate it from its current enslavement
to ruin; that 2 Peter describes not the dissolution of the cosmos but God's
judgment upon human evil; and that in Revelation to fear and worship God
necessarily requires the rejection and coming out of an oppressive idolatrous
system that is destroying the earth.

Moo argues that the diverse ways in which these texts portray the future of
the earth, taken together, rule out complacency in the face of environmental

degradation: the value of this creation to God and the future he has secured for it in Christ challenge us to take seriously our responsibility for its care in the present. The warnings in these texts of God's judgment upon human greed and idolatry ought to wake us up from our easy capitulation to the self-focused values of our societies; and these biblical visions of a new heaven and new earth, where righteousness makes its home, ought to inspire us to live even now as the 'new creations' we have already been made to be in Christ. At the same time, the emphasis on God's sovereignty in bringing in the new creation to come relieves us of the burden of thinking that it is all up to us, reminding us of our proper place within the household of God's creation. Above all, Moo argues that, in contrast to much secular environmentalism, a Christian ethos of creation care driven by faith and hope will be marked by love and joy.

Whereas Williamson and Moo both end up emphasizing the material continuity that biblical writers envision between the present world and the world to come, Sean McDonough's chapter, 'Paradise by Desolation Trail: De-Creation and the New Testament' (chapter 8), faces squarely the 'dismantling of the created order' that the NT portrays as preceding any such renewal or re-making of the earth. Combining exegesis with theological and practical reflection, McDonough's chapter makes the case that 'de-creation' is an important theme that ought not to be ignored by those interested in the Bible and ecology. He begins his investigation with those scenes in the Gospels that are perhaps most challenging for a 'green' reading of Scripture: Jesus' cursing of the fig tree and his 'apocalyptic discourse'. McDonough argues that these elements of Jesus' ministry are not anomalies but rather are of a piece with Jesus' radical 'disruption of Israel's corporate traditions', and McDonough reminds readers that the cosmic and social orders were seen as closely intertwined in the ancient world. It is above all in Jesus' death that the gospel writers reveal that just as Jesus 'has already in his life dissolved the traditional bonds of kinship, nation and cult', so too must the whole present creation be radically reconstituted at the coming of the kingdom of God.

This emphasis on the transitoriness of the present creation also emerges occasionally in the NT epistles. McDonough notes the important links between Romans 8 and 1 Corinthians 15, both of which echo Psalm 8's description of the role human beings are intended to have in creation. McDonough observes that the present subjection of creation to *futility* in Romans 8:20 suggests a 'nightmarish inversion of Psalm 8' and hence reveals the need for humanity's reconciliation to God if his purposes for creation are to be restored. Commenting on 2 Peter's vision of a new heaven and a new earth (which, McDonough notes, is only one of a number of images in this passage drawn from Isa. 63 – 66), he suggests, 'If the author deemed materiality as such a bad or inconsequential thing, it would make little sense for him to hold forth the prospect of *more* materiality'. This is a theme that McDonough returns to in his treatment of Hebrews, where he argues that the sharp contrast between this age and the age to come is not between a material creation and an immaterial reality but rather a sign of how this creation makes way 'for a new and better [material] creation'. This is also a central theme of the book of Revelation, where the present creation, in its dismantling, becomes an instrument of God's judgment upon human evil and where creation's renewal is seen as necessary if it is to bear the weight of the glory of God who comes to give life to his creation. McDonough concludes his chapter by positing four theological rationales for the NT's insistence on the transience of the present order of creation: it serves to teach us our dependence upon God ('Pedogogy'); to point towards the fulfilment of God's original plans to take creation to the perfection for which he has always intended it ('Progress'); to reveal the need for evil to be judged and the corrupted world itself to be renewed ('Purgation'); and to prepare for creation's liberation ('Preparation').

In chapter 9, 'Jürgen Moltmann: Creation and the Restructuring of Trinitarian Panentheism', David Rainey provides a wide-ranging engagement with the prolific writings of Moltmann on creation and eschatology. Rainey notes that, for these doctrines in particular, Moltmann is one of the most influential theologians of the last century. Much of Rainey's chapter is taken up with a consideration of Moltmann's overall theological programme; but Rainey also identifies a number of the ways in which Moltmann's thought is relevant for ecology and environmental ethics. Rainey begins by detailing the distinctively trinitarian shape of Moltmann's theology of creation. For Moltmann, he observes, 'the Father is the creating origin of creation, the Son the shaping origin and the Spirit is the life-giving origin'. Christ, as the Son and Wisdom of God the Father, is both the foundation of creation and its sustainer, his resurrection the promise of the future 'perfecting' of all of creation that God brings about by the life-giving Spirit. God indwells his creation by his Spirit, and it is God's Spirit that energizes and gives life to his creation. Moltmann finds the basis for his trinitarian panentheism in this conviction that God indwells the creation by the Spirit, both suffering with his creatures and enabling creation to participate in his life. Trinitarian panentheism, he claims, is able to account for and also to distinguish between God's immanence and God's transcendence in a way that is not possible within classical theism, deism or 'philosophical panentheism'.

Creation is for Moltmann an open system, created out of God's love and free will, and it was created with potentiality. Hence sin can represent a falling short of potential, a failure to reach the end God intends, 'the antithesis to eschatology', as Rainey describes it. Rainey notes that Moltmann is careful, however, to differentiate his trinitarian panentheism from process theology, despite the shared emphasis on the openness of creation to the future. Moltmann emphasizes that creation remains distinct from God and is contingent, created *ex nihilo*, not a part of God's being or nature. There is therefore no essential limitation in God's being; rather, he *chooses* to limit himself by creating 'space' for his creation, withdrawing his presence and restricting his power. Moltmann here borrows the concept of *zimzum* from Jewish mystical tradition to describe God's self-limitation. It is this limitation on the part of God that means that creation and the future are 'open and experimental', though God's promise that he one day will be all in all still stands.

Rainey summarizes several critiques that have been offered of Moltmann's theology, particularly of his panentheism and the notion that God must make space within himself in order to create (rather than, as Colin Gunton argues, making space 'without himself' in 'joyful giving of reality to the other'; see chapter 10). Rainey himself suggests that Nancey Murphy has perhaps provided a better model for creation and divine action in the world that avoids the problems of Moltmann's panentheism. Rainey concludes his chapter by considering the ways in which Moltmann's theology addresses questions of ecology and the environment. Among other things, Moltmann's view that God indwells an open creation contrasts with the 'subject–object dichotomy' of Cartesian dualism and the corresponding objectification of nature that Moltmann identifies as in part responsible for human domination and abuse of creation. As Rainey observes, Moltmann proposes that what is needed now is the recovery of a holistic, biblical perspective of creation if we are to respond to the 'crisis of scientific and technological civilization'. This task is not primarily about, Moltmann argues, studying the 'history of creation' or arguing for mere 'belief in creation' (see too Sam Berry's essay, chapter 11), but rather it involves the re-envisioning of all of creation for 'the praise of God's glory'.

In chapter 10, 'On Being Green Without Playing God: Colin Gunton's Environmental Ethic', Graham Watts engages with the environmental thought of another influential recent theologian, Colin Gunton. Gunton's 'distinctive doctrine of creation' has potentially important implications for contemporary environmental ethics, even if – as Watts points out – Gunton himself did not draw out many of these implications. Watts begins by observing how Gunton's trinitarian doctrine of creation, developed in dialogue with Irenaeus, conceives of God as intimately related to his creation. In this Gunton shares with Moltmann a strong critique of Cartesian dualism as well as of Western theism; but Gunton seeks to maintain God's distinction from creation in a way that Gunton claims Moltmann's panentheism fails to do. Gunton constructs a 'theology of trinitarian mediation' in which God's presence to his creation is mediated through the Son and the Spirit. Christ is the one in whom the unity of creation holds together; and the Spirit works to particularize and to act to bring all things to their eschatological fulfilment. In Gunton's view (echoing Irenaeus) the story of creation is not that of a perfect creation that is fallen and then restored in Christ; rather, the loss experienced in the 'fall' is the failure of humanity to take our proper part within God's purpose to bring his good creation towards its divinely intended fulfilment.

Watts explains that Gunton's understanding of the *imago Dei* is critical here: to be created in God's image is to be in relation to God, for which Christ is the archetype. To be 'authentically human' is thus to be in 'mutually constitutive relations to one another' (including with non-human creation) in a way analogous to the relations within the Trinity. Watts observes that 'Gunton seeks to apply concepts such as person and relation both to God and humanity in conceptually similar ways while nonetheless avoiding foundationalism'. But Watts raises a series of important questions about whether Gunton in fact presses this analogy too far; whether Gunton has appropriately interpreted the theology of the Cappadocians upon whom he depends at this point; and whether Gunton, as has sometimes been claimed, has a deficient doctrine of sin and the fall. Watts then goes on to engage critically yet appreciatively and constructively with Gunton's approach to ethics, proposing some ways in which Gunton's project can contribute in particular to a Christian environmental ethic.

Watts raises an important question about Gunton's thought that is also relevant for a number of the chapters in this volume: does a thoroughgoing emphasis on eschatology (and the corresponding development of an 'ethic of createdness' rather than a 'creation ethic') ultimately excuse a passivity in which we assume that human action (e.g. in caring for the earth) is relatively unimportant since God is the one who will bring all things to completion in Christ? In response to his own question, Watts returns to Irenaeus to reclaim the close link that Irenaeus perceives between 'the work of the Spirit and human co-operation in the coming of the kingdom of God'. This link reminds us that biblical eschatology is both about the present and the future, 'now' and 'not yet'. Watts also develops the ethical potential of the connections Gunton perceives between worship, sacrifice and the relationship between creation, the church and God. Does humanity's role as a 'royal priesthood' involve, as Paraskevè Tibbs has proposed, offering ourselves and creation itself back to God as a sacrifice of praise? In the end, though he makes some creative suggestions along these lines, Watts resists the overly hierarchical view of our relationship to creation that is engendered by such a focus on our role as 'priests'. Watts returns instead to Gunton's 'ethic of createdness', which – via virtue ethics and its emphasis on what it means to be 'good' – Watts suggests can be fruitfully combined with an understanding of our calling to be 'good' stewards of creation.

In chapter 11 geneticist and ecologist R. J. (Sam) Berry asks the controversial question 'Does Disputing Evolution Discourage Creation Care?'[9] Berry begins with a brief outline of the growing conflict between traditional natural theology and evolutionary science up to the time of Darwin's *Origin of Species* – though he notes that Darwin's ideas were accepted even among some conservative theologians, because they accorded with a strong view of providence. Evolution did, though, raise theological questions – not least because it appears to allow a system of natural processes in which God could be removed as unnecessary. This led to challenges to evolutionary theory and reluctance among some evangelicals to engage seriously with evolutionary science. For Berry the situation is complicated by varieties of 'creationism'. He includes in this the recent focus on 'Intelligent Design', which attempts to find a place for God within the complexities of biological processes and mechanisms. Berry suggests, however, that this may result in a too-small view of God, as one who is Creator but not Sustainer. Instead, he argues for the principle of 'complementarity', which has been used by a number of apologists, perhaps most successfully by Donald MacKay, to bring together religious and scientific explanations of the world. For Berry, accepting the operation of natural forces and processes is not necessarily to deny continued divine activity, and he affirms God's control over events in the natural world.

A significant issue in this chapter is how human beings relate to the environment. Berry is concerned that not engaging with the natural processes involved in evolution may result in a theology of creation that does not take sufficient account of God's immanence. That, in turn, can lead to a dualism that does not take creation care seriously enough. In Berry's view scientific enquiry, which includes the study of evolution, complements the Bible. It is not necessary to find a place for God within the evolutionary process or to deny that process because God cannot be somehow fitted into it. The Bible makes it clear that God is and remains intimately involved with the natural order. And we, too, are part of that order – with responsibility to study God's works, to delight in them and to care for the world that God has made.

The views presented in Berry's chapter will seem controversial to some. It is important, however, that they be represented in a volume of this kind. It is of

---

9. This chapter was first published in *SCB* 25.2 (2013), pp. 113–130, and is included here by permission of the editor.

value to note the way that Berry, as an eminent scientist, seeks to bring together scientific enquiry and a commitment to the integrity of the Bible, and to relate both to the issue of creation care. As the title of his chapter suggests, all too often evangelicals have let disagreements about the origins of creation or the nature of biological processes prevent us from working together to care for the world God has made.

Among other things, Berry's chapter reminds us of the challenges that can arise when those who are committed to Christ adopt very different ways of seeing the world. Howard Marshall's concluding Afterword, 'Ethical Decision-Making', raises the related practical question of how Christians are to handle differences among each other when we 'end up by upholding ethical positions that are mutually incompatible, contradictory, even intolerable' – including ethical positions that relate to how we live in, use and care for creation. Although Marshall concedes that he has no definitive answer to such a dilemma, he does suggest, on the basis of 1 Corinthians 10:31 – 11:1, several general biblical criteria for assessing our behaviours and attitudes. He also proposes two distinctions that can help us learn to live with each other even when we disagree over ethical issues: *mandatory* and *recommended*; and *clear* and *dubious* commandments. While rejecting as unscriptural the notion that there are two levels of Christian disciple, Marshall accepts that there remains

> a distinction between what may be regarded as scriptural categorical imperatives that are binding on all believers and what may be regarded as recommendations, in that they summon us to good actions that are not necessarily required actions (or prohibitions) for all believers.

We need to recognize, Marshall suggests, that those actions that fall into this latter category 'may be widely different from person to person and from one situation to another'. Moreover, there are some commandments that are clear and unambiguous, whereas others will remain less clear and require us to make space within the Christian church for different opinions and practices. In the end, Marshall acknowledges that though we are left with the practical difficulties of discerning which issues belong in which of these categories and learning how to live with each other and within secular society, we must 'get on with doing the best we can here and now without waiting for complete solutions'. To return, then, to our earlier observations, as we go on seeking to gain greater knowledge of creation and to sharpen our biblical and theological vision, we are called even with incomplete understanding and imperfect vision to enter into the joyful duty of love and care for all God has made.

The contributions summarized above represent a range of biblical and theological approaches to creation and the environment. In a volume of this kind it might seem inevitable that discussion begins with biblical and theological reflection and moves to its particular application in the 'real world'. And that is as it should be. Our commitment to the world we inhabit does not come primarily from an isolated desire to save the planet. We do recognize the importance of ecology, and the need to preserve the world for future generations. However, as Christians, our first responsibility must be to the God who has revealed himself in Christ, and who has called us to his service – and it is out of that calling to serve the Creator God within the world he has made that our environmental commitment arises. As noted already, a key aspect of our attitude towards creation and the environment is to see things as God sees them. That must not exclude reflection on the natural world – and aspects of God's majesty and glory are clearly evident within the created order (Rom. 1:20) and properly elicit praise. However, it is through the lenses of biblical and theological reflection that God's purposes both for creation and for human beings as part of creation come more clearly into focus. It is our earnest prayer as editors that this volume will contribute towards a clearer understanding of that divine purpose and will help to motivate us, as those who have been made in the image of God, to play our part in its fulfilment – and to share the divine commitment to creation and the environment for 'as long as the earth endures' (Gen. 8:22).

1. THE DOCTRINE OF CREATION: SOME THEOLOGICAL REFLECTIONS

Alister McGrath

It is my privilege in the opening chapter of this volume to offer a theological overview of some aspects of the Christian doctrine of creation. Sadly, I lack the space to engage with the doctrine to the extent that it deserves, and I must content myself with identifying and making some brief comments on issues and themes that remain of landmark importance in our thinking about the nature of the world, and our attitudes towards it. It is, I think, no accident that the canonical ordering of the Christian Bible leads to the reader's first encountering the idea of creation, and finally the idea of the 'new creation'.[1] It is one of the richest themes of the Christian metanarrative, the 'big picture' of reality, which lies at the heart of the Christian faith.

Doctrines and the 'big picture' of faith

The first task of Christian theology is to appreciate this 'big picture' in all its fullness. We need to be captivated by its comprehensiveness, by its richness, by

---

1. For some excellent reflections on how these ideas have been explored in the history of Christian theology, see Randall C. Zachman, 'The Universe as the Living Image of God: Calvin's Doctrine of Creation Reconsidered', *CTM* 61 (1997), pp. 299–312.

its capacity to make sense of things and to offer hope and transformation.[2] It discloses a glorious, loving and righteous God, who creates a world that goes wrong, and then acts graciously and wondrously in order to renew and redirect it, before finally bringing it to its fulfilment. And we ourselves are an integral part of this story, which discloses our true purpose, meaning and value – who we are, what is wrong, what God proposes to do about this, and what we must do in response.[3]

So what about Christian theology? How does it come into this? Perhaps I could begin by making an obvious point: as theologians, we must make sure that we have grasped – or, better, allow ourselves to be grasped by – this compelling vision of reality. This provides the context for our reflections. We are called upon to explore this vision of reality, to give an account of its coherence and contents, and explore how this gospel lens brings the reality of our experience and our world into sharper focus.

One of the best descriptions of this process of exploration of our faith comes from the pen of the English novelist Evelyn Waugh (1903–66), best known for *Brideshead Revisited* (1945). After his sudden conversion to Christianity in 1930, Waugh wrote to a friend describing how his new faith allowed him to see things clearly for the first time. Conversion, he wrote, was about stepping 'into the real world God made; and then begins the delicious process of exploring it limitlessly'.[4] Christian theology can be thought of as this process of exploring and reflecting, as we traverse the rich and wondrous landscape of faith that is laid out before us in the Bible.

It is clear, I think, that Christian beliefs are not a set of individual, unrelated ideas. They are interconnected, like a web, held together by the compelling and persuasive vision of reality that is made possible by the gospel. We see a breathtaking landscape, and marvel at its beauty; then we move on to take in its details. To understand the beliefs, we must first catch the vision. To make sense of the snapshots, we need to take in the panorama.

Now there is nothing wrong with snapshots, which often provide welcome detail of complex landscapes. Yet there is, I think, a danger that certain approaches to theology just offer us those snapshots, and fail to show us the

---

2. I explore these themes myself in Alister McGrath, *Surprised by Meaning: Science, Faith, and How We Make Sense of Things* (Louisville: Westminster John Knox, 2011).

3. For an influential exploration of this theme, see N. T. Wright, 'How Can the Bible Be Authoritative?', *VoxEv* 21 (1991), pp. 7–32.

4. Letter to Edward Sackville-West, cited in Michael de-la-Noy, *Eddy: The Life of Edward Sackville-West* (London: Bodley Head, 1988), p. 237.

panorama. The division of theology into *loci* too easily leads us to think of doctrines as self-contained, watertight compartments, each of which may be mastered without reference to anything else. This compartmentalizing mindset is encouraged by theology textbooks – and I must here confess my own complicity in this failure![5] – which break Christian theology down into segments. What ought to be understood as merely a pedagogical strategy, aimed at facilitating engagement with a vast subject in a manageable manner, too easily becomes misunderstood as a statement about the nature of the Christian faith. It is one thing to say – as I would say – that we have to find some way of teaching the Christian faith in an educationally realistic way. It is quite another to suggest that Christianity consists of a series of individual disconnected theological boxes, each of whose contents may be inspected at any time without needing to see what is contained in the others or considering the relationship between them.

Furthermore, it is too easy to detach these snapshots from the grand biblical narrative that gives them their full meaning and context. I am sure I am not the only one to be concerned about approaches to Christian theology that manage to detach them from a deep engagement with the themes of the Bible,[6] or that offer a superficial proof-texting, based on decontextualized biblical snippets, which is insensitive to the deeper logic of the Bible.

In thinking about the doctrine of creation, we are immediately confronted with the ineluctable fact of its interconnectedness with other leading themes of faith. One cannot speak of creation without reflecting on the nature of God, the identity of Jesus Christ, the role of the Holy Spirit, the nature of salvation, or sacramental theology – to mention just the more obvious themes, to which others can easily be added. There is a sense in which to study any single doctrinal theme is actually to study the whole web of faith, the 'grand narrative of the gospel', as it intersects at this node, or as it focuses on this theme.

And this is surely right, and an integral reason for rejoicing in the comprehensiveness and coherence of the Christian vision of reality. Our primary task is to grasp this 'big picture' and marvel at its capacity to explain, at the brilliance and radiance of the God who stands at its heart, and find ourselves captivated

---

5. See the highly organized presentation of the material in Alister McGrath, *Christian Theology: An Introduction*, 5th ed. (Oxford: Wiley-Blackwell, 2011).

6. The Enlightenment's disinclination to take narrative seriously has muddied the waters here: see the classic study of Hans Frei, *The Eclipse of Biblical Narrative: A Study in Eighteenth and Nineteenth Century Biblical Hermeneutics* (New Haven: Yale University Press, 1977).

by its overwhelming imaginative power. I often recall the words of C. S. Lewis, in describing his own intellectual and imaginative delight in his Christian faith: 'I believe in Christianity as I believe that the Sun has risen, not only because I see it, but because by it, I see everything else.'[7] His point is simple: there are good reasons for believing that Christianity is true and trustworthy – and one of them is its ability to light up the landscape of reality, illuminating the shadowlands and extending the reach of our vision.[8]

It is little wonder that many feel that Christian worship is one of the crucibles of theological reflection, as it challenges us to explore the landscape of faith without reducing it to rational categories – a reduction that would limit God to what we can understand, instead of allowing our capacity to grasp things to be expanded and enriched by the vision of God that stands at the heart of our faith.[9] Theologians who do not worship and pray – and I have to confess I know very few people in this category – seem to me to be missing out on something rather significant. And, inevitably, this leads to an impoverishment of the theological vision that we find in their writings.

So, as you will have gathered, I begin by insisting that we see the doctrine of creation not as some kind of hermetically sealed capsule, but as a node of the web of faith, a snapshot of the greater panorama of the gospel. To consider the doctrine of creation is really to define a point of entry to the theological labyrinth, in that its full exploration inevitably leads us to consider other themes and their positioning on a doctrinal map.

So what themes ought we to explore? Inevitably, I face the problem of limits on space, and must therefore offer either a superficial engagement with many things, or a more reflective consideration of only a few. One of the topics that

---

7. C. S. Lewis, 'Is Theology Poetry?', in *C. S. Lewis: Essay Collection* (London: Collins, 2000), p. 21. For Lewis's realization and enactment of the connection between theology and narrative, see Gilbert Meilander, 'Theology in Stories: C. S. Lewis and the Narrative Quality of Experience', *Word and World* 1.3 (1981), pp. 222–230; Peter J. Schakel and Charles A. Huttar (eds.), *Word and Story in C. S. Lewis: Language and Narrative in Theory and Practice* (Columbia: University of Missouri Press, 1991).

8. For the use of images of 'seeing' as metaphors for discerning truth, see the seminal essay by Hans Blumenberg, 'Licht als Metapher der Wahrheit', *Studium Generale* 10 (1957), pp. 432–447.

9. See the different and important perspectives on this point offered by David Peterson, *Engaging with God: A Biblical Theology of Worship* (Downers Grove: InterVarsity Press, 2002); Graham Hughes, *Worship as Meaning: A Liturgical Theology for Late Modernity* (Cambridge: Cambridge University Press, 2003).

a comprehensive treatment would embrace would be the question of how the work of God in redemption is to be correlated with the work of God in creation. Where is the emphasis to be placed? We might also consider the relation between creation and eschatology, focusing on the question of how the theme of a restored or renewed creation does justice to the Christian vision of hope, especially its Christological aspects.[10]

The doctrine of creation and 'natural theology'

So let me turn to consider some topics that I consider to be particularly pertinent. The first is both theological and apologetic in orientation: In what way, and to what extent, does the created order tell us something about the nature of God? Now we can easily pigeonhole this question as 'natural theology', and regard this as an old question that needs no further discussion.[11] But it cannot really be pigeonholed in this way, and it does require further discussion. I concede that, in some circles, 'natural theology' has come to mean 'proving God's existence without resorting to divine revelation',[12] but I need to point out that we find no such terminology and no such definition in Scripture. Perhaps we might try to explore this important question on biblical grounds, rather than imposing somewhat unhelpful dogmatic templates and historical stereotypes on the question.

Let's begin by looking at a biblical text, often cited in this discussion: 'The heavens are telling the glory of God' (Ps. 19:1).[13] This is sometimes interpreted,

---

10. A useful starting point is the excellent study of Moyer V. Hubbard, *New Creation in Paul's Letters and Thought* (Cambridge: Cambridge University Press, 2002). See also N. T. Wright, *Surprised by Hope: Rethinking Heaven, the Resurrection, and the Mission of the Church* (New York: HarperOne, 2008).

11. For some examples of this recent debate, see Laura L. Garcia, 'Natural Theology and the Reformed Objection', in C. Stephen Evans and Merold Westphal (eds.), *Christian Perspectives on Religious Knowledge* (Grand Rapids: Eerdmans, 1993), pp. 112–133; Jonathan Topham, 'Science, Natural Theology, and Evangelicalism in the Early Nineteenth Century: Thomas Chalmers and the Evidence Controversy', in D. N. Livingstone, D. G. Hart and M. A. Noll (eds.), *Evangelicals and Science in Historical Perspective* (Oxford: Oxford University Press, 1999), pp. 142–174.

12. As e.g. in William P. Alston, *Perceiving God: The Epistemology of Religious Experience* (Ithaca: Cornell University Press, 1991), p. 289.

13. Scripture quotations in this chapter are from the NRSV.

in a somewhat decontextualized manner, to provide a theological platform for forms of apologetics that 'prove' God from reflecting on nature.[14] I very much doubt that many reading this collection of essays will be inclined to think this. To begin with, it is philosophically dubious. But more importantly, it is not what the text itself is suggesting.

We need to remember that Israel already knew about the existence of its God. In fact, they knew rather more than this. The covenant between God and Israel rested on a firm conviction that such a God was trustworthy and truthful, and had chosen Israel as his covenant partner. The recognition that God's creation declares God's glory is not presented in this psalm as a mandate for deducing the existence and character of God by looking at the heavens. In a similar manner, Israel is often invited to reflect on what God has done in history – I think here of Psalm 136 – not as a proof of God's existence, but as a reassurance of his power and compassion. It is about reinforcing faith – fleshing out what it means to trust in God. In the same way, Psalm 19 seems to indicate that a God whose existence and properties were already known to Israel might be known in an aesthetically or imaginatively extended manner by reflection on what God has created.

This is a topic that I have found theologically, apologetically and spiritually fruitful.[15] The gospel transforms our view of reality, enabling us to see things as they really are. The scales fall from our eyes. The veil of the 'Spirit of the Age' is removed. Our blindness is healed. In every case the healing grace of God brings about something that argument cannot achieve. We may find ourselves persuaded that we are blind, and that our sight needs to be healed. But the salve, the cure, is something that only God can provide. There is clearly an interesting theological debate here about how we come to realize our need and appropriate the cure; my concern here is simply to emphasize that only God can heal our blindness.

Let us reflect on Romans 12:2: 'Do not be conformed to this world, but be transformed by the renewing of your minds, so that you may discern what is the will of God – what is good and acceptable and perfect.' It is a marvellous summary of Paul's vision of the transformative power of the gospel, including this theme of the 'renewal of our minds'. The gospel changes us; it renews

14. See James Barr, *Biblical Faith and Natural Theology* (Oxford: Clarendon, 1993), pp. 81–101; Cas J. A. Vos, *Theopoetry of the Psalms* (Pretoria: Protea Book House, 2005), pp. 92–116.

15. E.g. see Alister McGrath, *The Open Secret: A New Vision for Natural Theology* (Oxford: Blackwell, 2008).

us; it transforms us, enabling us to see, understand and value things in new ways. Perhaps we see this brilliant vision stated most clearly at Ephesians 1:17–19:

> I pray that the God of our Lord Jesus Christ, the Father of glory, may give you a spirit of wisdom and revelation as you come to know him, so that, with the eyes of your heart enlightened, you may know what is the hope to which he has called you, what are the riches of his glorious inheritance among the saints, and what is the immeasurable greatness of his power for us who believe, according to the working of his great power.

It's a long and complex sentence, but there's no doubting the point that is being made. The 'spirit of wisdom and revelation' leads to the 'eyes of our heart' – what a wonderful phrase! – being 'enlightened'.[16] Little wonder that Christian theologians reflecting on this passage have seen this as a key to the impact of the gospel. Theology is about seeing things for what they really are and drawing up a map of this new reality so that we may explore it further. We are given a new lens that brings things into sharper focus, an illuminating way of looking at things which casts light on and within the shadowlands.

So how does this affect our thinking about environmental ethics? The key point is that we see things – including the natural world – for what they really are, and are forced to re-evaluate them as a result. An analogy may help make this somewhat abstract point a little clearer. In 1923 an old country manor house in the south of England was purchased and renovated for educational use. The house had previously been owned by Sir Henry Layard (1818–94), a prominent Victorian archaeologist who had spent much of his time excavating ancient sites in Mesopotamia, and who was credited with the discovery of the 'lost' city of Nineveh in 1845.[17] The builders who converted the house into a school found a block of stone in one of the rooms. Under the terms of the sale, this block of stone was now the property of the school. But what were they to do with it? It was useless, apart from propping open doors.

---

16. For this theme in Augustine, see Roland J. Teske, 'Augustine of Hippo on Seeing with the Eyes of the Mind', in Craig J. N. de Paulo, Patrick Messina and Marc Stier (eds.), *Ambiguity in the Western Mind* (New York: Peter Lang, 2005), pp. 72–87.

17. See Mogens T. Larsen, *The Conquest of Assyria: Excavations in an Antique Land* (London: Routledge, 1996), pp. 34–39.

In 1994 a professor of art history at Columbia University who was researching a book about Layard visited the school.[18] After a close examination of this slab of stone, he made a trip to the British Museum in London. He was able to prove that it was really a 3,000-year-old carved panel that Layard had brought back to England from the throne room of the Assyrian King Assurnasirpal II (883–859 BC). It was sold at auction at Christie's later that year for a record $11.8 million.

When Russell first saw the stone, he assumed he was looking at a cheap plaster copy of an ancient Assyrian carving. Then his eyes were opened and he realized what the stone really was. He discerned its true significance. As a result, the way the object was understood and valued changed radically. What was once seen as a useless lump of rock was now recognized as an important historical relic, worth nearly $12 million.

The key point is that the stone *was seen with new eyes*. Russell displayed what the philosopher Iris Murdoch (1919–99) called 'attentiveness' – a careful, principled, committed attempt to perceive things as they really are, rather than as they merely appear to be.[19] Part of our 'discipleship of the mind' must be to learn to cultivate theological acuity, so that we see things as God sees them – and act accordingly.

Let me expand on this point briefly, as it is important apologetically. We can evaluate any 'grand narrative', any 'world view', any 'big picture' by asking two questions:

1. What is the evidence that might lead us to believe that it is correct?
2. How much sense does it make of what we actually observe?

As many of you know, I was originally a scientist, and this essentially scientific way of thinking continues to influence me. Like C. S. Lewis, I was drawn to Christianity mainly because of its ability to make sense of things. It is a far better way of seeing things than, for example, my youthful atheism. In one sense apologetics is about inviting people to see things our way – to step into the

---

18. John M. Russell, *From Nineveh to New York: The Strange Story of the Assyrian Reliefs in the Metropolitan Museum and the Hidden Masterpiece at Canford School* (New Haven: Yale University Press, 1997), pp. 173–189.

19. For the theological application of this idea, see Alister McGrath, 'The Cultivation of Theological Vision: Theological Attentiveness and the Practice of Ministry', in Pete Ward (ed.), *Perspectives on Ecclesiology and Ethnography* (Grand Rapids: Eerdmans, 2011), pp. 107–123.

Christian way of thinking and seeing, and realize how effective it is. There are excellent evidential reasons for believing that the Christian faith is true and trustworthy – and one of them is its capacity to integrate, correlate and unify what we see around us.

But how does this bold vision of reality affect the doctrine of creation? Put simply, it is an invitation to see nature in a new way. Not simply to look at it, but to behold it, to appreciate it for what it really is, and to act accordingly. This is about stripping away delusions and misunderstandings – such as any idea that nature is an autonomous entity, with which we may do as we please. You can see the obvious ethical implications of this. This is not our world, over which we have sovereignty; it is God's, and we are his stewards, appointed and called to tend his world as something that has been entrusted to us.

The beauty and order of the natural world does not prove that there is a God; it is, however, consistent with what we would expect if the Christian vision of reality is true. Perhaps we might draw on G. K. Chesterton here, as he explained why he, and so many, were rediscovering the intellectual vitality of Christianity back in 1903: 'We have returned to it because it is an intelligible picture of the world.'[20] Chesterton realized that testing a theory meant checking it out against observation. 'The best way to see if a coat fits a man is not to measure both of them, but to try it on.'[21] So what did he mean by this? Perhaps we should allow Chesterton himself to explain what he has in mind:

> Numbers of us have returned to this belief; and we have returned to it, not because of this argument or that argument, but because the theory, when it is adopted, works out everywhere; because the coat, when it is tried on, fits in every crease. . . . We put on the theory, like a magic hat, and history becomes translucent like a house of glass.[22]

Chesterton's argument is that Christianity offers a 'big picture' of things, and it is this vision of reality as a whole – rather than any of its individual components – which proves so compelling. Individual observations of nature do not 'prove' Christianity to be true; rather, Christianity validates itself by its ability to make sense of those observations. 'The phenomenon does not prove religion, but

---

20. G. K. Chesterton, 'The Return of the Angels', *Daily News*, 14 Mar. 1903. For an
    excellent account of Chesterton's return to belief, see William Oddie, *Chesterton and
    the Romance of Orthodoxy: The Making of GKC, 1874–1908* (Oxford: Oxford University
    Press, 2008).

21. Chesterton, 'Return of the Angels'.

22. Ibid.

religion explains the phenomenon.'[23] A good theory, for Chesterton, is to be judged by the amount of light it casts on what we see in the world around us and experience within us. 'With this idea once inside our heads, a million things become transparent as if a lamp were lit behind them.'[24]

Creation as event and process

But let me now ask another question. What do we mean by 'creation'? It is an English word that we often use uncritically, perhaps passing over the fact that it translates several Hebrew terms, with subtly different connotations. Does it mean 'form'? Or 'shape'? Or 'mould'? I mention this point simply because I can think of no text in the canonical OT which demands that the term 'create' be understood as 'create *out of nothing*'. Genesis 1, for example, clearly speaks of imposing order upon chaos. This theme of the imposition of order on chaos is found at many other points, and is often expressed in terms of God's defeat of chaotic forces, personified as great monsters.[25] It is certainly true that Jewish interpreters are increasingly coming round to the idea of *creatio ex nihilo*, a trend that I trace back to the sixteenth century.[26] Yet this doctrine is Christian in terms of its origins, reflecting some fundamental Christological convictions of the NT.

A further question is whether we understand the term 'creation' to designate a past act, now completed, or a process that is continuing. Early Christian writers explored this in some detail, and many readers will be aware of Augustine of Hippo's musings in his classic work *On the Literal Meaning of Genesis*, written between 401 and 415.[27] As the title makes clear, Augustine intended this to be a 'literal' commentary on the text ('literal' here means something like 'in the sense intended by the author'). So what literal interpretation does Augustine offer of the first two chapters of Genesis? Augustine draws out the following

---

23. Ibid.

24. Ibid. This general principle underlies the philosophy of 'inference to the best explanation': see e.g. Peter Lipton, *Inference to the Best Explanation*, 2nd ed. (London: Routledge, 2004).

25. Michael Deroche, 'Isaiah 45:7 and the Creation of Chaos', *VT* 42 (1992), pp. 11–21.

26. Hava Tirosh-Samuelson, 'Theology of Nature in Sixteenth-Century Italian Jewish Philosophy', *SiC* 10 (1997), pp. 529–570.

27. N. Joseph Torchia, *Creatio Ex Nihilo and the Theology of St. Augustine: The Anti-Manichaean Polemic and Beyond* (New York: Peter Lang, 1999).

core themes from these texts, set within the overall context of Scripture as a whole.

God brought everything into existence in a single moment of creation. Yet the created order is not static. God endowed it with the capacity to develop. Augustine uses the image of a dormant seed to help his readers grasp this point. God creates seeds, which will grow and develop at the right time. Using more technical language, Augustine asks his readers to think of the created order as containing divinely embedded causalities that emerge or evolve at a later stage. Yet Augustine has no time for any notion of random or arbitrary changes within creation. The development of God's creation is always subject to God's sovereign providence. The God who planted the seeds at the moment of creation also governs and directs the time and place of their growth.[28]

Augustine does not limit God's creative action to the primordial act of origination. He argues that God's work of creation includes both the initial origination of the world and its subsequent development. There are two 'moments' in creation: a primary act of origination, and a continuing process of providential guidance. Creation is thus not a completed past event. God must be recognized to be working even now, in the present, sustaining and directing the unfolding of the 'generations that he laid up in creation when it was first established'.[29]

Now there are many points of interest in what Augustine has to say, most notably the hermeneutical principles that he brings to bear on his OT texts. For Augustine, Genesis 1 is to be interpreted not simply in the light of Genesis 2, but in the light of the entire canon of Scripture. We cannot privilege Genesis 1 and give it some kind of hermeneutical priority in this matter. It is one of many passages that we are called upon to weave together into our understanding of the doctrine of creation. Augustine reads Genesis 1 in the light of an interpretative framework he finds in the biblical texts as a whole.

There are obviously many debates within evangelicalism over how to interpret Genesis 1, and I have no intention of resolving them in this chapter.[30] But I think it is fair to make two points. First, evangelicals tend not to be very good on the history of biblical interpretation, especially on the part of those who

---

28. For a full discussion of Augustine's views on this matter, see Alister McGrath, *A Fine-Tuned Universe: The Quest for God in Science and Theology* (Louisville: Westminster John Knox, 2009), pp. 95–108.

29. Augustine, *de Genesi ad litteram* 5.20.41 (my tr.).

30. For a somewhat polemical assessment, see Clark H. Pinnock, 'Climbing out of a Swamp: The Evangelical Struggle to Understand the Creation Texts', *Int* 43 (1989), pp. 143–155.

stood much closer historically to those texts than we do.[31] Augustine of Hippo – so prized by both Martin Luther and John Calvin – is a case in point. Might we not learn more from him?

Secondly, many of our debates over the doctrine of creation are covertly moulded by anxieties about biological evolution. It is often the elephant in the room, looming large over our discussions but not being mentioned out of fear or an excessively fastidious culture of theological politeness. Augustine knew nothing about big bangs or Darwin. His approach to the doctrine of creation has much to offer us – perhaps simply because it is *not* constructed as a defensive reaction against views seen to be threatening, but simply as an account of what he found in the biblical texts. There is a proper discussion to be had about how we understand the Bible in the light of science, and science in the light of the Bible, and I do not want to prejudice that. But I would point out that there is a well-credentialized way of thinking about creation that can fit in the 'big bang' and biological evolution without showing any strain. What Augustine would find unacceptable is any idea that the unfolding process of creation takes place without divine involvement and direction.

We find similar ideas being explored in the writings of the great evangelical theologian Benjamin B. Warfield, whose commitment to the authority of Scripture was unswerving.[32] But as Warfield rightly saw, belief in an inerrant text does not automatically ensure that it is interpreted correctly. The current discussions within evangelicalism about the interpretation of the biblical creation narratives are not about biblical *authority*, but about biblical *interpretation*.

For Warfield, the term 'creation' refers to God's primal act of bringing everything into being from nothing (*ex nihilo*).[33] It describes God's initial creation of the universe, with the potential for further development under God's sovereign providential guidance. To express this developmental aspect of things, Warfield introduces the notion of 'mediate creation', by which he means something intermediate between natural processes and divine providence. 'Mediate creation' refers to the direct action of God on material entities, in which God brings about novelty – that is, something that was not originally present in the primary act of creation itself. Warfield does not hold that

---

31. E.g. see Louis J. Swift, 'Basil and Ambrose on the Six Days of Creation', *Aug* 21 (1981), pp. 317–328.

32. As noted by David N. Livingstone and Mark A. Noll, 'B. B. Warfield (1851–1921): A Biblical Inerrantist as Evolutionist', *Isis* 91 (2000), pp. 283–304.

33. See further David N. Livingstone, *Darwin's Forgotten Defenders: The Encounter Between Evangelical Theology and Evolutionary Thought* (Grand Rapids: Eerdmans, 1987).

'naturalistic evolution' and 'divine creation' are identical; he does, however, insist that they are consistent with each other, provided both are interpreted correctly.

The place of humanity within creation

Any responsible Christian thinking about environmental ethics is likely to focus on two themes: a theologically attentive understanding of the natural world on the one hand, and of human nature on the other. A core theme here is that, while humanity is part of God's creation, this creation must be recognized to be *stratified* rather than uniform. Human beings are part of the created order; they have nevertheless been given a place of privilege and responsibility within that domain. This is traditionally articulated using the concept of the 'image of God' (Gen. 1:26–27).[34]

It must be said that the intricacies of the theological development of this theme substantially exceed the load-bearing capacity of its biblical foundations. Some recent theological interpretations of this idea are difficult to defend on the basis of the biblical witness – such as Emil Brunner's occasionally puzzling distinction between the 'formal' and 'material' aspects of the image of God.[35] Nevertheless, the theme has the potential to illuminate some themes of no small importance to the issue of environmental ethics – such as the limits of human authority, the issue of ethical responsibility, and the capacity of humanity to exist relationally with one another and with God.[36] For our purposes, the

34. A. Jónsson Gunnlaugur and S. Cheney Michael, *The Image of God: Genesis 1:26–28 in a Century of Old Testament Research* (Stockholm: Almqvist & Wiksell International, 1988); Philip Edgcumbe Hughes, *The True Image: The Origin and Destiny of Man in Christ* (Grand Rapids: Eerdmans, 1989).

35. Anthony A. Hoekema, *Created in God's Image* (Grand Rapids: Eerdmans 1994), pp. 52–58.

36. E.g. see Colin E. Gunton, 'Trinity, Ontology and Anthropology: Towards a Renewal of the Doctrine of *Imago Dei*', in Christoph Schwöbel and Colin E. Gunton (eds.), *Persons Divine and Human* (Edinburgh: T. & T. Clark, 1991), pp. 47–64; F. Leron Shults, 'Constitutive Relationality in Anthropology and Trinity: Shaping and *Imago Dei* in Barth and Pannenberg', *NZSTh* 39 (1997), pp. 304–322; Stanley J. Grenz, *The Social God and the Relational Self: A Trinitarian Theology of the Imago Dei* (Louisville: Westminster John Knox, 2001); Daniel K. Miller, 'Responsible Relationship: *Imago Dei* and the Moral Distinction Between Humans and Other Animals', *IJST* 13 (2011), pp. 329–339.

important point to appreciate is that bearing God's image is not primarily about entitlement and privilege; it is about accountability and stewardship.

The doctrines of creation and the Trinity

But let me move on, and look at a fourth area of the doctrine of creation, which seems to me to be profoundly interesting. I have in mind a trinitarian approach to creation.[37] Like many others, I am in two minds about the resurgence of trinitarian thinking in the twentieth century.

On the one hand, I welcome this, taking great pleasure in getting away from the sort of deistic view of God that was so characteristic of both Christian theology and popular piety in the nineteenth century. Yes, I know they believed in the Trinity then. It was just that most of them did not really know what to do with it. For example, William Paley's classic work *Natural Theology* plods along quite happily talking about a God who creates a world wisely and keeps a benign eye on it. But, as his many critics of that period pointed out, it was a severely deficient notion of God. Irenaeus of Lyons offered us a much more compelling vision when he described the Holy Spirit and Jesus Christ as 'the two hands of God' through whom the works of creation and redemption were achieved.

As many readers will know, a new interest in the theology of Jonathan Edwards – which I greatly welcome – has seen attention being paid to his trinitarian theology of beauty, which allows him to approach the 'reading' of nature in a rich and revealing manner.[38] The trinitarian revival has enriched the theological vision of God by insisting that the limiting constraints of rationality that so often impeded theological statements about God in the eighteenth and nineteenth centuries be seen for what they really are – a reflection of human limitations, and a most unfortunate tendency to conceive God in terms that human beings can cope with, rather than try to enlarge and enrich our vision of God in the light of the biblical testimony.

So I welcome this trinitarian revival. But as an evangelical, I am also worried about it. Why so? Let me try to explain. My evangelical instinct is that we keep our theological language and concepts as close to those of Scripture as possible. I fully take the point Athanasius made years ago in his letter to Serapion – that

---

37. E.g. see Roderick T. Leupp, *The Renewal of Trinitarian Theology: Themes, Patterns, & Explorations* (Downers Grove: InterVarsity Press, 2008).

38. See e.g. Beldan C. Lane, 'Jonathan Edwards on Beauty, Desire and the Sensory World', *TS* 65 (2004), pp. 44–68.

to make biblical points, we sometimes have to use non-biblical language. Yet I cannot help but feel that there is a degree of trinitarian inflationism going on that places theological reflection at some distance from the biblical texts.[39] Athanasius was perfectly capable of stating his doctrine of creation simply and succinctly, like this: 'The Father creates all things through the Word in the Spirit.'[40] I worry – I hope needlessly – that we are losing contact with the biblical witness when we begin to use the arcane vocabulary of trinitarian theology and think in terms of an internal trinitarian logic.

I do not see this as a massive problem, but simply as a trend that may need to be addressed and corrected. My own view is that when theology is seen as an interconnected web of ideas and themes, then *every* doctrine has a trinitarian dimension, precisely because of the interconnectedness of these ideas. The doctrine of creation – like the doctrine of atonement or the church – is located within a context and set of conceptual relationships, which ensure that its trinitarian aspects are both secured on the one hand, and given their due – but not improper or exaggerated – weight.

There is much that such a trinitarian way of seeing creation ensures. Creation is seen as integrally related to the work of redemption and final consummation, especially when viewed through the lens of the 'economy of salvation'.[41] The work of God as creator is here immediately – and naturally – seen as linked with God's providence, God's acts of revelation and God's work of restoration and renewal. It's like telling a story. There are multiple possible points of entry. There are several ways of arranging the material for best effect. But the outcome is more or less the same, in that the same story is told. To speak of creation, redemption or final consummation is about breaking into the 'grand narrative' of faith at a certain point. We might have a very useful discussion about the pedagogical advantages of using the traditional creedal order; we might equally have a good discussion about which approach is most effective apologetically. My point is this: theology aims to ensure that the full story is told, however it is narrated in practice. To use the classic language of theology, the purpose of the doctrine of the Trinity is to 'preserve the mystery' – that is to say, to prevent

---

39. For my concerns about the inflation of trinitarian vocabulary far beyond its biblical foundations, see Alister McGrath, 'The Doctrine of the Trinity: An Evangelical Reflection', in Timothy George (ed.), *God the Holy Trinity: Reflections on Christian Faith and Practice* (Grand Rapids: Baker Academic, 2006), pp. 17–35.

40. Athanasius, *Ad Serapion* 1.24 (my tr.).

41. J. Patout Burns, 'Economy of Salvation: Two Patristic Traditions', *TS* 37 (1976), pp. 598–619.

us from reducing God to our level of thinking, and to enable our thinking to rise as near as possible to his level, no matter how much mental discomfort this may cause.

Creation and context: shifting emphases

Finally, I would like to touch on the way in which the profile of the doctrine of creation varies from one cultural situation to another. For example, consider the ongoing discussion within OT scholarship about whether pre-exilic Israel privileged the narrative of God's acts in history over that of God's work of creation, and the related suggestion that the doctrine of creation became of particular importance during the exilic age.[42] These are interesting discussions, and I have no intention of irritating OT scholars among my readers by making any sophomoric judgments here. The general point that I wish to make is simply this: often the cultural circumstances in which we find ourselves cause us to give a higher profile to certain doctrines of the faith than to others. Changing situations lead to different articulations, though not to different conceptions, of our vision of the gospel.

It is my judgment that the profile of the doctrine of creation has risen within evangelicalism in the last few decades. I would like to suggest that there are three reasons that might contribute to the doctrine of creation assuming such a higher profile.

1. The new interest in science and religion has caused many theologians – and I include myself here – to reassert that the doctrine of creation allows us to affirm the rationality and ordering of creation, which is fundamental to the scientific enterprise.[43] Furthermore, the widespread adoption of the standard cosmological model – which asserts that the universe came into being at some point in the distant past – is clearly harmonious with a Christian doctrine of creation. The exploration of these areas continues to be both apologetically and theologically fruitful.

---

42. E.g. see Rolf Rendtorff, '"Where Were You When I Laid the Foundations of the Earth?" Creation and Salvation History', in Rolf Rendtorff (ed.), *Canon and Theology: Overtures to an Old Testament Theology* (Minneapolis: Fortress, 1993), pp. 92–113.

43. A good example is John Polkinghorne, *Science and Creation: The Search for Understanding* (London: SPCK, 1988).

2. A Christian doctrine of creation reminds us that the world is God's, not ours. We are its stewards, not its owners; it has been entrusted to us, who bear God's image.[44] The new (and welcome) awareness of environmental concerns within evangelicalism is grounded in such fundamental theological beliefs.[45] It is very easy to develop a coherent environmental ethic on the basis of the opening chapters of Genesis, with important implications for Christian attitudes and outlooks.[46] We see nature not as something that exists for our convenience, but as God's precious possession, entrusted to us for safe-keeping. And once we see nature in that light and in that manner, our behaviour towards it changes. Perhaps our reflections on these themes have been stimulated by concerns about our planet's well-being. Yet this merely provides the context for our reflections; their substance is shaped by Scripture itself.

3. A growing awareness of the importance of apologetics has seen the emergence of approaches that start out from human interest in the beauty of creation, and then construct a navigable channel from the works of creation to the wisdom of the Creator. This is not apologetically opportunistic, as it is deeply rooted in a theology of creation. 'The heavens are telling the glory of God' (Ps. 19:1). Paul's remarkably sophisticated line of apologetic argument at the Areopagus, described in Acts 17,[47] must surely alert us to the importance of a doctrine of creation in enabling us to connect the gospel with what I fear is an increasingly biblically illiterate culture, yet which still retains a fundamental interest in questions of meaning and value.

Conclusion

My space has run out, and I have only been able to touch on some of the themes attending a doctrine of creation. There is, I think, much more that needs to be

---

44. See Jürgen Moltmann, *God in Creation: A New Theology of Creation and the Spirit of God* (Minneapolis: Fortress, 1990).

45. See e.g. Richard Bauckham, *Bible and Ecology: Rediscovering the Community of Creation* (London: Darton, Longman & Todd, 2010).

46. Katharine K. Wilkinson, *Between God and Green: How Evangelicals Are Cultivating a Middle Ground on Climate Change* (New York: Oxford University Press, 2012).

47. See the still valuable study of Bertil Gärtner, *The Areopagus Speech and Natural Revelation* (Uppsala: Almqvist & Wiksell, 1955).

considered. But that, after all, is to be expected. We are all on a journey of discovery in our walk of faith, as we reflect on the richness of our faith. When Paul speaks of the 'boundless riches of Christ' (Eph. 3:8), he is not forbidding us to explore, but *encouraging* us to do so, in the knowledge that there will always be more to discover about Christ, the focus and centre of our faith. That applies to the doctrine of creation as much as to any great theme of our faith. As Evelyn Waugh put it, let us continue 'the delicious process of exploring it limitlessly'!

© Alister McGrath, 2014

2. 'IN THE BEGINNING IT WAS VERY GOOD': GENESIS 1 – 2 AND THE ENVIRONMENT

David L. Baker

Introduction

In the beginning, the environment – as all of creation – was good. That is the unequivocal message of Genesis 1. In the account of events on the first day we read, 'God saw that the light was good; and God separated the light from the darkness' (v. 4).[1] This is the first of seven occurrences of the 'approval formula' (see also vv. 10, 12, 18, 21, 25, 31). The common word 'good' (*ṭôb*) is theologically significant in the OT. Unlike some other ANE deities,[2] the God of Israel is good (Pss 100:5; 136:1) and his goodness is reflected in his works (Job 12:7–10; Pss 19:1–6; 104; cf. Acts 14:27; Rom. 1:20). Ken Gnanakan draws three further conclusions from this point:[3]

- Evil is not part of creation at the beginning, but a later development.

---

1. I have made my own translation from Hebrew of the Genesis texts cited in this chapter.
2. Cf. John H. Walton, *Ancient Near Eastern Thought and the Old Testament: Introducing the Conceptual World of the Hebrew Bible* (Grand Rapids: Baker, 2006), p. 109.
3. Ken Gnanakan, *God's World: Biblical Insights for a Theology of the Environment* (London: SPCK, 1999), p. 43.

- Creation has value in itself, not simply because it is useful to human beings.[4]
- The goodness of creation implies its beauty.[5]

The seventh and last occurrence of the approval formula is found at the end of the chapter: 'Then God saw everything that he had made, and indeed it was very good; and there was evening and there was morning – the sixth day' (v. 31a). This time it is applied to the whole of creation, not just one part. And it has two extra words compared with the earlier occurrences to emphasize the perfect goodness of creation at the beginning of time: 'indeed' (*hinnēh*) and 'very' (*mě'ōd*).

The conviction that the world God created is good should motivate us to protect it from exploitation and pollution.[6] Ellen Davis suggests that Genesis 1 may be seen as a contemplation reflecting on the goodness of the world created by God, and portraying 'God's action and perception as the model for our own'.[7] The God in whose image we are made is delighted with his work. 'Appreciation and enjoyment of the creatures are the hallmark of God's dominion and therefore the standard by which our own attempts to exercise dominion must be judged.'[8]

John Stott asks, 'To whom does the earth belong?', and answers that it belongs both to God as landlord (Pss 24:1; 50:10–12) and to humanity as tenant (Ps. 115:16).[9] This is elaborated in Genesis 1 – 2, making it clear that God has ultimate rights over the earth as its creator but that he has delegated its

---

4. Cf. Christopher J. H. Wright, '"The Earth Is the Lord's": Biblical Foundations for Global Ecological Ethics and Mission', in Noah J. Toly and Daniel I. Block (eds.), *Keeping God's Earth: The Global Environment in Biblical Perspective* (Downers Grove: Inter-Varsity Press, 2010), pp. 216–241. Wright points out that the earth is already declared good before human beings are created. See also Jonathan Burnside, *God, Justice, and Society: Aspects of Law and Legality in the Bible* (Oxford: Oxford University Press, 2010), p. 146.

5. Cf. Victor P. Hamilton, *The Book of Genesis: Chapters 1–17* (Grand Rapids: Eerdmans, 1990), who translates *ṭôb* in these chapters as 'beautiful'.

6. James Barr, 'Man and Nature – The Ecological Controversy and the Old Testament', *BJRL* 55 (1972), pp. 9–32, esp. 31.

7. Ellen F. Davis, *Scripture, Culture, and Agriculture: An Agrarian Reading of the Bible* (Cambridge: Cambridge University Press, 2009), pp. 46–48.

8. Ibid., pp. 64–65.

9. John R. W. Stott, *Issues Facing Christians Today*, 4th ed. (Grand Rapids: Zondervan, 2006; rev. Roy McCloughry and John Wyatt), pp. 146, 150.

management to human beings (cf. Lev. 25:23). It follows that we should care for God's property and treat it with respect, not abuse, pollute or destroy it.[10]

The material on creation and the environment in Genesis 1 – 2 may be grouped under four main topics: biodiversity, dominion, food and agriculture. We will discuss them one by one.

Biodiversity (Gen. 1:11–12, 21, 24–25)

The idea of biodiversity is discernible at the earliest stage of the creation of life (vegetation), on the third day in the scheme of Genesis 1:

> Then God said, 'Let the land sprout vegetation: plants yielding seed, and fruit trees[11] bearing fruit with the seed in it, according to their kinds,[12] on the land'; and it was so. So the land produced vegetation: plants yielding seed according to their kinds, and trees bearing fruit with the seed in it according to their kinds; and God saw that it was good. (Vv. 11–12)

It reappears in the next two great stages by which life comes into being, in the sea:

> So God created the great sea monsters; and every other living creature that moves, with which the waters swarm, according to their kinds, and every winged creature according to their kinds; and God saw that it was good. (V. 21)

---

10. Wright, 'Earth Is the Lord's', p. 219.

11. The Hebrew here is singular; the noun has a plural form (*'ēṣîm*) used elsewhere for trees (e.g. Ps. 104:16), but the singular can also be used for the plural (e.g. Lev. 26:20) and that is clearly the meaning here. Many nouns in this chapter are singular in form but plural in meaning (e.g. *deše'*, *'ēśeb*, *'ôp*).

12. Again, the Hebrew is singular (lit. 'fruit tree according to its kind') but clearly intended to be plural in meaning. This is the traditional understanding of the expression, as in 'each according to its kind' (RSV, ESV; cf. *DCH*, vol. 5, p. 262; Mark D. Futato, *'mîn'*, in *NIDOTTE*, vol. 2, pp. 934–935), 'according to their various kinds' (NIV; cf. NET), 'each corresponding to its own species' (NJB), 'according to their types' (Gordon J. Wenham, *Genesis 1–15* [Waco: Word, 1987], p. 21). Alternative translations suggested include 'of every kind' (NRSV, NJPS; cf. Hamilton, *Genesis 1–17*, p. 124), 'for its kind' (Barry Bandstra, *Genesis 1–11* [Waco: Baylor University Press, 2008], p. 60), 'of its kind' (Claus Westermann, *Genesis 1–11* [London: SPCK, 1984], p. 77).

And on the land:

> Then God said, 'Let the land produce living creatures according to their kinds: cattle and reptiles[13] and wild animals[14] according to their kinds'; and it was so. So God made the wild animals according to their kinds, and the cattle according to their kinds, and everything that moves on the ground according to their kinds; and God saw that it was good. (Vv. 24–25)

The key phrase is 'according to their kinds'. The Hebrew word *mîn* (kind) is roughly equivalent to 'species',[15] though perhaps closer to the broader terms 'genus' or 'family'.[16] It is only found in this distinctive expression. It occurs 31 times in the OT – in Genesis 1:11–25 (10 times), 6:20 (3 times), 7:14 (4 times), Leviticus 11:14–29 (9 times), Deuteronomy 14:13–18 (4 times) and Ezekiel 47:10 – always in connection with plants and animals.[17]

Reflection

Genesis 1 reflects a simple division of vegetation and animals into broad categories, emphasized by the ten times repeated phrase 'according to their kinds'. The second account of creation has less detail than the first, but it is evident that there is a variety of flora and fauna, and this is appreciated by the first man (2:9, 19–20). A much more detailed categorization is found in the food laws of Leviticus 11 and Deuteronomy 14. We are later told that Solomon makes a careful study of the natural world (1 Kgs 4:33), though the details are not reported. Joel 1:4 distinguishes four kinds of locust.

Clearly this diversity of animal and vegetable life is part of God's ongoing plan for his good world. Noah is portrayed as a conservationist, who builds an ark to preserve various species of life on earth from the destruction of the flood (Gen. 6:20; 7:2–3).[18] OT poets celebrate the wonder of God's creative activity,

---

13. Lit. 'moving things', often translated 'creeping things'; includes reptiles and other small animals.

14. Lit. 'living [creatures] of the land/earth'.

15. *DCH*, vol. 5, p. 262.

16. Westermann, *Genesis 1–11*, p. 126; Hamilton, *Genesis 1–17*, p. 126; cf. Futato, *'mîn'*, p. 934.

17. Also Sir. 13.16, and three times in DSS (see Paul Beauchamp and Heinz-Josef Fabry, *'mîn'*, in *TDOT*, vol. 8, pp. 288–291), with a broader meaning than in the OT (applying to human beings and things, as well as animals and plants).

18. Cf. Ian Bradley, *God Is Green: Christianity and the Environment* (London: Darton, Longman & Todd, 1990; repr. Image, 1992), pp. 20–21.

with a particular interest in life on earth (Job 38 – 39; Ps. 104). Scientists have already identified more than a million kinds of animals and plants on the earth, and new species are still being discovered. But sadly, extinction rates have accelerated in recent years as a result of habitat destruction, especially of tropical forests; and unless preventative action is taken in the near future, it is probable that global warming will lead to the extinction of many more species in the future.[19]

Dominion (Gen. 1:26–28)

There has been extended discussion about the idea of human dominion over the rest of creation and how it relates to human responsibility for climate change and other ecological problems. Before entering into such discussion, however, it is important to see what the key text in Genesis 1 actually says:

> Then God said, 'Let us make human beings[20] in our image, according to our likeness; and let them have dominion[21] over the fish of the sea and over the birds of the sky and over the cattle and over all[22] the earth, and over every reptile that moves on the land.'

> So God created human beings in his image,
>   in the image of God he created them;
>   male and female he created them.

---

19. For more detailed discussion of biodiversity, with biblical-theological reflections, see Fred Van Dyke, 'The Diversity of Life: Its Loss and Conservation', in Toly and Block, *Keeping God's Earth*, pp. 93–115; and Daniel I. Block, 'To Serve and to Keep: Toward a Biblical Understanding of Humanity's Responsibility in the Face of the Biodiversity Crisis', in ibid., pp. 116–140.

20. So GNT, REB, TNIV, NLT2. The Hebrew word *'ādām* is grammatically singular, as in the traditional translation 'man' (still used by ESV, NJB, NJPS). Several versions have a singular form with more gender-inclusive language (e.g. 'humankind' in NRSV and NET; 'mankind' in NIV 2011). But the meaning is plural (see v. 27), so the plural translation is justifiable, as for the various kinds of animals in the preceding verses.

21. So NRSV, ESV; or 'rule' (NIV, NJPS); 'be masters' (NJB).

22. NRSV and NJB add 'the wild animals of', on the basis of the Syriac, though neither MT nor other ancient versions have these words. Westermann, *Genesis 1–11*, p. 79, accepts the emendation (cf. Richard Bauckham, *Bible and Ecology: Rediscovering the Community of Creation* [Waco: Baylor University Press, 2010], p. 181, n. 33).

Then God blessed them, and God said to them, 'Be fruitful and multiply, and fill the earth and subdue it; and have dominion over the fish of the sea and over the birds of the sky, and over every living creature that moves[23] on the land.' (Vv. 26–28)

There are three major points in this text: human beings as the image of God, human dominion over other creatures, and God's blessing of human beings.

First, we read about God's plan to make human beings in his image and likeness (v. 26), followed by its enactment (v. 27). This is obviously an important statement about humanity, though its meaning is not entirely self-evident. In what way are we like God? Some have understood the statement quite literally to mean that human beings resemble God in physical appearance, and this might be supported by some of the appearances and visions of God in the OT (e.g. Gen. 3:8; 18:1–2; Isa. 6:1; Ezek. 1:26). However, there are also references to God's 'wings' (e.g. Ruth 2:12; Ps. 36:7), which surely are not intended to be taken literally. Traditional Christian exegesis has understood this statement about the image of God with reference to human spirituality and rationality, distinguishing us from other creatures.[24] Many alternative suggestions have been made, but perhaps the best is that of David Clines, who argues that human beings are appointed as God's representatives in this world.[25] This representation takes place on God's authority, and demands behaviour consistent with that of the one who is represented.

In a similar vein, Walter Houston shows that the text makes human beings 'God's responsible representatives on earth', an idea that is comparable to the ANE ideology of kingship, in which the king was understood to be the image of his god and to rule on behalf of the god.[26] Here this ideology is democratized, so that all human beings are seen in principle as representatives of God's rule on earth, and this is realized specifically in the role of Israel as God's holy people.[27] God entrusts us with the task of representing him and implementing

---

23. So NRSV, NIV, ESV, NET; cf. NJB; lit. 'creeps' (cf. NJPS); cf. 'scurry' (NLT2).

24. Barr, 'Man and Nature', p. 19; cf. Stott, *Issues*, p. 147.

25. David J. A. Clines, 'The Image of God in Man', *TynB* 19 (1968), pp. 53–103.

26. Walter J. Houston, '"And Let Them Have Dominion . . .": Biblical Views of Man in Relation to the Environmental Crisis', in E. A. Livingstone (ed.), *Studia Biblica 1978*, vol. 1: *Papers on Old Testament and Related Themes*, JSOTSup 11 (Sheffield: JSOT Press, 1979), pp. 161–184, esp. 165.

27. Davis, *Scripture*, p. 56; Burnside, *God, Justice, and Society*, pp. 153–154.

his will. We are to rule *on behalf of* God, not *instead of* God'.[28] Human rule in the world should therefore be modelled on divine rule. For example, God's rule is portrayed as that of a shepherd (Ps. 23; cf. John 10:1–18), and the same picture is used with reference to human leadership (e.g. Ezek. 34; 1 Pet. 5:1–4). God is merciful and gracious (Exod. 34:6), and this is the basis of his rule over his creatures (Ps. 145:8–16).[29]

So if the first point is God's creation of human beings in his image, the second is God's plan that human beings should exercise dominion over all other living creatures – in sea and sky, and on the land (v. 26). Human beings are created for a purpose. As God's representatives on earth, they are responsible for managing the rest of his creatures, ruling on God's behalf. This is significantly different from the Mesopotamian creation stories, where human beings are created to serve the gods, relieving them of the tiresome burden of labour.[30] The verb 'have dominion' (*rādâ*) is elsewhere concerned with relationships between people (e.g. Lev. 25:43; 1 Kgs 5:16 [Hebr. v. 30]) and nations (Lev. 26:17; 1 Kgs 4:24 [Hebr. 5:4]); Ps. 110:2; Isa. 14:2), and only here applied to dominion over the non-human creation. The use of force is implied in some of these texts, but this is to be accompanied by compassion (Lev. 25:43, 46, 53; Ps. 72:8, cf. vv. 12–14). Solomon's dominion is explicitly described as peaceful (1 Kgs 4:24).[31]

In verse 28 the verb 'have dominion' (*rādâ*) is repeated and supplemented with 'subdue' (*kābaš*). The meaning is not very different. The latter verb almost always implies the use of force, sometimes in connection with the triumph of good over evil (e.g. Mic. 7:19; Zech. 9:15), though also in more negative contexts (e.g. Esth. 7:8; Jer. 34:11, 16). In connection with the land, it elsewhere refers to occupation (e.g. Num. 32:22, 29; Josh. 18:1; 1 Chr. 22:18), so perhaps has the connotation here of taking possession.[32] Alternatively, it may be a reference to the hard work of agriculture (cf. Gen. 2:5, 15),[33] bearing in mind the struggle

---

28. Bauckham, *Bible and Ecology*, p. 30 (his italics).

29. See also Margaret Barker, *Creation: A Biblical Vision for the Environment* (London: T. & T. Clark, 2010), p. 195; Douglas J. Green, 'When the Gardener Returns: An Ecological Perspective on Adam's Dominion', in Toly and Block, *Keeping God's Earth*, pp. 267–275.

30. Walton, *Ancient Near Eastern Thought*, pp. 214–215.

31. Cf. Barr, 'Man and Nature', p. 22; Barker, *Creation*, p. 215.

32. Davis, *Scripture*, pp. 59–63, following a suggestion of Norbert Lohfink; cf. Bauckham, *Bible and Ecology*, p. 16.

33. Barr, 'Man and Nature', p. 22; Bauckham, *Bible and Ecology*, pp. 17, 22.

between man and earth that follows from human sin (cf. Gen. 3:17–19). In any case, to quote James McKeown, 'rather than implying empowerment to exercise dictatorial rule over the rest of creation, the verbs in this context of creation and blessing should be understood as indicating a supremacy that is harmonious and mutually beneficial'.[34] Davis suggests translating the preposition *bĕ* in verse 28b as 'among', understanding the kind of dominion envisaged as firm rather than harsh, indicating the unique role of human beings without separating them from the rest of creation.[35]

The third point is that God blesses human beings with a promise of descendants (v. 28). Although God's words seem to be a command ('Be fruitful and multiply . . .'), the emphasis is on divine blessing rather than human obedience. God-implanted instincts will ensure that men and women play their part in procreation, but without God's blessing the desired end will not be achieved. This point is also evident from narratives later in Genesis about several ancestors of Israel who were unable to have children without the intervention of God. Here it is the blessing of descendants that enables human beings to increase in number so there will be enough of them to exercise dominion over the earth.

Reflection

The theme of ruling or dominion is mentioned in connection with two days of creation. Sun and moon are to rule day and night respectively (day 4 – vv. 16–18; cf. Ps. 136:7–9). And human beings are to have dominion over all other creatures (day 6 – vv. 26–28). This may suggest that human dominion over the animal world is parallel to the rule of the heavenly lights over day and night.[36] It is presumably not meant in terms of literal rule, as of a king over his subjects, but perhaps indicates the keeping of order and being the dominant bodies in the sky and on the earth respectively.[37]

It is human dominion over creation that we consider here. Human beings are commissioned with the task of leading and organizing the rest of the created

---

34. James McKeown, *Genesis* (Grand Rapids: Eerdmans, 2008), p. 27; cf. Christoph Uehlinger, 'The Cry of the Earth? Biblical Perspectives on Ecology and Violence', in Leonardo Boff and Virgil Elizondo (eds.), *Ecology and Poverty: Cry of the Earth, Cry of the Poor*, Concilium 1995.5 (London: SCM, 1995), pp. 41–57, esp. 51–53; Burnside, *God, Justice, and Society*, pp. 156–157.

35. Davis, *Scripture*, pp. 54–55.

36. The Hebrew verbs are different, but the idea is similar.

37. Cf. Westermann, *Genesis 1–11*, pp. 132, 159.

world, in accordance with God's authority and power.[38] Made in God's image (1:26–28), we are his representatives on earth with the responsibility of managing the fish and birds, livestock and wild animals, and the whole earth (2:15). And since we are God's representatives, we are expected to care for the earth and its occupants in the way God would if he were physically here. We are not kings ruling our own land, but viceroys ruling on behalf of the true King.[39] This has implications for the way we treat the earth, including the amount of carbon we pour into the atmosphere, how we treat animals that provide us with food, and so on.

Dominion over the earth is not intended as permission for exploitation. That would be contrary to the OT concept of kingship, which is intended to be for the benefit of those ruled rather than the ruler himself (Deut. 17:16–20; Ps. 72, esp. vv. 12–14). This understanding of dominion is emphasized even more strongly in the NT, with Jesus' teaching on and example of servant leadership (Mark 10:42–45; Phil. 2:6–8). 'Dominion over the animals certainly does not mean their exploitation by humans,' to quote Claus Westermann, because 'people would forfeit their kingly role among the living . . . were the animals to be made the object of their whim'.[40]

Psalm 8 expresses the idea of human dominion poetically, using a different verb (*māšal*) but with no significant change in meaning:

> You have given them dominion over the works of your hands;
> you have put all things under their feet,
> all sheep and oxen,
> and also the beasts of the field,
> the birds of the air, and the fish of the sea,
> whatever passes along the paths of the seas. (Vv. 6–8, NRSV)

---

38. Gen. 2:19–20 may be the first recorded example of human dominion over the animals, here shown in giving them their names. If so, it may be noted that the animals – though under human authority – are pictured as companions rather than subjects (Wenham, *Genesis 1–15*, p. 33). However, George W. Ramsey, 'Is Name-Giving an Act of Domination in Genesis 2:23 and Elsewhere?', *CBQ* 50 (1988), pp. 24–35, esp. 34–35, argues that this is an act of discernment rather than domination (cf. Burnside, *God, Justice, and Society*, p. 160). Bauckham (*Bible and Ecology*, pp. 22–23) suggests that the man is simply 'recognising them as fellow-creatures with whom he shares the world'. Cf. Westermann, *Genesis 1–11*, pp. 228–229.

39. Stott, *Issues*, p. 150.

40. Westermann, *Genesis 1–11*, p. 159.

This psalm is quoted in the NT to suggest that human dominion of the world has not fulfilled God's purposes as intended, and will be perfected only by the dominion of the perfect man (1 Cor. 15:24–28; Heb. 2:6–9).[41] James points out that human beings are able to tame the natural world, but less able to tame their own tongues (3:7–8). Stott comments, 'human beings find it easier to subdue the earth than they do to subdue themselves'.[42]

So how does all this relate to human dominion over the earth today? In 1967 an American historian by the name of Lynn White published an article in *Science* magazine, in which he blames Christianity for the ecological crisis because it transformed humanity from being part of nature to become the exploiter of nature.[43] He argues that our 'implicit faith in perpetual progress'[44] was unknown to antiquity, where time was viewed as cyclical, and is a result of the linear view of time in Judeo-Christian theology. He traces this view back to the Genesis account of creation, in which 'God planned all this explicitly for man's benefit and rule: no item in the physical creation had any purpose save to serve man's purposes.'[45] As a result, he claims, 'Christianity is the most anthropocentric religion the world has seen.'[46] This leads White to conclude that 'modern science is an extrapolation of natural theology' and 'modern technology is at least partly to be explained as . . . realization of the Christian dogma of man's transcendence of, and rightful mastery over, nature'.[47] In the nineteenth century science and technology 'joined to give mankind powers which, to judge by many of the ecologic effects, are out of control. If so, Christianity bears a huge burden of guilt.'[48] So, '[d]espite Copernicus, all the cosmos rotates around our little globe. Despite Darwin, we are *not*, in our hearts, part of the natural process. We are superior to nature, contemptuous of it, willing to use it for

---

41. Derek Kidner, *Genesis*, TOTC (Leicester: Inter-Varsity Press, 1967), suggests on the basis of Rom. 8:19–23 and what is known of the pre-human world that 'there was a state of travail in nature from the first, which man was empowered to "subdue" (1:28) . . . until he relapsed instead into disorder himself' (p. 73).

42. Stott, *Issues*, p. 155.

43. Lynn White, 'The Historical Roots of Our Ecologic Crisis', *Science* 155 (1967), pp. 1203–1207; repr. in R. J. Berry (ed.), *The Care of Creation: Focusing Concern and Action* (Leicester: Inter-Varsity Press, 2000), pp. 31–42.

44. Ibid., p. 37.

45. Ibid.

46. Ibid., p. 38.

47. Ibid., p. 40.

48. Ibid.

our slightest whim.'[49] 'What we do about ecology depends on our ideas of the man–nature relationship. More science and more technology are not going to get us out of the present ecologic crisis until we find a new religion, or rethink our old one.'[50] White himself does not propose a new religion, but suggests rethinking Christianity with Francis of Assisi as a model, the saint who 'tried to depose man from his monarchy over creation and set up a democracy of all God's creatures'.[51] 'Since the roots of our trouble are so largely religious, the remedy must also be essentially religious, whether we call it that or not.'[52]

This is strong stuff, and requires serious consideration, but it is actually quite weak on biblical exegesis, as well as inadequate in terms of history. James Barr has shown that White overstates the connection between biblical faith and modern science.[53] It is true that some – though not all – of the great scientists have been Christians, and their faith was an inspiration in their discoveries. But it does not follow that they or their religion should be held responsible for the exploitation of nature by later generations. On the contrary, the biblical foundations of Jewish-Christian creation theology tend towards a duty to respect and protect the earth rather than a licence to exploit it. Barr points out that the exploitation of nature derives from liberal humanism, which does not take account of God and his purposes. The biblical ideal of dominion is leadership rather than exploitation.[54]

In a similar way Ronald Sider argues that modern consumerism is founded in individualism and materialism, originating in the Enlightenment, whereas biblical faith allows us to 'both enjoy material abundance and understand its limits', and therefore 'provides a solid foundation for caring for the creation entrusted to us by the Creator'.[55] 'Created in the divine image, we alone have been placed in charge of the Earth. At the same time, our dominion must be the gentle care of a loving gardener, not the callous exploitation of a self-centred

---

49. Ibid. (his italics).

50. Ibid., pp. 40–41.

51. Ibid., p. 41.

52. Ibid., p. 42.

53. Barr, 'Man and Nature', pp. 10–30. For another critique of White's proposal, from a different perspective, see Lawrence Osborn, *Guardians of Creation: Nature in Theology and the Christian Life* (Leicester: Apollos, 1993), pp. 24–32.

54. Barr, 'Man and Nature', p. 31; cf. Houston, 'Dominion', p. 167.

55. Ronald J. Sider, 'Biblical Foundations for Creation Care', in Berry, *Care of Creation*, pp. 43–49, esp. 48–49.

lordling . . .'[56] 'Dominion in this context is the exercise of God-given authority for the ultimate good of all.'[57] Only human beings are made in the image of God; but that means responsibility rather than rights.

It is true that anthropocentrism is at the heart of the environmental crisis, as indicated by White, but it is quite mistaken to claim that the Bible is anthropocentric. On the contrary, human beings are one of many kinds of creatures made by God. Like the heavenly lights, they have dominion over others. Like the fish and birds, they are blessed by God and encouraged to be fruitful and multiply. Other biblical creation texts are even less anthropocentric (Job 38 – 39; Ps. 104).[58] It would be more accurate to say the Bible is theocentric: Genesis 1 begins with God, Revelation 22 ends with God, and the chief actor in between is God.[59] Most biblical scholars today agree that Genesis gives us the responsibility for looking after the world God has created, not the right to exploit it selfishly.

Have human beings achieved dominion over the earth as intended by God? Stott considers that human beings have generally obeyed God's command to subdue the earth, in the research, discovery and invention that have enabled them to progress from food-gathering to agriculture to animal domestication to industrialization.[60] On the other hand, Davis points out that God's commands and actions in Genesis 1 are usually followed by a note confirming that his intention is fulfilled ('and it was so'), but this is not the case with the command to human beings to exercise dominion, perhaps leaving open the question of how far this command has been fulfilled in accordance with his intention.[61] In any case, we should not forget that our dominion takes place in cooperation with natural processes instituted and maintained by God.[62]

Food (Gen. 1:29–30; 2:8–9)

The third topic relating to creation and the environment in Genesis 1 – 2 is the

---

56. Ibid., p. 48.

57. McKeown, *Genesis*, p. 332.

58. As pointed out by Uehlinger, 'Cry', p. 50.

59. Cf. Carl E. Armerding, 'Biblical Perspectives on the Ecology Crisis', *JASA* 25.1 (1973), pp. 4–9.

60. Stott, *Issues*, p. 148.

61. Davis, *Scripture*, p. 59.

62. Stott, *Issues*, pp. 148–149.

provision of food for God's creatures. There are two complementary statements. In the first creation account we read:

> Then God said, 'See, I have given you every plant yielding seed that is on the face of all the earth, and every tree that has fruit yielding seed in it; they will be yours for food. And to every wild animal, and to every bird of the sky, and to everything that moves on the land – everything that has the breath of life – I have given every green plant for food'; and it was so. (1:29–30)

In the second account animals are not yet in the picture, so their diet is obviously not mentioned, and the focus is on one man and the garden in which he is placed:

> Then the LORD God planted[63] a garden in Eden, in the east; and he put there the man whom he formed. And the LORD God made all kinds of trees grow out of the ground, desirable[64] to the sight[65] and good for food; also the tree of life in the midst of the garden, and the tree of the knowledge of good and evil. (2:8–9)

It is interesting to note that God's provision of food for human beings contrasts with the Mesopotamian belief that humans were created to provide food for the gods.[66]

According to Davis, Genesis 1:29–30 (together with vv. 11–12) represents the plant world known to people living in the hill-country of Canaan and surrounding countries, emphasizing plants that produce seed.[67] Just as the location of Canaan at the meeting point of three continents was strategic in politics and economics, so it was genetically significant with a mixture of flora and fauna from Europe, Africa and Asia. Among this diversity of animal and

---

63. The translation 'planted' (NRSV, ESV, NJB, NJPS, NLT2; Wenham, *Genesis 1–15*, p. 61) is better than 'had planted' (NIV). While the pluperfect is possible linguistically, there is no indication that it is intended here, and it appears to be used by NIV in order to harmonize the order of creation with ch. 1. In any case, the planting of the garden is closer to God's provision of food in Gen. 1:29–30 than to the creation of plants in 1:11–12 (Westermann, *Genesis 1–11*, p. 208).

64. Cf. 3:6. Or 'pleasing' (NIV, NJPS; cf. NRSV, ESV). NJB translates *neḥmād* as 'enticing', which includes something of the connotation of 'covet' (cf. Exod. 20:17; Deut. 5:21; the word there is from the same root).

65. So NRSV, ESV, NJPS; or 'in appearance'; or 'to look at' (NJB, NET).

66. Cf. Walton, *Ancient Near Eastern Thought*, p. 215.

67. Davis, *Scripture*, pp. 48–53.

plant life there was an abundance of seed-bearing plants such as cereals and legumes. And in relation to food supplies seed was a key factor because it facilitated both storage of food and – in due course – agriculture.

The Garden of Eden (Gen. 2:8–9) is often viewed as an orchard, and it is true that fruit trees are the main focus in chapter 3, but it does not follow that there were *only* fruit trees in the garden. The description of the trees mentions variety ('all [kinds]'), beauty ('desirable to the sight') and nutrition ('good for food'). Ezekiel 31:8 alludes to a tradition that there were cedars and other great trees in Eden, designed to provide wood rather than food. Like the man (Gen. 2:7) and the animals (v. 19), the trees are made from the ground (v. 9).

Reflection

An interesting question that arises from these texts is whether the original diet God designed for humans and animals was vegetarian. At first sight, this is the implication of Genesis 1:29–30 and 2:9, 16; though there appears to be a distinction between the vegetarian food given to humans and to animals.[68] The former eat grain and fruit, whereas the latter eat green plants. Victor Hamilton understands these verses as a statement that both humans and animals were created vegetarian, just as they will be in the messianic age (Isa. 11:7; 65:25).[69] Westermann cites various Mesopotamian and Greek traditions that humanity was once vegetarian, unlike ancient Egyptian texts that mention meat as human food.[70] According to Derek Kidner, however, the assigning of every plant and tree for food to all creatures does not necessarily mean all creatures were once herbivorous, nor that all plants were once edible.[71] Rather, it is a general statement that God provides food for all his creatures from the earth.

After the flood God gives humanity permission to eat meat (9:3), in words that echo 1:29–30.[72] This permission apparently implies that humans have previously been vegetarian, though Gordon Wenham points to indications that meat may have been eaten earlier than that:[73]

68. Westermann, *Genesis 1–11*, p. 162.

69. Hamilton, *Genesis 1–17*, p. 140; cf. Westermann, *Genesis 1–11*, pp. 162, 208; Barr, 'Man and Nature', p. 21; William P. Brown, *The Ethos of the Cosmos: The Genesis of Moral Imagination in the Bible* (Grand Rapids: Eerdmans, 1999), p. 42.

70. Westermann, *Genesis 1–11*, pp. 162–164.

71. Kidner, *Genesis*, p. 52.

72. Three expressions in 9:3 are also found in the earlier text: 'they will be yours for food' (*lākem yihyeh lĕ'oklâ*); 'green plant[s]' (*yereq 'ēśeb*); 'I have given you' (*nātattî lākem*).

73. Wenham, *Genesis 1–15*, p. 34.

- God makes garments of skin for the first man and woman, presumably involving killing an animal (3:21)
- Abel keeps and sacrifices sheep (4:2–4)
- Noah distinguishes between clean and unclean animals (7:2).

According to this line of reasoning, Genesis 9:3 is legitimating meat-eating rather than beginning something new. It may be noted, however, that these possible allusions to meat-eating all refer to the period after the first sin, and there is no evidence of meat-eating in Genesis 1 – 2. Also, Noah takes all kinds of (implicitly vegetarian) food into the ark (6:21), for his family and the animals, and there is no indication that the animals themselves are to be eaten.

In any case, whatever conclusion we may draw about whether human beings were originally designed to be vegetarian, it is reasonable to conclude from the first two chapters of Genesis that their primary diet in the beginning was plants and fruits rather than animals. And in most later societies with which we are familiar, eating meat has been kept for special occasions, unlike affluent societies today where many eat meat almost every day. We should be aware that producing meat (and milk) has a significant effect on the atmosphere, since cows and other livestock release vast quantities of methane, even worse than carbon dioxide in terms of the greenhouse effect. Moreover, beef cattle consume vast quantities of grain and soybeans that could otherwise be eaten by human beings; not to mention the fact that in many cases these animals are kept in atrocious conditions.[74]

Agriculture (Gen. 2:5–7, 15–17)

There is an allusion to the beginning of agriculture in the second creation account. A negative statement about the absence of agriculture before the creation of human beings sets the scene:

> There was not yet any wild shrub[75] on the earth, nor had any wild plant sprung up; for the LORD God had not sent rain on the earth, and there was no one[76] to work the ground.

---

74. As pointed out by Davis, *Scripture*, pp. 97–99.
75. Cf. NJB, NLT2; lit. 'shrub of the field'. The expression is parallel to the terms for 'wild animal': *ḥayyat haśśādeh* (lit. 'living [creature] of the field') in 3:1, 14, and *ḥayyat hāʾāreṣ* (lit. 'living [creature] of the land/earth') in 1:25, 30 (cf. 1:24).
76. Lit. 'no man' or 'no human being'.

But a stream[77] used to come up from the earth and water the whole surface of the ground. Then the LORD God formed man[78] with dust from the ground, and breathed into his nostrils the breath of life; and the man became a living creature.[79] (2:5–7)

At the beginning of this account the earth is empty, without any plants or animals. There is moisture, though its exact nature is uncertain, but no vegetation. The repeated word 'any' (*kol*) emphasizes this point (v. 5).

Some scholars contrast the primeval desert landscape in verse 5 with the watery chaos of 1:2, while others argue that the first creation account is presupposed here and this passage is describing agricultural land before farming. Still others see a contrast between the situation before (2:5–6) and after (3:17–24) the creation and disobedience of human beings. In the absence of rain, and without human beings to irrigate the land, the stream is limited in value.[80] Kidner rejects the common view that verse 5 indicates dryness and verse 6 refers to a new development, arguing that both describe how things were at the beginning.[81] He points to a similar use of the verb translated 'water' (hiphil of *šāqâ*) in Ezekiel 32:6, where it means 'inundation'. If this is correct, the picture given here is not so very different from that in 1:2. The earth was not initially the hospitable place we know, but a watery waste.[82]

---

77. So NRSV; *DCH*, vol. 1, p. 118; cf. NIV; Westermann, *Genesis 1–11*, pp. 200–201. Alternatively, 'mist' (ESV, NIV marg.) or 'springs' (NET, NLT2). Wenham, *Genesis 1–15*, p. 58, suggests 'fresh water ocean', on the basis of Mesopotamian etymology.

78. So NRSV, NJB, NJPS; Hamilton, *Genesis 1–17*, p. 150; or 'a man' (NIV 2011); lit. 'the man' (so ESV, NET, NLT2, NIV 1984; Westermann, *Genesis 1–11*, p. 181). Alternatively, perhaps, 'a human being' (cf. 1:26–27) – since the question of gender has not yet arisen at this point.

79. So ESV; cf. Gen. 1:20–21, 24; 2:19; 9:10, 12, 15–16. Alternatively, 'living being' (so NRSV, NIV, NJB, NJPS, NET) or 'living person' (NLT2). However, it seems unnecessary to translate the expression here differently from its normal use in Genesis. The one place where it clearly has a different meaning is 1:30, where it means 'breath of life' – a concept here expressed by the phrase *nišmat ḥayyîm*.

80. Wenham, *Genesis 1–15*, pp. 57–59. On the first man as irrigationist, see Brown, *Ethos*, pp. 139–140.

81. Derek Kidner, 'Genesis 2:5, 6: Wet or Dry?', *TynB* 17 (1966), pp. 109–114.

82. Cf. David Toshio Tsumura, *Creation and Destruction: A Reappraisal of the Chaoskampf Theory in the Old Testament* (Winona Lake: Eisenbrauns, 2005), pp. 77–84; 'A Biblical Theology of Water: Plenty, Flood and Drought in the Created Order', in Toly and Block, *Keeping God's Earth*, pp. 165–184, esp. 169.

There is a play on words in verses 5–7 between man/human being (*'ādām*) and ground (*'ădāmâ*). *'Ādām* is made from *'ădāmâ*. An oft-cited English equivalent to the pun is 'human from the humus'. The two words appear again in close proximity in verses 8–9 and 19, and in 3:17–19, 22–24. This suggests a special relationship between human beings and the ground, which is developed further as the first man is placed in a garden, with the responsibility of looking after it and an invitation to enjoy its produce:

> The LORD God took the man; and he put him in the Garden of Eden, to work[83] it
> and to keep[84] it. And the LORD God commanded the man, 'You may freely eat from
> every tree of the garden. But from the tree of the knowledge of good and evil you
> shall not eat; for when[85] you eat from it you shall surely die.' (Vv. 15–17)

Verse 15 repeats the essence of verse 8 (that God planted the garden), with similar language but a new focus:

- Verse 8 focuses on God's role as planter of the garden.
- Verse 15 focuses on the man's role as gardener.

At the beginning, human beings are created for life in this world, with the task of working (*'ābad*) and keeping (*šāmar*) the land. The first verb is often used of cultivating the ground (e.g. 2:5; 3:23; 4:2, 12; Deut. 28:39; Prov. 12:11), and of work in a broader sense (e.g. Exod. 20:9), and is closely connected with the idea of service (e.g. 14:4; 15:14; Num. 3:7–8), having the same root as the noun 'servant/slave' (*'ebed*). The second denotes watchful preservation, often with the plain meaning of guarding something (e.g. Gen. 3:24; 4:9; 30:31) but also keeping God's covenant and commandments (e.g. 17:9–10; 18:19; 26:5) and God's caring for his people (e.g. 28:15, 20). Neither gives a licence for selfish exploitation: on the contrary, the connotation of 'service' in the first verb implies

---

83. So NIV, ESV; or 'till' (NRSV, NJPS); 'cultivate' (NJB); 'tend' (NLT2).

84. So NRSV, ESV; or 'take care of' (NIV, NJB); 'tend' (NJPS); 'maintain' (NET); 'watch over' (NLT2).

85. So NIV, NET; cf. NLT2; lit. 'on the day' (cf. NRSV, ESV, NJB). *Běyôm* is probably better translated 'when' than 'on the day', as in 2:4 and 5:1, because the man and woman do not die on the actual day they eat the fruit. This is confirmed by the similar expression in 1 Kgs 2:37, 42, which emphasizes urgency and certainty but does not indicate death on the precise day of the offence. So Hamilton, *Genesis 1–17*, p. 172; Westermann, *Genesis 1–11*, p. 224; contra Wenham, *Genesis 1–15*, p. 68.

that human beings work the land for the benefit of the latter, or at least for their mutual benefit; and that implication becomes explicit in the concept of 'preservation' in the second verb.[86]

It is clear here that work is part of human life from the first, not a result of sin. Some interpreters have disputed this, taking the last few words of verse 15 to be an addition to the text, viewing paradise as a place of perfect bliss where work would be unnecessary, but this idea is foreign to Genesis 2.[87] On the contrary, work is an essential part of human existence, just as it is an essential part of the divine rhythm in Genesis 1:1 – 2:3. Unlike the drudgery of work in Mesopotamian myths, imposed on humans to relieve the burden of the gods, the work assigned to human beings in Genesis is intimately related to the land on which they live and from which they draw their sustenance, and should be a joyful participation in God's creative work.[88]

The land is to be the source of food (v. 16; cf. 1:29; 3:17–19), and thus of continuing life. It has already been stated that the trees are good for food (v. 9); now the man is given permission to take advantage of this. But there is one exception (v. 17). The prohibition is stated very strongly in apodictic form ('you shall not . . .', as in the Decalogue), and followed by a motive clause. The latter is not a death sentence (which would be expressed by an infinitive with hophal, 'be put to death', e.g. Gen. 26:11; Exod. 21:12), but a warning of future punishment (infinitive with qal, 'die', e.g. Gen. 20:7; 1 Sam. 14:39; Ezek. 33:14). God does not give reasons for the prohibition, but simply warns of fatal consequences if the man disobeys. The fruit is apparently not poisonous, since the couple do not get sick or die as a direct result of eating it. Some have suggested the reference is to spiritual death, but there is no indication of that in the text. It seems more likely that the warning refers to physical death, as a punishment for disobedience.

Reflection

What does it mean to 'work' and 'keep' the earth (Gen. 2:15)? On the one hand, the word 'work' may be understood as giving human beings the right to use natural resources for their own benefit and that of others. At the same time, we should remember that the word 'work' in Hebrew includes the idea of service, which provides a balance to the idea of dominion in chapter 1. In any case, the

---

86. Sider, 'Biblical Foundations', p. 48; Davis, *Scripture*, pp. 29–32; cf. Block, 'To Serve and to Keep', p. 130.

87. Westermann, *Genesis 1–11*, p. 220; Brown, *Ethos*, pp. 140–141.

88. Cf. Westermann, *Genesis 1–11*, p. 222.

word 'keep' implies that the earth is to be worked responsibly, taking due consideration of the good of the earth itself. In other words, there is to be a balance between making the most of the good earth that God has created, and ensuring that the earth remains good for the benefit of all his creatures.

In relation to agriculture, one concern in today's world is the control of the global seed market by multinational corporations.[89] A few years ago Syngenta tried – unsuccessfully – to patent the flowering sequences of certain plants, to prevent farmers using their own crops to produce seed for the following year! Another control strategy, developed by the American government in conjunction with the seed industry, is sterile seed. This is produced by so-called 'Terminator' technology that makes the second generation of seed sterile so that farmers have to buy new seed each year instead of growing it themselves. Obviously Genesis does not envisage the ability to exercise this degree of control over crops, and therefore does not give ethical guidelines on the matter. However, it is clear that strategies of this kind are designed for the benefit of the wealthy, mostly in developed countries, without concern for the welfare of farmers and their customers. In contrast, OT law repeatedly advocates generosity to the poor, especially in connection with the produce of the land (cf. Exod. 23:10–11; Lev. 19:9–10; 23:22; 25:1–7; Deut. 14:28–29; 23:24–25; 24:19–22; 26:12–13).

Conclusion

To conclude, we may reflect on the beauty of nature as designed by God, the environment of its first human occupants. In the beginning it is good – very good indeed. There is a diversity of species, with food provided for all by the Creator. One species in particular – *Homo sapiens* – is created in the image of God, and given the duty and privilege of care for other creatures. They are to increase in number, work and keep the land, and exercise dominion over the animals.

The first account of creation concludes with a day of rest. However we envisage its value for God himself, the Sabbath clearly provides human beings with time to rest and opportunity for worship. And surely one of the ways we can best worship God is to appreciate the amazing world in which he has placed us. Spectacular views from mountain tops, fields of wild flowers stretching as far as the eye can see, desert dawns and seaside sunsets, walks through woods and by rivers – these are just a few reminders of the greatness of God.

---

89. Davis, *Scripture*, pp. 52–53.

Bible readers are well aware that the idyllic situation described in the first two chapters of Genesis does not last very long, and the entry of sin into the world brings toil and trouble (Gen. 3:17–19). The harmonious relationship between human beings and their environment is fundamentally changed as a result of the first man and woman's disobedience to their Creator (cf. Rom. 8:19–23).

Human pride and greed seemingly know no limits. While ultimate judgment on such hubris is undoubtedly in the hands of God (Gen. 11:1–9; Rev. 20:11–15), that does not absolve us from our present responsibility of caring for God's good creation. Christians should be deeply concerned about the degradation of the environment by people and their projects, and take whatever steps they can to reduce pollution, protect wildlife and mitigate climate change. At the same time, we can live in hope, remembering the promise of a new heaven and new earth (Rev. 21 – 22), where everything will not only be very good but 'far more than all we can ask or imagine' (Eph. 3:20 NRSV).

3. CURSING AND CHAOS: THE IMPACT OF HUMAN SIN ON CREATION AND THE ENVIRONMENT IN THE OLD TESTAMENT

Robin Routledge

Introduction

It is a popular view of Christian theology that when the first human beings sinned, not only did they 'fall', but because they had been given authority to rule over the earth as God's representatives, they were responsible for a 'cosmic fall' affecting the whole of the created order. The cursing of the ground in Genesis 3:17 as a consequence of human sin is seen to provide evidence for this idea, as is Paul's description of creation being 'subjected to futility' and in 'bondage to decay' (Rom. 8:20–21).[1]

This view implies that God's judgment in Genesis 3 brought a fundamental change in the order of creation, and the imposition into God's very good world (Gen. 1:31) of both moral and natural 'evil'. The latter is sometimes taken to include the introduction of 'thorns and thistles' (Gen. 3:18); and – if the picture of the harmony of the messianic kingdom in Isaiah 11:6–9 with its reference to the lion eating straw like the ox is viewed as a return to the way things were originally intended to be – predation and savagery within the animal kingdom: Tennyson's 'nature red in tooth and claw'.[2] A fallen world also faces natural disasters. Thus Calvin, in reference to Genesis 3:19, maintains that

---

1. Unless stated otherwise, all Scripture translations in this chapter are from the NRSV.

2. Alfred Lord Tennyson, 'In Memoriam A. H. H.' (LVI).

all the evils of the present life . . . proceeded from the same fountain. The inclemency of the air, frost, thunders, unseasonable rains, drought, hail and whatever is disorderly in the world, are the fruits of sin . . . the whole order of nature was subverted by the sin of man.[3]

John Stott, commenting on Romans 8:20–21, notes that 'nature shared the curse' of Genesis 3:17–19 and goes on, 'nature is out of joint because under judgement'.[4] Douglas Moo, in what he admits is a simplistic statement, notes that 'the first humans, created in God's image, failed to obey the Lord their God and brought ruin on themselves and the entire world'.[5]

In the light of current environmental debates there is a need here for circumspection. Natural disasters, and natural evil in general, are so called because they are not directly causally related to human activity. Increased understanding of the effect human beings have on the environment means that what we term 'natural' in this context will need to be modified. Nevertheless, there remain some things that cannot be blamed entirely on human beings; and such things are seen as the result of a cosmic fall that has affected the whole of the created order.

This view, though, has recently been called into question.[6] One reason is that it raises serious scientific issues. It is incompatible with an evolutionary view of the cosmos; and while a literal interpretation of Genesis 1 – 3 may allow for a fundamental ontological change in the order of creation, that is not how many Christians view those chapters. It seems significant that several recent theological discussions of the 'origin' of natural evil are set, also, within the context of scientific discussion. One such is the kenotic view of John Polkinghorne and others,[7] that in creating the world God limited himself. This so-called 'free will' or 'free process' defence maintains that God could not create any

---

3. John Calvin, *Genesis* (Edinburgh: Banner of Truth Trust, 1975), p. 177.

4. John R. W. Stott, *The Message of Romans*, BST (Leicester: Inter-Varsity Press, 1994), pp. 238–239; see also e.g. C. E. B. Cranfield, *The Epistle to the Romans*, vol. 1 (Edinburgh: T. & T. Clark, 1975), p. 413; Jonathan A. Moo, 'Continuity, Discontinuity, and Hope: The Contribution of New Testament Eschatology to a Distinctively Christian Environmental Ethos', *TynB* 61.1 (2010), pp. 21–44 (26–29).

5. Douglas J. Moo, 'Nature in the New Creation: New Testament Eschatology and the Environment', *JETS* 49.3 (2006), pp. 449–488 (457).

6. E.g. John J. Bimson, 'Reconsidering a "Cosmic Fall"', *SCB* 18.1 (2006), pp. 63–81.

7. E.g. John Polkinghorne (ed.), *The Work of Love: Creation as Kenosis* (Grand Rapids: Eerdmans, 2001).

world he chose, for example a world free from evil, without also removing creaturely freedom, and with it the potential for good.[8] Polkinghorne argues that 'the same biochemical processes that allow cells to mutate and produce new forms of life will allow other cells to mutate and become malignant'.[9] More recently, Bonting has argued that creation is God's continuing transformation of initial chaos. As such, it is not a single completed act followed by a 'fall', but an ongoing process, which will be brought to fulfilment at the end of time. This allows for both cosmic and biological evolution; and natural and moral evil is the result of the chaos that remains, before its final, eschatological, defeat.[10]

It is not my intention here to engage in that (albeit important) scientific discussion. It may be helpful, apologetically, to have an understanding of origins that is compatible with current scientific enquiry; however, when looking at the *theological* outlook of *the OT writers*, the discussion needs to be set against their particular (non-scientific) world view; and focusing too much on the scientific may detract from a proper understanding of *theological significance*.

More important for the purpose of this discussion, is whether or not the idea of a cosmic fall is compatible with the OT. John Bimson, for example, argues that the OT writers do not refer to such an event to explain the world as they saw it; in fact they imply '*nothing at all about the natural world being fallen or distorted in any way*',[11] and instead regard the creation as being as good as when God made it – continuing to reveal his glory. However, while the idea of a

---

8. According to Plantinga, 'a world containing creatures who are significantly free (and freely perform more good than evil actions) is more valuable . . . than a world containing no free creatures at all' (Alvin C. Plantinga, *God, Freedom, and Evil* [Grand Rapids: Eerdmans, 1974], p. 30).

9. John Polkinghorne, *Scientists as Theologians* (London: SPCK, 1996), p. 48; cf. his *Science and Religion in Quest for Truth* (London: SPCK, 2011), p. 61. Some 'process theologians' argue that 'free process' is the result of God's *actual*, rather than *self* limiting: creaturely freedom is an eternal metaphysical reality that even God cannot override; see e.g. Ian G. Barbour, *Nature, Human Nature and God* (Minneapolis: Augsburg Fortress, 2002), pp. 104–116; see also John B. Cobb, Jr., and David Ray Griffin, *Process Theology: An Introductory Exposition* (Philadelphia: Westminster, 1976); Jay Bird McDaniel and Donna Bowman (eds.), *Handbook of Process Theology* (Atlanta: Chalice, 2006).

10. Sjoerd L. Bonting, *Creation and Double Chaos: Science and Theology in Discussion* (Minneapolis: Fortress, 2005).

11. Bimson, 'Reconsidering', p. 71 (his italics).

cosmic fall has limitations, and some OT passages do indicate that God's glory continues to be reflected in creation (e.g. Pss 8; 19:1–4a),[12] there is the indication, too, of a significant change in the created order as a result, not only of sinful humans, but also of human sin.

A world 'out of joint'

Acknowledgment that the world is not as it should be appears to be reflected in several parts of the OT. The problem of innocent suffering raised in the book of Job, as well as other aspects of theodicy, indicate a sense of dissatisfaction with the world as it is. And though, in Job's case, God responds by emphasizing his role as Creator and pointing out Job's very limited understanding of the world, Job's suffering is not just part of 'the way things are'. Indeed, with the emphasis, in Job 38 – 41, on God's inscrutability as Creator, this might be a good place to make such a claim; but the Prologue offers a different explanation. There are things that Job is unaware of, but there is no sense that his suffering is built, intentionally, into the order of creation. Ecclesiastes, too, reflects on the imperfections in creation. In what may be the longest *inclusio* in the OT, the writer declares life, the universe and everything, to be 'meaningless'. The world is unfair; life is unfair; and human beings need to recognize that and find happiness and fulfilment where they can. Again, the overwhelmingly negative tones of the writer indicate that, for him, this is not the way it should be; and there is the hope that God's justice will ultimately prevail.

In their view of the coming kingdom of God, the prophets also anticipate a transformation of the natural order. The picture in Isaiah 11:6–9 of natural enemies living side by side, and even of the lion eating straw like the ox is, in my view, figurative;[13] it points to peace and harmony in the era of salvation. But for that figure to be meaningful, it must be seen to represent not a distortion of the natural order, but a recognizable and welcome move to something better: to an ideal to which the present, natural, order of things

---

12. Though that potential may be lessened by human sinfulness; see e.g. Terence E. Fretheim, *God and World in the Old Testament: A Relational Theology of Creation* (Nashville: Abingdon, 2005), p. 284.

13. It seems unlikely that this is a literal description of the new age; see e.g. John Goldingay, *Isaiah*, NIBC (Peabody: Hendrickson, 2001), pp. 85–88; John N. Oswalt, *Isaiah 1–39*, NICOT (Grand Rapids: Eerdmans, 1986), pp. 283–284.

does not attain. The prophets' vision of abundance in the coming age again represents an ideal that contrasts with the possibility of drought and famine in the present age,[14] and similarly indicates that the world as it is is not all that it could be. And if, as is often suggested, that coming age, with its peace, harmony and abundance, is in a sense a 'return to Eden',[15] then this would further suggest that not only is the world not as it could be, *but it is not as it was when God made it.* The OT writers may not attribute that change directly to a cosmic fall, and they continue to celebrate the goodness of God's creation, and rejoice in his present blessing; but there is a recognition, too, that all is not as God intended.

We see a significant indication of a world gone wrong in the change in God's expressed intentions for human beings between the blessings of Genesis 1:28 and 9:1–3; the first addressed to Adam and Eve; the second to Noah – who stands, essentially, where Adam stood, in the new beginning that follows the flood.[16] The relationship between these passages has been discussed in some detail by Lawrence Turner,[17] who notes that of the three imperatives in the former blessing – namely, 'be fruitful and multiply, and fill the earth', 'subdue' (*kābaš*) the earth, and 'have dominion (*rādâ*) over the fish of the sea and over the birds of the air and over every living thing that moves upon the earth' – the first is repeated verbatim (Gen. 9:1) to Noah; while the other two have been substantially revised in the light of intervening events.[18]

---

14. E.g. Isa. 32:14–20; 51:3; Joel 2:18–27.

15. Commenting on Isa. 11:6–9 Clements suggests that the imagery is traditional, representing 'a return to the conditions of a paradise that will be enjoyed in the idyllic future age' (R. E. Clements, *Isaiah 1–39*, NCB [London: Marshall, Morgan & Scott, 1980], pp. 121–124 [122]); Childs also suggests that it refers to 'the restoration of creation by a new act of God' (Brevard S. Childs, *Isaiah*, OTL [Louisville: Westminster John Knox, 2001], p. 104). See also John Goldingay, *The Message of Isaiah 40–55: A Literary-Theological Commentary* (London: T. & T. Clark, 2005), pp. 422–423; R. N. Whybray, *Isaiah 40–66*, NCB (London: Marshall, Morgan & Scott, 1975), p. 155; Gordon Wenham, 'The Old Testament and the Environment: A Response to Chris Wright', *Transformation* 16.3 (1999), pp. 86–92 (88, 90).

16. See e.g. Victor Hamilton, *Genesis 1–17*, NICOT (Grand Rapids: Eerdmans, 1990), p. 313; Gordon J. Wenham, *Genesis 1–15*, WBC 1 (Dallas: Word, 1987), p. 192.

17. Lawrence A. Turner, *Announcements of Plot in Genesis*, JSOTSup 96 (Sheffield: JSOT Press, 1990), pp. 21–49.

18. See also Walter J. Houston, 'Sex or Violence? Thinking Again with Genesis About Fall and Original Sin', in Nathan MacDonald, Mark W. Elliott and Grant Macaskill

The term *rādâ* (have dominion) may refer to domination over (or by) enemies;[19] and an interpretation of the relationship between human beings and the environment along those lines has been held responsible for the alleged view, within Western Christendom, that the earth and its resources exist for the sole benefit of human beings – thus excusing both exploitation of the environment and indifference towards environmental issues.[20] Maybe partly as a (right) response to that criticism, commentators play down this aspect of *rādâ* – noting that, in the OT, such dominion should not be harsh;[21] and that the term is used to refer to the beneficent rule of the ideal king (Ps. 72:8) whose goal is to maintain security, peace and prosperity,[22] and to defend, rather than exploit,

---

(eds.), *Genesis and Christian Theology* (Grand Rapids: Eerdmans, 2011), pp. 140–151 (143–145). Houston suggests that Gen. 9:2–3 reflects the world as it is, while Gen. 1:2–30 expresses the ideal; though he notes further that while Gen. 1:28–30 points to the ideal past, the future ideal is reflected in Isa. 11:6–9.

19. E.g. Lev. 26:17; Neh. 9:28; Ps. 110:2; Isa. 14:2, 6; see John Goldingay, *Old Testament Theology*, vol. 1: *Israel's Gospel* (Downers Grove: IVP Academic; Milton Keynes: Paternoster, 2003), p. 110; James McKeown, *Genesis* (Grand Rapids: Eerdmans, 2008), p. 27. More generally, see Philip J. Nel, '*rdh*', in *NIDOTTE*, vol. 3, pp. 1055–1056; H.-J. Zobel, '*rādâ*', in *TDOT*, vol. 13, pp. 330–336.

20. E.g. Lynn White, 'The Historic Roots of Our Ecologic Crisis', *Science* 155 (1967), pp. 1203–1207. For comments on White's position, see e.g. R. J. Berry, 'A Christian Approach to the Environment', *Transformation* 16.3 (1999), pp. 73–74; Walter Brueggemann, *Genesis*, Interpretation (Atlanta: John Knox, 1982), pp. 32–33; David E. Engel, 'Elements in a Theology of Environment', *Zygon* 5.3 (1970), pp. 216–228; Hamilton, *Genesis 1–17*, p. 138; Hugh Montefiore, 'Why Aren't More People Interested in the Environment?', *Transformation* 16.3 (1999), pp. 74–77 (75–76); Alister McGrath, 'Recovering the "Creation": A Response to Hugh Montefiore', *Transformation* 16.3 (1999), pp. 78–80; D. J. Moo, 'Nature in the New Creation', pp. 449–452; Chris Wright, 'Theology and Ethics of the Land', *Transformation* 16.3 (1999), pp. 81–86 (82).

21. E.g. Lev. 25:43, 46, 53; cf. Isa. 14:6; Ezek. 34:4.

22. E.g. Ps. 72:8; 1 Kgs 5:24–25. For discussion of links between *rādâ* and the relationship between king and people, see James Limburg, 'The Responsibility of Royalty: Genesis 1–11 and the Care of the Earth', *WW* 11.2 (1991), pp. 124–130 (125–126). This view is reflected regularly in commentaries; see e.g. Hamilton, *Genesis 1–17*, pp. 137–138; Wenham, *Genesis 1–15*, p. 33; Claus Westermann, *Genesis 1–11* (London: SPCK, 1984), pp. 158–159; though see Goldingay, *Israel's Gospel*, p. 110.

those in his care (e.g. Ezek. 34:4). In my view the gentle, nurturing aspect of *rādâ* is overplayed.[23] However, it can be argued from the usage of the term in the OT that 'dominion' does not need to be harsh, aggressive or exploitative; and the link with kingship does suggest concern for the well-being of those over whom dominion is exercised.[24] This dominion is also linked with being made in God's image (Gen. 1:26),[25] indicating that human beings rule not in their own right but on God's behalf. As such, *rādâ* points to the significant role of human beings who, as God's representatives, exercise rule over, and responsible stewardship towards, the created order.

In contrast, Genesis 9:2–3 points to a despotic reign over other creatures based on fear and dread,[26] in which animals, birds and fish are delivered into

---

23. Limburg suggests that the emphasis of *rādâ* 'is on gentleness and on an active program of caring that results in *shalom*' ('Responsibility of Royalty', p. 126); and notes that Solomon's 'dominion' over the whole region west of the Euphrates (1 Kgs 4:24) led to Judah and Israel living in safety (v. 25). But was his rule over the other nations devoted equally to *their* safety? In the 'dominion' of the ideal king in Ps. 72:8, 'foes bow down before him and his enemies lick the dust' (v. 9) – again suggesting that not all benefit equally from his reign (though cf. Brueggemann, *Genesis*, pp. 32–33). Goldingay argues that *rādâ* points to mastery and coercion, though allows that this does not need to be harsh or exploitative. He maintains that a 'dog eat dog' world is not God's intention, but nor is it the result of a 'fall'; and suggests that human dominion includes working towards the ideal represented by Isa. 11:6–9 (Goldingay, *Israel's Gospel*, pp. 110–111); though in my view that argument is not convincing.

24. Brueggemann suggests that 'the task of "dominion" does not have to do with exploitation and abuse. It has to do with securing the well-being of every other creature and bringing the promise of each to full fruition' (*Genesis*, p. 32); see also Joseph Blenkinsopp, *Creation, Un-Creation, Re-Creation: A Discursive Commentary on Genesis 1–11* (London: T. & T. Clark, 2011), p. 26. See also Richard Bauckham, 'First Steps to a Theology of Nature', *EvQ* 58.3 (1986), pp. 229–244 (235–238); 'Humans, Animals, and the Environment in Genesis 1–3', in MacDonald, Elliott and Macaskill, *Genesis and Christian Theology*, pp. 175–189 (179–183); Ken Gnanakan, *God's World: A Theology of the Environment* (London: SPCK, 1999), pp. 51–59.

25. For further discussion of this, see Robin Routledge, *Old Testament Theology: A Thematic Approach* (Nottingham: Apollos, 2009; Downers Grove: IVP Academic, 2009), pp. 139–141.

26. Commentators note a significant negative change from Gen. 1:28 in the relationship between human beings and animals; see e.g. Hamilton, *Genesis 1–17*, pp. 313–314; John E. Hartley, *Genesis*, NIBC (Peabody: Hendrickson, 2000), p. 109; McKeown, *Genesis*,

the hands of human beings, as food. Thus the text points to a fundamental change, both in the relationship between human beings and the animal kingdom, and in human eating habits.[27] Whereas previously green plants seem to have been provided as humankind's staple diet (Gen. 9:3; cf. 1:29), now, quite literally, everything is on the table!

A further significant change in the relationship between human beings and creation is evident in the total omission of the reference, in Genesis 9, to 'subduing (*kābaš*) the earth'.[28] Like *rādâ*, *kābaš* may indicate hostile domination,[29] and some have taken that to portray the relationship between human beings and the created world as a struggle from the start. It seems reasonable, though, in this context, to take *kābaš* in a similar way to *rādâ*,[30] to indicate responsible dominion over the earth.

Gordon Wenham points to the need for human beings to 'control their environment';[31] an example of which might be working or tilling the

---

pp. 63–64; Gerhard von Rad, *Genesis*, rev. ed. (London: SCM, 1972), pp. 131–132; Wenham, *Genesis 1–15*, p. 192; Westermann, *Genesis 1–11*, pp. 462–463 (though Westermann challenges the extent of the change as represented by von Rad). Cassuto takes a more positive view: as a result of being saved from the flood, animals 'would realise more clearly the superiority of the human species'; see Umberto Cassuto, *A Commentary on the Book of Genesis*, pt. 2 (Jerusalem: Magnes, 1964), p. 125.

27. See e.g. Wenham, 'Old Testament and the Environment', p. 88.

28. Turner, *Announcements*, pp. 33–41.

29. See e.g. Philip J. Nel, '*kbš*', in *NIDOTTE*, vol. 2, p. 596; S. Wagner, '*kābaš*', in *TDOT*, vol. 7, pp. 52–57. It is used in the OT to refer to subduing enemies (2 Sam. 8:11; Zech. 9:15), subjection of slaves (Neh. 5:5; 2 Chr. 28:10; Jer. 34:11, 16), and, possibly, rape (Neh. 5:5; Esth. 7:8). It also refers to the subjugation of the 'land' (*hā'āreş*), linked with the conquest (Num. 32:22, 29; Josh. 18:1) and with David's reign (2 Chr. 28:10). This appears to refer, primarily, to defeating enemies; but the similarity of the language may indicate a conscious allusion to Gen. 1:28; and may relate to the 'rest' that is associated with creation and the institution of the Sabbath (Gen. 2:2–3), and also with the possession of the land (e.g. Deut. 3:20; Josh. 1:15; 21:44; 24:4), and David's reign (2 Sam. 7:1; 1 Chr. 23:25; cf. 1 Kgs 5:4; 8:56).

30. See e.g. Westermann, *Genesis 1–11*, p. 161.

31. Wenham, 'Old Testament and the Environment', p. 89. Bauckham, too, suggests that human mastery over nature involves what all creatures need to do: adapt the environment to meet their needs ('First Steps', p. 236). In Fretheim's view, referring to the creation as 'very good' does not imply that there was no possibility of further development (*God and World*, p. 41).

ground,[32] which was still a requirement in the garden (Gen. 2:15), in order to produce crops that are beneficial for human beings. Genesis 2:5 further points to the centrality of cultivating the ground (*hā'ădāmâ*),[33] noting the absence of anyone to fulfil that function, and so anticipating the role, within the wider created world, of soon-to-be-created human beings. It could be argued that this corresponds to the directive in Genesis 1:28 to 'fill the earth and subdue it',[34] and so points to God's intention for the Edenic ideal to be extended to the whole world. This intention might be reflected further in Genesis 2:10, where the river that waters Eden spreads out to water the rest of the earth.[35]

---

32. The Hebrew verb *'ābad*, translated in Gen. 2:5, 15 as 'work' (NIV) or 'till' (NRSV), also means 'serve'. Ellen F. Davis, *Scripture, Culture, and Agriculture: An Agrarian Reading of the Bible* (Cambridge: Cambridge University Press, 2009), argues that *'ābad* is not an agricultural term, and in the light of its wider meaning refers to human beings 'serving' the soil (pp. 28–30); see also Fretheim, *God and World*, p. 53. This has been taken to indicate that 'dominion' over the earth entails non-exploitative stewardship and care for the well-being of the natural order. However, as in the discussion of *rādâ* above, this should not be pressed too far. According to Ringgren, in this context, with an inanimate object, *'ābad* means 'to work on, develop, cultivate' (H. Ringgren, "*'ābad*', in *TDOT*, vol. 10, pp. 376–390 [382–383]); see also Eugene Carpenter, "*'bd*', in *NIDOTTE*, vol. 3, pp. 304–309. Nevertheless, though human beings do not 'serve' the earth, cultivating the earth may be viewed as part of the service of human beings to God; thus Carpenter describes working the ground as 'an inherently religious act when done to fulfil the Creator's purposes' (p. 304).

33. For further discussion of the centrality of agriculture within the Genesis creation account(s), see e.g. Davis, *Scripture*, pp. 42–65.

34. Turner argues that tilling the soil may be subsumed under the command to 'subdue the earth' (*Announcements*, pp. 34–35). Fretheim, similarly, suggests that 'the point made about the role of the human in 1:26–28 is essentially the same as that stated in 2:5' (*God and World*, p. 53). Bauckham also takes 'subduing the earth' to refer to agriculture; he suggests a close connection between 'subduing' and 'filling' the earth and notes that 'the only way humans are able to fill the land is to cultivate it and so make it yield more food than it would of its own accord' ('Humans, Animals', p. 180).

35. Gen. 2:10–14 is generally regarded as an insertion (see e.g. Wenham, *Genesis 1–15*, p. 64; Westermann, *Genesis 1–11*, p. 194), suggesting narrative significance. It is not certain from the text of v. 10 whether the river rose in or just outside the garden (see e.g. Westermann, *Genesis 1–11*, p. 216); it does seem clear, though, that the same river that watered the garden extended beyond it. Its division, outside the garden,

In the blessing of Genesis 9:2–3, however, there appears to be the recognition that such control over the environment, and with it the wider extension of Edenic blessing, has been severely limited. This does, though, need to be seen in relative terms. Cultivation and agriculture continue outside the garden – though now with increased difficulty. It may no longer be appropriate to describe that struggle as 'subduing the earth'; but it is reasonable to suppose that elements of that mandate remain – particularly as it relates to human beings seeking to control their environment through tilling the soil.

Cursing the ground

A crucial question here is: What has accounted for the change between Genesis 1:28 and 9:1–3? One answer is provided by the narrative in Genesis 3, which culminates in divine judgment, including the cursing of the ground (*hā'ădāmâ*). Turner suggests that all three elements in Genesis 1:28 are affected by God's judgment in Genesis 3:17–19;[36] though, as already noted, the most serious impact is on human ability to 'subdue the earth'. If, as seems widely agreed, this may be related, primarily, to cultivating the ground, then it stands in direct relationship to the curse in Genesis 3:17, which also affects the ground. This takes us back to the idea of a 'fall' that affects not only human beings, but also has a direct impact on the rest of the created order.[37] As noted already, the OT writers do not refer explicitly to a universal fall to explain the current state of the world, any more than they note the continuing impact of the sin of the first pair on subsequent generations of human beings. However, while that latter event is not described explicitly as a 'fall', many scholars do take the narrative of Genesis 3 to point to a decisive event that

---

into four further rivers might suggest completeness and universality: the fruitfulness associated with the garden flows to the four corners of the earth. See Wenham, *Genesis 1–15*, pp. 64–65; Westermann, *Genesis 1–11*, pp. 216–217; however, cf. Cassuto, *Genesis*, pt. 2, pp. 114–121.

36. Turner, *Announcements*, p. 23.

37. In Gen. 3 Adam and Eve are not cursed directly. The terms of the curse on Cain (Gen. 4:11) are similar, the ground will not yield its fruit, but in this latter case the curse is directed at the offender. This variation may reflect Cain's more serious sin; but might also indicate that the curse in Gen. 3:17 is not simply to punish the first human pair, but has wider implications.

had a lasting impact on human beings; what Eichrodt describes as 'a falling out of line of the development willed by God'.[38] Might the same reasoning not be applied to the wider impact of human sin and the divine curse on the rest of the created order – even without an explicit reference to creation's 'fall'?[39]

An important consideration here is the effect of the curse. Cursing in the

---

38. Walther Eichrodt, *Theology of the Old Testament*, 2 vols. (London: SCM, 1961–7), vol. 2., p. 406. Goldingay doubts the appropriateness of the term 'fall', though he acknowledges that 'at the beginning of the human story something happened that brought about a once-for-all negative change to humanity's situation' (*Israel's Gospel*, pp. 144–148 [145]). Eichrodt points, further, to 'a decisive event, by which God's plan for Man in his creation was frustrated and human history came to be branded with the stamp of enmity towards God. This event has the character of a "Fall", that is a falling out of line of the development willed by God' (Eichrodt, *Theology*, vol. 2, p. 406). The location of this narrative at the beginning of the primeval history might also be viewed as significant: setting the scene for all that follows, and particularly the continuing decline into sin. Cf. Terence E. Fretheim, *The Pentateuch*, IBT (Nashville: Abingdon, 1996), pp. 76–81; *God and World*, pp. 70–75. See also Routledge, *Old Testament Theology*, pp. 154–156.

39. While recognizing the difficulties in assessing how much of the evil in the world can be attributed to the 'fall of humanity', Christopher Wright notes that 'the event described in Genesis 3 is certainly portrayed as having radically distorted and fractured our relationship with the earth itself, and also . . . as having frustrated the creation's function in relation to God' ('Theology and Ethics', p. 82); see also Christopher J. H. Wright, *The Mission of God: Unlocking the Bible's Grand Narrative* (Downers Grove: IVP Academic, 2006), pp. 432–433. Bauckham also notes that the fall of human beings has had an impact on the environment ('First Steps', p. 240); and while expressing reservations about the traditional view that 'the fall of Adam and Eve led to the fall of nature', he goes on to suggest that 'in terms of the effects of the human fall on our relationship with nature . . . this sequence still has validity' (p. 241). Though cautious about referring to a 'fall', Houston acknowledges that there is 'fallenness': 'that creation has fallen from the intention of God is shown with the utmost clarity' ('Sex or Violence?', p. 146). Gnanakan, too, points to the 'sin and fall of human beings from God's originally intended purposes', and this leads to 'environmental complications and ecological disasters' (*God's World*, p. 47).

OT is generally presented as the antithesis of blessing;[40] in this case it results in the increased difficulty that human beings will have extracting a living from the soil, in contrast to the blessings of life in the garden. This appears to have significant parallels with the blessings and curses associated with breaking the Sinaitic covenant: obedience to the covenant results in blessing in the land (e.g. Deut. 28:1–14); conversely, disobedience results in curses (e.g. Deut. 28:15–68), which include *hardship in the land* (in which the failure of agriculture plays a large part) and eventual *removal from the land* (Deut. 28:63–68). These treaty curses culminate in the exile; and that seems to be reflected in the judgment in Genesis 3, particularly in the expulsion from, and hardship of life outside, the garden. It is not clear whether the *thorns and thistles* that will contribute to that hardship came into existence only as a result of the curse.[41] In my view these are not inherently evil and do have a role within the created order – *but in the right place*. The problem here appears to be not their existence, but the fact that following the cursing of the ground they will now grow among crops and will have an adverse effect on the task of cultivating the soil, thus impinging, negatively, on human welfare and well-being. The result is a 'dissonance in creation' between toil and reward, which, according to von Rad, 'is not accounted for by God's original ordinance'.[42]

And what about animal predation? Was this, too, the result of 'the falling out

---

40. See e.g. Robin Routledge, 'Blessings and Curses', in *Dictionary of the Old Testament: Prophets* (Downers Grove: IVP Academic, 2012), pp. 60–64; see also Herbert Chanan Brichto, *The Problem of 'Curse' in the Hebrew Bible* (Philadelphia: SBL, 1963); Robert Gordon, 'Curse, Malediction', in *NIDOTTE*, vol. 4, pp. 491–493; Josef Scharbert, ''ālâ', in *TDOT*, vol. 1, pp. 261–266; ''rr', in *TDOT*, vol. 1, pp. 405–418; 'brk', in *TDOT*, vol. 2, pp. 279–308; 'qll', in *TDOT*, vol. 13, pp. 37–44.

41. Gen. 2:5 points to the general absence of vegetation before God planted the garden, and notes two groups in particular: *śîaḥ* and *'ēśeb*, maybe corresponding to wild shrubs that require only rain to grow, and cultivated plants that require human care. The general view is that this verse depicts arid desert, with Eden planted as an oasis; though Kidner takes the reference to a river watering the earth (Gen. 2:6) to suggest a watery scene, corresponding to Gen. 1:2; see Derek Kidner, 'Genesis 2:5, 6: Wet or Dry?', *TynB* 17 (1966), pp. 109–114. In either case, the absence of plant life may suggest an early stage in the creation process; and does not rule out the later existence of non-cultivated plants outside the garden. Although there is no further mention of rain until the flood narrative, we might suppose that there was beneficial rain in the meantime, making such plant life possible.

42. Von Rad, *Genesis*, p. 95.

of line of the development willed by God'? Genesis 1:30 gives reason to suppose that animals, like humans, were, originally, vegetarian.[43] Perhaps more significant for the OT writers would have been their concern for their own welfare and that of their domesticated animals – and the threat posed to both by predators. That threat is the primary focus of Isaiah's vision of the 'peaceful kingdom'; and if this vision recalls, and points to a restoration of, the Edenic ideal, we can infer that predation – particularly as it affects human well-being – was not seen as part of the intended order of creation.

It has been suggested that these hardships already existed outside the garden, and that the curse consists, primarily, in removing human beings from a cossetted setting into a more hostile environment.[44] That, though, seems to be putting things the wrong way round. I have argued that Genesis 1:28 and 2:5 point to God's intention to extend the blessings associated with life in Eden, as human beings 'subdue' the earth, primarily through what appears from the text to be a key task in relation to creation: cultivating the ground (Gen. 2:5, 15). The cursing of that same 'ground', however, prevents human beings from fulfilling that goal. The curse, then, lies not primarily in *removal to a hostile environment*, but in the fact that an environment that might otherwise have been 'subdued' will remain hostile and will continue to resist humankind's best efforts. Because the world at large is not as it should be, the reversal of the curse may be viewed, figuratively, as a return to Eden. As already noted, this is particularly relevant to the Babylonian exile: expulsion from the land corresponds to expulsion from

---

43. The provision of vegetation for human beings and animals in Gen. 1:29–30 does not specifically exclude eating meat and so does not explicitly confirm that they were vegetarian. However, Gen. 9:3 seems to imply that eating meat in contrast to 'green plants' is something new, suggesting that human beings at least may have had an exclusively vegetarian diet. By extension, it does not seem unreasonable to take the similar reference to providing animals with 'every green plant for food' (Gen. 1:30) also to indicate an exclusively vegetarian diet.

44. Bimson e.g. argues that following the curse, 'the chief contrast [Adam] is to experience is between life in a "garden" (*gan*) – implying a specifically modified environment – and life among unmodified nature, where the ground brings forth "thorns and thistles" (Gen. 3:17)' ('Reconsidering', p. 68). Brueggemann seems to imply something similar: he suggests that relief from the curse through Noah (Gen. 5:29) would 'end the banishment of the man and woman . . . and cause a homecoming' (*Genesis*, p. 70); though Brueggemann also relates this (figuratively) to the return from exile: 'Noah would do for humanity just what Second Isaiah announced for Israel then in exile (cf. Isa. 54:9–17)' (ibid.).

the garden; and the return to Eden thus corresponds to physical relocation back in Judah. More generally, though, this kind of language may be taken to point to the restoration of Edenic blessings to the whole created order.[45]

In the light of this discussion, it is my contention that the OT writers saw the world as being, to some extent, 'out of joint' – particularly in relation to those things that affected human life and welfare directly. In Genesis 3 that disjunction is attributed to a decisive event that had the impact of a primeval 'fall', which was the consequence of human sin, and resulted in the cursing of the ground. This includes increased difficulties associated with farming and threats from wild animals – and those would be the things that had the most impact on everyday life and so would most need to be explained – but it is, in my view, broad enough to explain other 'natural' disasters that also contributed to the hardship of human existence outside the garden.

Cursing the ground and a 'return to chaos'

Another key event between these two expressions of God's purpose for the relationship between human beings and the created order is the flood, which is sometimes viewed as a 'return to chaos'. I have argued elsewhere that while the act of creation is effected by God, who alone existed 'in the beginning', it is also portrayed as the transformation of something 'formless and empty' (*tôhû wābôhû*, Gen. 1:2), which in the OT has generally negative associations, into something positive and very good (Gen. 1:30).[46] However, human sin can allow primeval chaos and disorder to return,[47] as in the flood, where the waters again cover the earth.[48] Jeremiah uses the same expression, *tôhû wābôhû*, to refer

---

45. National restoration is described in this way in e.g. Isa. 51:3; Ezek. 36:35.

46. See e.g. Robin Routledge, 'Did God Create Chaos? Unresolved Tension in Genesis 1:1–2', *TynB* 61.1 (2010), pp. 69–88 (73–74). However, cf. David T. Tsumura, *Creation and Destruction: A Reappraisal of the Chaoskampf Theory in the Old Testament* (Winona Lake: Eisenbrauns, 2005); Rebecca S. Watson, *Chaos Uncreated: A Reassessment of the Theme of 'Chaos' in the Hebrew Bible* (Berlin: de Gruyter, 2005).

47. See also Routledge, *Old Testament Theology*, pp. 135–136.

48. Clines notes the 'Creation – Uncreation – Recreation' theme in Gen. 1 – 11; see David J. A. Clines, *The Theme of the Pentateuch*, JSOTSup 10 (Sheffield: JSOT Press, 1978), p. 73–76; see also Blenkinsopp, *Creation*; Bernard W. Anderson, *From Creation to New Creation: Old Testament Perspectives*, OBT (Minneapolis: Fortress, 1994), pp. 34–36; Fretheim, *God and World*, pp. 79–83.

to the impact of the Babylonian exile (Jer. 4:23), suggesting that it was also viewed as 'uncreation';[49] and the same terms, *tôhû* and *bôhû*, appear in Isaiah 34:11, again in the context of 'uncreation' (cf. v. 4), here in connection with God's judgment on Edom. Zephaniah 1:2–3, which also has links to the flood narrative, appears, too, to depict divine judgment on sin as a reversal of creation.[50]

The view that creation involves bringing order out of disorder is sometimes linked with the role of human beings to 'subdue the earth'. Fretheim, for example, suggests that 'in some sense "chaos" persists', as a necessary part of God's good, though not perfect, creation; and that 'a key human responsibility set out in the command of Gen. 1:28 is *to work creatively with that disorder*'.[51] He also recognizes, however, that this disorder is limited; and human irresponsibility can move things back towards the undesirable situation of Genesis 1:2. In my view, though, chaos remains negative and

---

49. For discussion of Jer. 4:23 as 'uncreation', see e.g. Walter Brueggemann, *Jeremiah: Exile and Homecoming* (Grand Rapids: Eerdmans, 1998), pp. 59–60; Michael Fishbane, 'Jeremiah IV 23–26 and Job III 3–13: A Recovered Use of the Creation Pattern', *VT* 21.2 (1971), pp. 151–167; Hetty Lalleman, 'Jeremiah, Judgement and Creation', *TynB* 60.1 (2009), pp. 15–24 (18–20).

50. See e.g. John Goldingay, *Old Testament Theology*, vol. 2: *Israel's Faith* (Downers Grove: InterVarsity Press; Milton Keynes: Paternoster, 2006), pp. 307–308; O. Palmer Robertson, *The Books of Nahum, Habakkuk and Zephaniah*, NICOT (Grand Rapids: Eerdmans, 1991), pp. 257–260; see also Michael DeRoche, 'Zephaniah i 2–3: The "Sweeping of Creation"', *VT* 30.1 (1980), pp. 104–109. DeRoche also sees a reversal of creation in Hos. 4:1–3; see Michael DeRoche 'The Reversal of Creation in Hosea', *VT* 31.4 (1981), pp. 400–409. Murray describes Isa. 24 in a similar way as 'the undoing of creation and its order' (R. Murray, *The Cosmic Covenant: Biblical Themes of Justice and Peace and the Integrity of Creation* [London: Sheed & Ward, 1992], p. 19). See also, Routledge, *Old Testament Theology*, pp. 133–136. Brueggemann sets the creation account in Gen. 1 against the background of exile: 'the land which God now creates for his people is contrasted with chaos . . . the text contrasts Israel's land of future, characterized by all of Yahweh's blessings, with the land of the present, described as formless and void' (Walter Brueggemann, *The Land: Place as Gift, Promise and Challenge in Biblical Faith*, 2nd ed. [Minneapolis: Augsburg Fortress, 2002], p. 135). For the way this theme is developed in the New Testament, see chapter 8 in the present volume: Sean McDonough, 'Paradise by Desolation Trail: De-Creation and the New Testament'.

51. Fretheim, *God and World*, p. 44 (his italics).

undesirable;[52] and the designation of creation as 'very good' requires God's prior transformation of chaotic elements. The initial removal of chaotic elements does not, though, rule out the need for human beings to seek to control their environment – as indicated by the imperative 'subdue the earth' – particularly if that is concerned, primarily, with cultivating the land.

While these two things – the return of chaos/uncreation and cursing the ground – have different emphases, there are close links between them. Genesis 8:21 – 'I will never again curse the ground because of humankind, for the inclination of the human heart is evil from youth; nor will I ever again destroy every living creature as I have done' – seems particularly significant in this regard. The interpretation of the verse is debated. One issue is the relation of the evil inclination of human beings, which in Genesis 6:5 is given as the reason for the flood, to this context.[53] On this point, despite other key differences in interpretation, there appears to be general agreement that Genesis 8:21 points to a change in the way God will deal with human beings and the world in the future, and that the writer recalls Genesis 6:5 deliberately, to indicate that this is not because of any alteration in the human condition.[54] The common

---

52. It is not necessary to go so far as Levenson, who sees chaos as a pre-existent evil power, which, though restrained by God, is seeking an opportunity to break loose; see Jon. D. Levenson, *Creation and the Persistence of Evil: The Jewish Drama of Divine Omnipotence* (Princeton: Princeton University Press, 1994). Levenson sees the creation account in Gen. 1 as a late stage in the development of creation theology, from which the combat motif has been largely purged. Chaos is confined but not eliminated, and, as 'God's primal challenger' (p. 16), it remains a threat. However, the OT writers focus less on the threat and more on God's victory: chaos may return only with God's permission and remains under his control. See Routledge, 'Did God Create Chaos', p. 75.

53. See e.g. Cassuto, *Genesis*, pt. 2, pp. 119–120; Hamilton, *Genesis 1–17*, pp. 309–311; R. W. L. Moberly, *The Theology of the Book of Genesis* (Cambridge: Cambridge University Press, 2009), pp. 111–118; David L. Petersen, 'The Yahwist on the Flood', *VT* 26.4 (1976), pp. 438–446 (442–444); R. Rendtorff, 'Gen. 8:21 und die Urgeschichte des Jahwisten', *KD* 7 (1961), pp. 69–78; John H. Sailhamer, *The Meaning of the Pentateuch: Revelation, Composition and Interpretation* (Downers Grove: InterVarsity Press, 2009), pp. 598–599; von Rad, *Genesis*, pp. 122–123; Wenham, *Genesis 1–15*, pp. 190–191; Westermann, *Genesis 1–11*, pp. 454–457.

54. Moberly sees the 'evil thought' clause in Gen. 8:21 as an addition intended to point not only to the promise not to add to the curse and destroy all life, but also to a change in God's attitude: 'if corrupt humanity will not change, then God will

reference to the evil inclination of human hearts in relation both to the flood and to the cursing of the ground suggests a close relationship between the two. This connection is reinforced in the parallelism, in Genesis 8:21, between the divine promises never again to curse the ground and never again to destroy every living creature 'as I have done', which seems to be a clear, if implicit, reference to the flood.

If there is a connection between cursing the ground and the flood, an important question is: What is the nature of that connection? It seems unlikely that God's decision in Genesis 8:21 never again to curse the ground refers to nullifying the curse.[55] The hardships associated with the curse are all still present after the flood; and, as already noted, the key factor of subduing the earth is now missing. More likely, it refers to not *adding to* those things,[56] in the sense of not bringing into effect the full implications of the curse.[57] The correspondence, here, between cursing the ground and the destruction caused by the flood, and, more particularly, between 'not again' cursing the ground and 'not again' bringing such a global judgment, suggests that the flood may be seen as an outworking of the original curse. That might be seen, too, in the narrative link between Genesis 8:21 and Genesis 5:29, which expresses the hope that, through Noah, there will be some relief from the pain caused by the cursing of the ground: 'out of the ground that the LORD has cursed this one shall bring us relief from our work and from the toil of our hands'.[58] This anticipates Noah's role in the rest of the narrative and suggests that relief from the effects of the curse is closely associated with the new order that will exist after the flood. Within the wider narrative, the fulfilment of that expectation appears to be the removal of the threat of global destruction, indicating that the potential for such devastation was viewed as part of the original cursing of the ground – since there would

---

change in not enacting on humanity the judgement that such corruption might be expected to bring onto itself' (Moberly, *Theology*, p. 116).

55. See Rendtorff, 'Gen. 8:21'; von Rad, *Genesis*, pp. 122–123. Petersen's view ('Yahwist on the Flood', pp. 442–444) that this is ironic, indicating that the flood was ineffectual in addressing the problem of human sin and that in the end nothing has changed, seems equally unlikely.

56. E.g. Wenham, *Genesis 1–15*, p. 190; Cassuto, *Genesis*, pt. 2, pp. 119–120.

57. See the discussion of Gen. 5:29 below.

58. Some see this as an insertion by J into the genealogy of Gen. 5, which is usually ascribed to P (see e.g. Wenham, *Genesis 1–15*, p. 129; Westermann, *Genesis 1–11*, pp. 359–360). The view that it is important enough for the narrator to want to include it adds weight to its narrative significance.

be little relief in the promise that God will merely not add further hardships to that curse. As well as looking back to Genesis 5:29, in its canonical setting, Genesis 8:21 also has forward links to Genesis 9:11, suggesting that relief from the cursing of the ground is a result of God's renewed commitment to creation embodied within the Noahic covenant.[59] Here too, though, the main focus is the promise that global devastation of the kind seen in the flood will not recur, and again indicates that the possibility of such destruction was linked with the curse.

But, as already implied, it is not just the flood that is in view here. The promise that God will not again curse the ground and not again destroy every living creature is, in Genesis 8:22, accompanied by the promise of stability in the natural order – 'as long as the earth endures, seedtime and harvest, cold and heat, summer and winter, day and night, shall not cease'. This could refer back to the decision not again to send a flood – but then why not simply say that! And why give such a wide-ranging assurance, which includes elements that are unlikely to have been affected by the flood – such as the continuation of day and night? In my view, this is because it relates not only to the flood but also (and primarily) to what the flood represents: namely a return to chaos – a going back to something like the pre-creation state in Genesis 1:2. And, in my view, the cursing of the ground is linked with that too. A small point in relation to that is that while Genesis 8:21 clearly refers to the flood, the link is not made explicit, thus leaving open the possibility of a more general application.

In the light of this I want to suggest that the cursing of the ground in Genesis 3:17 opened the way for chaos and disorder to return. It disrupted God's purpose for human beings in relation to the environment (cf. Gen. 1:28), but also resulted in a disjunction within the created order itself. The promise in Genesis 8:21–22 does not remove the elements of the curse pronounced in Genesis 3:17; but it will result in a renewed stability in the created order that was disrupted as a consequence of the curse. And God's renewed expression of divine commitment to the created order and with it the promise to limit the extent to which chaos is allowed to return, constitutes the relief from the effects of the cursing of the ground anticipated in Genesis 5:29.

A further connection in the primeval history between the return to chaos (represented by the flood) and the cursing of the ground may be evident in the

---

59. See e.g. Wright, 'Theology and Ethics', p. 83. Wright also includes the hope of a new creation in the relief anticipated in Gen. 5:29. Hope of a new creation, seen in part, in the re-creation that follows uncreation, is an important aspect of the 'return to chaos' motif – see the discussion below.

repetition of 'saw ... good ... took' in Genesis 3:6 and Genesis 6:2. This provides a narrative link between the human action that led to God's initial curse, and the events leading to the flood. Significantly, the latter includes the withdrawal of God's Spirit (Gen. 6:3).[60] The only other place in the primeval history where the Spirit is specifically designated as belonging to God is Genesis 1:2, where the Spirit appears to have a role in controlling the waters of chaos; and the withdrawal of God's Spirit in Genesis 6:3 opens the way for that chaos to return.

Links between cursing and chaos are also evident in prophetic books, where they are associated with divine judgment. So, for example, Isaiah 24:6 refers to 'a curse' (*'ālâ*), which 'devours the earth' as a result of human beings breaking the 'everlasting covenant' (v. 5), which is probably a reference to the covenant with Noah.[61] The result is what Seitz describes as 'a return to the days of Noah'[62] and to the devastation of the earth associated with the flood. This connection is reinforced by the reference later in the passage to the 'windows of heaven' being opened (Isa. 24:18; cf. Gen. 7:11); and the suggestion, already implicit in the language, that this is an 'uncreation' – or a reversal of creation – may be further indicated by the reference to *tōhû* in verse 10. There is no direct link between the curse here and the cursing of the ground in Genesis 3:17.[63] However, if as I have argued, the flood and the potential for further global devastation is part of that original curse, there may be an indirect link. Following

---

60. See Robin Routledge, '"My Spirit" in Genesis 6:1–4', *JPT* 20.2 (2011), pp. 232–251.

61. See e.g. Robin Routledge, 'Mission and Covenant in the Old Testament', in Rollin G. Grams, I. Howard Marshall, Peter F. Penner and Robin Routledge (eds.), *Bible and Mission: A Conversation Between Biblical Studies and Missiology* (Schwarzenfeld: Neufeld, 2008), pp. 8–41 (16–17); Oswalt, *Isaiah 1–39*, p. 446.

62. Christopher R. Seitz, *Isaiah 1–39*, Interpretation (Louisville: John Knox, 1993), pp. 179–184; see also Childs, *Isaiah*, p. 179.

63. In Isa. 24:6 the noun *'ālâ* (curse) occurs, whereas Gen. 3:17 and 5:29 use the verb *'ārar* (to curse). The basic meaning of *'ālâ* is 'oath' and it appears to have become linked with the curse associated with breaking an oath. In the context of Isa. 24:5–6, which refers to breaking 'the everlasting covenant', *'ālâ* is the more appropriate term. However, the semantic ranges of the terms overlap; thus, while the word used (*'ālâ*) is determined by the context, its meaning is not substantially different from *'ārar*. See further Routledge, 'Blessings and Curses'; Brichto, *Problem of 'Curse'*; Gordon, 'Curse, Malediction', in *NIDOTTE*, vol. 4, pp. 491–493; Scharbert, '*'ālâ*', in *TDOT*, vol. 1, pp. 261–266; '*'rr*', in *TDOT*, vol. 1, pp. 405–418; '*brk*', in *TDOT*, vol. 2, pp. 279–308; '*qll*', in *TDOT*, vol. 13, pp. 37–44.

the flood, the mitigation of the curse was embodied in the Noahic covenant; with the breaking of that covenant by human beings, the curse is again allowed to have a greater impact. As noted, the exile is viewed by Jeremiah as a return to the chaos of Genesis 1:2; and Zephaniah describes divine judgment in terms of a reversal of creation. These passages do not specifically refer to a curse, though the devastation of exile is linked with a curse (*'ālâ*) in Jeremiah 23:10. In that verse the effect of the curse is that 'the land mourns' (*'āblâ hā'āreṣ*) and a similar expression occurs in the context of 'uncreation' language in Jeremiah 12:4 (cf. v. 10) and Hosea 4:3. Again, there is no immediate link to Genesis 3:17; but if that original curse is linked with the return of chaos, the reversal of creation portrayed here, also as the result of a curse, might further suggest a (significant) connection between them. That connection is reinforced by the reasonable assumption that Jeremiah has in mind the Deuteronomic curses, associated with breaking covenant promises, which are, in turn, reflected in the judgment in Genesis 3, and which point to a link between the exile and expulsion from the garden.

One final passage to consider here is Job 3:1–13. Here, Job *curses* the day of his birth; and, following Fishbane, it seems reasonable to take the rest of the passage – which uses language that suggests the reversal of the creative events of Genesis 1 – to express the content of that curse.[64] Some take the view that Job's wish that he had never been born is a 'counter-cosmic incantation',[65] aimed at undoing the process of creation – and particularly his own origins. If the day of his birth had never been created, then he might be freed from his sufferings

---

64. See Fishbane, 'Jeremiah iv 23–26'; see also e.g. David J. A. Clines, *Job 1–20*, WBC 17 (Dallas: Word, 1989), pp. 67–105; D. N. Freedman, 'The Structure of Job 3', *Bib* 49 (1968), pp. 503–508; Fretheim, *God and World*, pp. 221–229; Robert S. Fyall, *Now My Eyes See You: Images of Creation and Evil in the Book of Job*, NSBT (Leicester: Apollos, 2002), pp. 141–145; Norman C. Habel, *The Book of Job*, OTL (Philadelphia: Westminster, 1985), pp. 98–112; John E. Hartley, *The Book of Job*, NICOT (Grand Rapids: Eerdmans, 1991), pp. 88–95; Valerie Forstman Pettys, 'Let There Be Darkness: Continuity and Discontinuity in the "Curse" of Job 3', *JSOT* 98 (2002), pp. 89–104. There are some differences over the structure of the passage. Habel divides it into two (vv. 1–10, Job's curse; and vv. 11–26, Job's lament), others (e.g. Clines and Freedman) suggest three strophes (vv. 1–10, 11–19, 20–26). While the precise division is not vital to the current discussion, in my view Fishbane's argument that the content of the curse is found in vv. 3–13 is convincing; see Hartley, *Job*, pp. 88–89; Pettys, 'Let There Be Darkness'.

65. E.g. Fishbane, 'Jeremiah iv 23–26', p. 153; Hartley, *Job*, p. 91.

by slipping into non-existence.[66] Pettys gives a wider significance: Job can no longer make sense of his situation within traditional wisdom teaching about divine justice, and, disorientated, calls for a return to chaos: 'creation, now a parody of divine order, will be negated'.[67] Fretheim also links this with the wider theme of divine justice: he suggests that Job's experience is universalized in order to demonstrate 'that the world is not a just order; his birth was the result of creation in disarray and his own personal "day" and night participated in that disorder'.[68] The significance of this passage for the present discussion is twofold. First, the language of cursing is closely associated, here, with the language of uncreation and chaos; and that correlation further reinforces the view that the idea of linking these two concepts was not unfamiliar to the OT writers. Secondly, following Pettys and Fretheim, the passage links the return to chaos with the problem of divine justice (or the lack of it). Elsewhere, this is associated primarily with acts of judgment: notably the flood and the exile. Here, though, the significance of chaos is widened, and appears to include natural evil, including the unfairness of life, more generally.

To reiterate, then, I have argued that there is evidence that the OT writers see that the world is not as God intended it to be. That is explained, in Genesis 3:17, in terms of the cursing of the ground, which is also closely related to the idea of a return to chaos, seen in the flood (and also evident elsewhere in the OT). The curse disrupted God's purpose for human beings in relation to the environment (cf. Gen. 1:28) and also resulted in a disjunction within the created order itself, thus opening the way for the return of chaos.

Final observations

This association of curse and chaos seems to be significant in several ways.

First, it allows the view that cursing the ground is not only punishment for sin, but also represents a frustration of the divine purpose in creation,

---

66. See e.g. Fishbane, 'Jeremiah iv 23–26'; Habel, *Job*, pp. 107–110; Hamilton, *Job*, p. 91. Some (e.g. Fishbane, Habel) suggest that a curse had magical power to bring about the destruction expressed; see also H. H. Rowley, *Job*, NCB (London: Marshall, Morgan & Scott, 1970], pp. 38–39). However, see Clines, *Job 1–20*, p. 79; Anthony C. Thiselton, 'The Supposed Power of Words in the Biblical Writings', *JTS* 25 (1974), pp. 281–299.

67. Pettys, 'Let There Be Darkness', p. 92.

68. Fretheim, *God and World*, p. 229.

particularly as that purpose relates to the role of human beings. As such its impact may be seen to extend beyond increased difficulties in agriculture, to include natural disasters more generally.

Secondly, it reinforces the promise of future restoration, following the curse and its effects. The hope of God's final victory that will finally eliminate chaos and bring a new creation features prominently in the return to the chaos motif. Several scholars have pointed to the significance of an eschatological perspective on ecological and environmental issues,[69] and this contributes to that discussion from an OT point of view.

Thirdly, linking the return to chaos motif with cursing the ground suggests that returning chaos may not only be evident in major acts of divine judgment – such as the flood and the exile – but also has an impact on everyday life. While Genesis 1:30 suggests the initial transformation of chaotic elements, the reality of the current situation is that aspects of primeval chaos are now present, causing a disruption in the created order. So far as the OT writers are concerned the impact of chaos continues to be under God's authority. It is, nevertheless, a part of human experience, evident both in natural disasters and in the observable 'unfairness' of life (as in Job 3) and natural evil more generally.

Finally, recognizing that a key factor in the disjunction of the created order is the presence of chaos – which, while controlled by God remains, essentially, at odds with the divine intention – gives incentive to those who are made in God's image, and who are called as his representatives to exercise responsible stewardship over the world, to seek to limit that disorder: in this context in terms of environmental and ecological awareness.[70] The task of subduing the earth may have become more difficult – but the challenge to human beings to seek to bring order into the present chaos remains.[71]

© Robin Routledge, 2014

---

69. E.g. Francis Bridger, 'Ecology and Eschatology: A Neglected Dimension', *TynB* 41.2 (1990), pp. 290–301; D. J. Moo, 'Nature in the New Creation'; J. A. Moo, 'Continuity, Discontinuity, and Hope'.

70. Contra Bimson, 'Reconsidering', p. 81.

71. See e.g. Gnanakan, *God's World*, p. 47.

4. CREATION AND KINGSHIP: ENVIRONMENT AND WITNESS IN THE YAHWEH *MĀLĀK* PSALMS

Jamie A. Grant

Introduction

The Yahweh *mālāk* collection (Pss 93 – 100) is, at one and the same time, a great statement of faith and a great challenge to the faith of its original hearers. The statement of faith is grounded in the vision that Yahweh still reigns over the whole earth, despite every indication to the contrary. The challenge to the faith practice of Israel is that *all nations* are called to join in the worship of Yahweh. The tenor of these psalms reflects a remarkable fideism that reminds Israel of the universal reign of their God despite the cognitive challenges to that world view rooted in the loss of the holy land, the holy city and the holy temple. There is a strong sense of paradigm challenge in this collection. The challenge is one of perspective. Psalms 93 – 100 suggest that the people's understanding of their God is too small and, at the same time, the voice of these psalms suggests that Israel's understanding of the covenant community is also wholly inadequate. In presenting this corrective, the psalmists draw upon several evidences to support their call for fuller understanding of God and Israel: (1) the character and works of Yahweh; (2) testimony drawn from Israel's dealings with Yahweh; and (3) the voice of creation and the created order that testifies both to Yahweh's universal rule and also calls all peoples to worship him as a result. The tone of these psalms is both inspirational and missional, lifting the eyes of the people from the pressures of present circumstance and pointing them to a far greater spiritual reality that is no less 'real' because of the fact that it is spiritual. To that extent the voice of the Yahweh *mālāk* psalms is remarkably contemporary in an age where, for Western Christianity at least, the faith community seems to be in decline and biblical norms and understandings are challenged by aggressively secularist agendas.

A spot of context

In order to understand the full impact of the message of the Yahweh *mālāk* collection a spot of contextualization is needed. I have, elsewhere, given some consideration to the challenges and opportunities of dealing with indeterminate texts.[1] On one level it is virtually impossible to suggest a historical setting for the Yahweh *mālāk* psalms that is in any way definitive. Reference to the post-exodus desert experience in Psalm 95, Moses, Aaron and Samuel in Psalm 99 and the existence of Zion in Psalms 97 and 99 do little to provide any sense of historical setting from the text of the psalms themselves.

Thus we are left to probe the historical origins of these compositions from their semantic content. The evidence from the individual psalms is mixed. Hossfeld, for example, suggests that Psalm 93:1–4 is a

> preexilic praise to the King of the Jerusalem Temple; this praise was made current in the exilic or postexilic period with v. 5. The cosmic character of Yhwh's kingship is diverted toward law and Temple, or made concrete in those terms.[2]

Although Goldingay suggests simply that the psalm 'gives no indication of a historical or liturgical context', he goes on to voice the possibility that the psalm may be read consistently with passages from Second Isaiah and, therefore, dated to the early post-exilic period.[3] Equally, some commentators read Psalm 93's

---

1. Jamie A. Grant, 'Determining the Indeterminate: Issues in Interpreting the Psalms', *STR* 1.1 (2010), pp. 3–14.

2. Frank-Lothar Hossfeld and Erich Zenger, *Psalms 2: A Commentary on Psalms 51–100*, Hermeneia (Minneapolis: Fortress, 2005), p. 448. Similarly, Samuel Terrien sees the origins of the claim that Yahweh reigns as being derived from 'the early days in the Promised Land', but the psalm reached 'its final formulation at the birth of Judaism during and after the Babylonian exile' (*The Psalms: Strophic Structure and Theological Commentary*, Eerdmans Critical Commentary [Grand Rapids: Eerdmans, 2003], p. 660).

3. John Goldingay, *Psalms*, vol. 3: *Psalms 90–150*, BCOTWP 3 (Grand Rapids: Baker, 2008), p. 65.

title in the LXX, 'when the land was inhabited' (*hote katōkistai hē gē*),[4] as a reference to the repopulation of the land following the return from Babylonian exile.[5] However, just to maintain the delightfully consistent inconsistency in assessing psalmic historical settings, Eaton comments confidently that 'It is now widely acknowledged that this is an ancient psalm, dating from the early monarchy, as both style and content indicate.'[6]

We could continue such historical deliberations throughout the whole collection with similar results. Two themes seem to come to the fore in the consideration of the historical contexts of Psalms 93 – 100 in the secondary literature. First, there is consistent reference to the 'ancient' roots of the theology of the Yahweh *mālak* psalms. These compositions draw upon the imagery of the exodus (95:7–11; 99:6–7; possibly 93:3–4) and Deuteronomistic covenant theology (93:5; 94:10–15; 95:6–11; 100:5), as well as grounding themselves in a strong creation ideology (93:3–4; 95:4–5; 96:11–12; 97:4–6; 98:7–8; etc.). There is a sense in which the Yahweh *mālak* psalms go back to the formative roots of Israel's theological understanding of Yahweh and their relationship with him.[7] The second theme seems to be one of recontextualization for the post-exilic period. These poems call for a return to foundational understandings, but it does seem to be *a return* that is advocated. There are subtle indications of rereading in a new context. For example, the dual reference to Israel being the sheep of Yahweh's pasture seems to reflect the covenantal nomenclature of the exilic period (used elsewhere in Jer. 23:1 and Ezek. 34:31 as well as in the clearly exilic Pss 74 and 79). Also the 'worthless idols' (*'ĕlîlîm*) of Psalms 96 and 97 arguably take on a particular resonance for the people who have seen that worship in practice in the exile.[8] The reminders not to be disobedient like previous generations, again, take on a particular significance in the context of

---

4. All Scripture translations in this chapter are my own.

5. A. F. Kirkpatrick, *The Book of Psalms* (Cambridge: Cambridge University Press, 1910), p. 563.

6. John H. Eaton, *The Psalms: A Historical and Spiritual Commentary with an Introduction and New Translation* (London: T. & T. Clark International, 2003), p. 331.

7. Even on a very superficial level, it is interesting to note that the divine name is used 53 times in these eight psalms, *'ădōnāy* not at all and *'ĕlōhîm* only 11 times to refer to God and, on almost every occurrence, *'ĕlōhîm* is used in conjunction with the divine name ('the LORD our God', 'the LORD is our God', etc.). Clearly, the psalmists' focus is on Yahweh and Israel's relationship with him.

8. Intertextually, it is Isaiah who focuses most on the uselessness of the *'ĕlîlîm* (see e.g. Isa. 2, 10, 19).

the exile and return from exile. While none of these factors would conclusively establish a setting for the Yahweh *mālak* psalms in the return from exile, they do seem to combine to point to a social setting for the collection in the (early) post-exilic period.

While explicit historical indications in the text are sparse, the *canonical* setting of the psalter clearly points to a reading of the Yahweh *mālak* psalms as being a response to the crisis of exile. Gerald Wilson was the first to describe the differences between Books 1–3 and Books 4–5 in terms of both content and style of editing.[9] He also pointed to a kind of canonical 'narrative' in the psalter that marked the rise and fall of the Davidic king through the placement of royal psalms at key junctures of the psalter (Ps. 2 – establishment of the Davidic king; Ps. 72 – continuation of the line to the next generation; Ps. 89 – loss of the king and failure of the line).[10] Wilson then argues that Book 4 turns away from the kingship of David and refocuses the reader's attention on the kingship of Yahweh. He describes Book 4 as the 'editorial "centre" of the final form of the Hebrew psalter' and suggests that it provides

> the 'answer' to the problem posed by Psalm 89 as to the apparent failure of the Davidic covenant with which Books One – Three are primarily concerned. Briefly summarised the answer given is: (1) YHWH is king; (2) He has been our 'refuge' in the past, long before the monarchy existed (i.e., in the Mosaic period); (3) He will continue to be our refuge now that the monarchy is gone; (4) Blessed are they that trust in him![11]

While we may quibble with elements of Wilson's reconstruction (specifically revolving around the importance of the Davidic psalms to Books 1–3 and *the rejection* of the Davidic king in favour of Yahweh as King in Books 4–5[12]) his broader argument has a great deal to commend it and has acquired a broad degree of acceptance. Essentially, Book 3 *as a whole* is dominated by the language and imagery of loss and exile. It deals not just in Psalm 89 with the loss of the Davidic line but with the loss of faith (Ps. 73), the loss of the temple (Ps. 74),

---

9. Gerald H. Wilson, *The Editing of the Hebrew Psalter*, SBLDS 76 (Chico: Scholars Press, 1985).

10. Gerald H. Wilson, 'The Use of Royal Psalms at the "Seams" of the Hebrew Psalter', *JSOT* 35 (1986), pp. 85–94.

11. Wilson, *Editing*, p. 215.

12. Several of the chapters in Philip S. Johnston and David G. Firth (eds.), *Interpreting the Psalms: Issues and Approaches* (Leicester: Apollos, 2005), draw out these elements of critique in more detail.

the fall of the city (Ps. 79), the disobedience of the people (Ps. 78), the pain and mockery of exile (Ps. 83) and the exacerbated torment of divine absence in the midst of pain (Ps. 88). Book 3 as a collection focuses on the totality of exile in all of its bleakness. Book 4 responds by pointing to the universality of Yahweh's rule. Holistic loss is met and matched by the completeness of God's rule. The losses lamented in Book 3 (temple, city, land, king) were all outward signs of the reign and rule of Yahweh. Their loss would, in the ancient world, have been taken as the defeat and demise of Israel's God at the hands of the gods of the nations. Book 4 responds to the loss of the *external signs* of Yahweh's dominion by asserting the continuing, universal reality of the kingdom of God in the human realm. The trappings of divine rule may be gone but the underlying reality remains undiminished.

So, in terms of context, there is some historical indication that this collection finds its voice as an encouragement to the post-exilic generation of God's people to return to the basics of loving Yahweh and walking in his ways. Certainly, from a canonical perspective, this collection serves as part of the response to the crisis of exile. Exile was, of course, a huge personal, social and geopolitical tragedy for Judah. However, it was also more than that. It was a *spiritual* tragedy that struck at the very heart of their belief system. The common presuppositions of the ANE implied that a defeated nation means a weak god. Book 4 as a whole, and the Yahweh *mālāk* psalms in particular, point to a different reality – a deeper reality – that denies such conclusions. This collection calls for a faith perspective to triumph over appearance because that faith perspective better reflects reality than does that which is visible. What is more, the collection places a responsibility upon those who see with the eyes of faith to present that reality to others who otherwise fail to recognize the telling signals that are sent in and through the created order. The natural environment affirms the collection's statement of faith and provides a communicative bridge to those who are invited to join the worshipping community.

The statement of faith

That the Yahweh *mālāk* psalms require the exercise of faith is beyond doubt. The contextual setting – both historical and canonical – places the reader in the post-exilic setting of defeat but with some small degree of hope. Psalms 93 – 100 challenge their readers to adopt a much more expansive view of the world around them. The people of God are not just some insignificant people group sitting in a political backwater far removed from all that is important in the world. They are the representatives of the universal King over all creation and are called on both to recognize and proclaim his reign. James Mays is helpful here:

> The declaration 'the Lord reigns' involves a vision of reality that is the theological centre of the Psalter. The cosmic and worldly action to which it refers is the aetiology of the psalmic situation. The psalmic understanding of the people of God, the city of God, the king of God and the law of God depends on its validity and implications. The psalmic functions of praise, prayer and instruction are responses to it and articulations of its wonder, hope and guidance. The organising role of the declaration does not ignore or obviate the plurality of thought about God in the psalms. It does announce a metaphor that transcends and lies behind the variety. It is what every reader and user of the psalms may know as the code for understanding all of them.[13]

Mays's description of the Yahweh *mālāk* ideology as a 'vision of reality' provides an insightful perspective on the collection. The historical setting seems to present a view of reality where Israel's God is weak and defeated, one of the many deities to fall at the hand of Marduk and the might of Babylon. However, these psalms call for an understanding of reality that belies the circumstances. Yahweh reigns, not Marduk (93:1; 96:10; 97:1; 99:1). Yahweh sits enthroned above *all* gods (93:2; 95:3; 96:4–5; 97:9; 98:6; 99:1–3). Yahweh is pictured as the great, cosmic author, the creator of all things, and therefore both owner and ruler over all things (93:3–4 [defeat of the primordial seas in creation?]; 94:9–10; 95:4–6; 100:3). The 'offices' of Creator and King automatically confer the role of Judge to Yahweh (94:1–2; 96:13; 98:9).

The Yahweh *mālāk* collection is – understandably, given this broadly accepted descriptor – replete with the language, imagery and trappings of kingship. The implications of the divine kingdom are outworked in some detail for the reader:

- Psalm 93: Yahweh is King by dint of being Creator (cf. creation narratives in Gen. 1 – 2).
- Psalm 94: kingship implies the highest judicial function, and Yahweh's reign is characterized by social justice.
- Psalm 95: Yahweh, as Creator, reigns over all gods and, as covenant God, must be obeyed by his people.
- Psalm 96: Yahweh is the true God, the absolute Monarch and the ultimate Judge of the whole universe, and therefore he is worthy of praise.

---

13. James L. Mays, *The Lord Reigns* (Louisville: Westminster John Knox, 1994), p. 22.

- Psalm 97: Yahweh reveals his sovereignty by way of cosmic theophany.
- Psalm 98: Yahweh is King and Judge who intervenes in the affairs of humanity to outwork his purpose.
- Psalm 99: Yahweh is enthroned over the cosmos and dwells in unblemished holiness.
- Psalm 100: given that all this is true, worship and serve the covenant God!

This collection of psalms creates a theological construct that points to the absolute rule of Yahweh in every way possible. This all-encompassing rule requires an all-encompassing response. The worshipping community responds in praise and with obedience. Furthermore, that worshipping community cannot be limited simply to ethnic Israel . . . it must encompass the whole earth and all nations and peoples.

The missional call

So, effectively, the Yahweh *mālak* psalms present a construct of reality that is, on the one hand, complete and inescapable, yet, on the other, it is a construct of reality that is not entirely obvious. These poems succinctly encapsulate the universal and all-encompassing reign of Yahweh – his kingly rule simply *is*. It is a brute fact that brooks no debate. We must remember the constant focus of this collection: Yahweh, Yahweh, Yahweh. There are fifty-three occurrences of the divine name in eighty-eight verses. The focus is absolutely resolute: Yahweh and no other is Creator, Yahweh and no other is King, Yahweh and no other is Judge, and so on. The gods of the nations are not *'ĕlōhîm*; they are *'ĕlîlîm* – not gods at all, but worthless idols, deceptions (96:5; 97:7). Yahweh alone is Israel's God (95:6–7), and, what is more, Yahweh alone is the high God above all other gods (95:3; 96:4; etc.).[14] So the exclusive claim of this collection is that Israel's God alone is worthy of fealty and worship.

---

14. The question of the understanding of monotheism in the psalter is an interesting one. It is not uncommon for the psalmists to use the imagery of the celestial pantheon, where Yahweh sits unchallenged as the high God. Of course, the use of such imagery does not necessarily mean that the psalmists and their hearers accepted the validity and existence of lesser gods. The language was common currency in the ancient world and the metaphor was adopted to make the poets' particular point rather than as an ontological statement.

The totality of this construct suggests that this reality should be blindingly obvious. If Yahweh's rule is so complete and absolute, then one would assume that it is also clearly observable. However, as we have seen from our discussion of context, the general observations of the watching world would lead to quite different conclusions. For a Babylonian or an Assyrian or an Egyptian looking on, the claim of Yahweh's universal kingdom would seem laughable. Perhaps during the reigns of David or Solomon such discussion would have appeared more credible to Israel's watching neighbours, but following the sacking of Jerusalem and the destruction of the temple, Yahweh's seat on earth, this vision of reality would by and large seem absurd to them.[15] So the Yahweh *mālak* psalms include another vital focal point for the overall argument of the collection to make sense: namely, the missional call to all the earth to join in the worship of Yahweh.

We must briefly work out the dynamic in order to grasp the thrust of the collection. Psalms 96 – 98 provide one of the most explicit missional challenges found in the OT. Chris Wright comments on Psalm 96:

> What makes [Ps. 96] a new song is *where* it is sung (in all the earth) and *who* is going
> to be doing the singing (all peoples). What was an old song for Israel becomes a new
> song as it is taken up by new singers in ever expanding circles to the ends of the earth.
> Psalm 96 in particular recognizes the polemical or confrontational nature of such a
> universal vision, for it must inevitably transform the religious landscape. Other gods
> must be recognized for what they are, 'nothings' (Ps. 96:5), and the nations must
> instead ascribe all glory to Yhwh alone and bring offerings to him (96:7–9).[16]

As Wright points out, these psalms present a 'polemical' or 'apologetic' task. All nations are called to worship but who is the primary audience of this call? It is, of course, the covenant community of Israel. So, while the call to worship

---

15. Granted the dynamic of restoration to Zion provides 'evidence' of renewed vigour on Yahweh's part (Ps. 98), and Zion continues to play a significant role in the psalmic vision of universal praise of Yahweh (see e.g. Ps. 87, which is placed in a collection dominated by images of exile and loss). However, even taking into account Yahweh's ability to restore his people to their land, the claims of the Yahweh *mālak* psalms would still strike a dissonant chord for observers viewing reality from a purely geopolitical perspective.

16. Christopher J. H. Wright, *The Mission of God: Unlocking the Bible's Grand Narrative* (Nottingham: Apollos, 2006), p. 480 (his italics).

of Psalm 96 is directed to 'all the earth', the charge to 'declare his glory among the nations' speaks to the listening community of faith.[17]

So we see how the construct works:

- The Yahweh *mālak* psalms present a holistic vision of Yahweh's absolute and universal rule.
- They call on all peoples and all nations to recognize that supremacy and join the worshipping community of faith.
- The nations are not present to hear that call, so the restored community of Israel in Zion is reminded of their responsibility to declare the message of Yahweh's rule, thus drawing others into the worshipping community of faith.[18]

Almost inevitably this leads to a question of means and mechanisms. How is Israel to take the Yahweh *mālak* message to the nations and peoples of the earth?

The environmental voice

While it is doubtful that Israel was called to engage in what has been described as centrifugal mission ('going into all the world'), the Yahweh *mālak* psalms give clear indication that the people of God are to declare the message of Yahweh's universal rule in some way. Many commentators ignore this commission,

---

17. 'Who speaks in this psalm, who is addressed, and to what end? Of course, the opening makes clear that the psalm directly addresses earth and its peoples, inviting the whole world in its day to come to worship Yhwh. This longing and possibility does not await Christ's coming. But then there is the formal oddity about the relationship between the two opening tricola as the earth is both singer (v. 1b) and the recipient of the proclamation (v. 3). Verses 11–13 also bring out the question of who actually hears the psalm, because the heavens and the earth are spoken of, not spoken to. It is Israel in its worship that hears the psalm's declaration that the creation is to rejoice, and its bidding to the earth and its peoples in vv. 1–10. There is no immediate way in which the nations themselves hear it' (Goldingay, *Psalms*, vol. 3, p. 108).

18. Goldingay's conclusion that Ps. 96 'perhaps . . . implies a missionary commission to Israel' seems rather weak given the logical progression of his argument up until that point (ibid.).

assuming that the psalm refers to some sort of eschatological event, but, as Goldingay points out, there is no compelling reason to do so:

> When the Jews in the Dispersion came to commend Yhwh to the Gentile world, consciously or unconsciously, deliberately or incidentally, then they were living out the implications of this psalm. It helps us understand the Jewish people's enthusiasm about spreading the knowledge of the true God.[19]

There is, of course, much debate over the extent of this Hebraic 'missional' activity in historical reality, but Goldingay's comments reflect well the implied dynamic of Psalm 96 and the other poems in this collection. The rhetorical challenge presented to the covenant community is clearly to take the message of Yahweh's kingdom to the nations.[20] There is no explicit discussion of how this will happen, but the expectation that it should happen is clearly present in this collection.

The second question begged by the vision of reality in the Yahweh *mālāk* psalms is a 'why' question rather than a 'how' question. Why would the Gentile nations pay any credence to this construct of reality? Yahweh was, in the eyes of the watching world, a defeated God, so why should they believe in this vision of reality that presents him as universal King?

It is here, with apologies for tardiness, that we finally arrive at our environmental discussion. The environment plays an essential role in adding a sense of conviction to the global message of the Yahweh *mālāk* psalms. Psalm 97:6 is something of a hermeneutical key in this dynamic: 'The heavens declare his righteousness, and all the peoples see his glory!' (*higîdû haššāmayîm ṣidqô wĕrā'û kol-hā'ammîm kĕbôdô*). The dynamic is clear: there is something in the created order that reveals the true nature of Yahweh to an otherwise sceptical, Gentile audience. The heavens speak; the peoples see.[21] The environment plays a clear role in the invitation to worship that Israel is meant to extend to the nations. Let me unpack some of the environmental factors that come into play in the apologetic presentation of the Yahweh *mālāk* psalms.

---

19. Ibid.

20. Obviously, Jesus' teaching about the kingdom of God in the Gospels does not appear from nowhere. There is a strong kingdom theology in the OT that provides the ideological backdrop to this collection of psalms.

21. The common verb *r'h* used in Ps. 97:6 can have the connotation of 'seeing', as in 'understanding' (*HALOT*, p. 8580).

Yahweh is Creator, therefore King

Challenging the ANE cosmogonies that present the formation of the universe as an accidental by-product of conflicts between squabbling deities, Psalm 93 presents Yahweh as King who established and establishes the world (93:1–2). His rule is pre-existent, and is evidenced by his triumph over the primordial waters (93:3–4). Some commentators want to see this as an exodus reference where Yahweh triumphed in a god-conflict with the Egyptian deities by proving that he is 'mightier than the sea'. However, given the contextualization in 93:1–2 ('robing in majesty', 'throne is established from of old'), it seems more likely that the starting point of the apologetic that justifies the 'vision of reality' presented in this collection is the very fact that Yahweh made everything, and therefore he is Ruler over everything.[22]

The centrality of this apologetic is seen by the lovely concatenation that follows through the next few psalms, focusing in on Yahweh as Creator. We move from 93:3–4 to the following:

- 'The Planter of the ear, does he not hear? The One who formed the eye, does he not see?' (94:9) – Yahweh as Creator of humanity.
- 'The sea belongs to him, for he made it, the dry ground his hands formed' (95:4) – creation confers ownership.
- 'Let us kneel before Yahweh our Maker!' (95:6) – Yahweh as Creator of the covenant community as well as all of humanity.
- 'All the gods (*'ĕlōhîm*) of the peoples are *'ĕlîlîm* but Yahweh made the heavens' (96:5) – why is Yahweh better than the gods? Because he created the environment around us.

So Yahweh's worth is attested by the assertion that he purposefully created the universe and humanity for the purpose of relationship with him. In most cosmogonies of the ancient world the creation of the earth was accidental and humanity was the plaything of fickle and nasty gods. There is a qualitative difference to the presentation of Yahweh in these compositions.

Creation's natural desire to worship Yahweh

Psalms 96 – 98 are something of a unit within the 93 – 100 collection. Most commentators acknowledge the close association between Psalms 96 and 98, with Psalm 97 inevitably being drawn into the discussion by dint of its placement

---

22. It was a common notion in the ANE that ownership implied rule. Therefore, Yahweh as Creator of the earth and its peoples automatically implies that he is Lord.

and certain similarities of theme.[23] Following the declarations of Yahweh's authorship of the world in which we live, the psalmists move to the natural consequence of this scenario. Just as humanity is tied to its Creator (Ps. 95), so too is the created order itself. This is seen in the use of jussives in Psalms 96 and 98.

Psalm 96:11–13 sets the tone. Heaven/earth, sea/its inhabitants, field/its inhabitants, forest/its inhabitants, 'are glad', 'rejoice', 'roar', 'exult' and 'sing for joy'. Why? Because Yahweh is coming to Judge the earth in righteousness and faithfulness. Similarly, in Psalm 98:7–9 the sea/inhabitants, the world/inhabitants, the rivers, the hills, respectively 'roar' (both sea and earth), 'clap their hands' and 'sing for joy', once again, before the judgment of Yahweh. Normally, judgment is not something that we consider positively. Judgment and singing for joy are not really cognates in the semantic world in which we dwell! Yet that is precisely the vision of reality presented in this section of the collection. How so?

Jannie Du Preez is helpful here:

> We associate God's judgement with all manner of dread expectations. Yet his judgement does not consist only in calling his opponents to account. It may be thought of with joyful anticipation, for everything that is now in disarray and disharmony, suffering from injustice and violence shall be set right. This is the broader aspect of judgement which the Old Testament saints embraced and in which they rejoiced . . . In a very special way *nature* will rejoice in the restoration of all things, for God's coming will put an end to the violence that nature had to suffer. . . . In a glorious way Psalm 96 and its twin, Psalm 98, remind the believing community that God's purpose with creation is nothing less than a new heaven and a new earth in which justice will be at home.[24]

Nature rejoices in divine judgment because it brings restoration. Just as humanity can rejoice in forgiveness and restoration, so the environment in some sense awaits the cleansing and renewal that will result from the appearance of Yahweh in righteous, faithful and equitable judgment. Just as the land of Canaan was 'polluted' by the offensive acts of the Amorites and, later, of the Israelites themselves (see e.g. Num. 35:33–34 or Ps. 106:37–38), so there is a sense in which the created order is 'polluted' by all of the injustice perpetrated upon it.

---

23. Hossfeld and Zenger, *Psalms 2*, p. 477.

24. Jannie Du Preez, 'Reading Three "Enthronement Psalms" from an Ecological Perspective', *Missionalia* 19.2 (1991), p. 127 (his italics).

Judgment cleanses of pollution and restores the proper order, so the environment anticipates this eschatological act with much joy.

Creation proclaims Yahweh's glory

Therefore, the logical conclusion of this construct of reality is that the created world itself declares the kingship of Yahweh (97:6). The subtle implication, therefore, seems to be that contemplation of the environment plays a vital role in the apologetic presentation of Yahweh's kingship to those outside the covenant community.[25] Contemplation of creation affirms the greater worth of the Creator. Other gods may claim to do various and different things but, whatever their empty claims, that which is created in some way reflects the glory of the one who created it. That link is unbreakable and the reflection is, in some sense, undeniable, according to the Yahweh *mālāk* psalms. The rhetorical thrust of the collection is that even those who have no 'natural' reason to accept or acknowledge the kingship of Yahweh are convinced by the powerful testimony of the existence of created order. It may be tarnished and 'awaiting renewal' but the natural environment is a powerful witness to the character, goodness, power, lordship and coming judgment of Yahweh, the Creator and covenant God.

Conclusion

Where does that leave us in terms of conclusions? Obviously, these can be no

---

25. This, of course, should not be understood simplistically. The psalmists are not implying that anyone who contemplates the created order will somehow instantly and magically become a believer in Yahweh. For many who observed the natural order then, as is also true now, this was simply not the case. However, the tone of what the psalmists have to say in this collection points the reader inevitably to the conclusion that the created order can and does lead interested observers to seek out a Creator. The implication is that design and order observed in the natural realm (note the torah-type language that is often applied to the environment, e.g. Job 38:33 or Ps. 119:89, etc.) can lead those who ponder it to ask who this Designer might be. For many in antiquity the world came into being as the accidental by-product of a god conflict, and humanity was no more than the plaything of the gods. Many in the modern world have a similarly 'random' view of the world and the place of humans within it. The Yahweh *mālāk* psalms suggest that the environmental realm can and does speak to inquisitive human hearts, leading some to hope that there may be something more than happenstance governing the realm in which we live.

more than observations, as time and space do not allow further consideration; however, the following points seem to me, at least, to be worth making.

Creation reflects the glory of the Creator

If the power, might, goodness and righteousness of God are displayed in the created realm, then anything that damages the natural environment in some way tarnishes not the glory of God itself but humanity's ability to perceive the worth and glory of God. There are, of course, all sorts of biblical reasons for the protection, preservation and care of the environment, but this is one of the less well-recognized ones among Christians. The natural environment fulfils an apologetic role. Our desire should be to keep that voice as clear as possible.

Creation 'speaks' in sceptical settings

The setting for the Yahweh *mālāk* psalms is not positive. Whether read historically or canonically, the context of this collection points to an environment in which its claims would not naturally seem convincing. Yet somehow the mighty work of Yahweh in creation is assumed to speak convincingly even against this unreceptive backdrop. There is something telling for the contemporary community of faith here. The gospel presents a 'vision of reality' that is difficult to swallow for the watching world, yet there seems to be a natural bridge between the biblical construct of reality and the sceptical world views of today: the natural environment round about us. Alister McGrath describes apologetics as the art of 'bridgebuilding', and contemplation of the created order is a shared conversation that can be built into a bridge. Obviously, this is not something to be practised flippantly or insensitively, but who among us – Christian or not – has *never* looked up into the night sky and thought, 'This cannot possibly have been an accident!' The first stanchion of a bridge is built.

The importance of the worshipping community

The natural world sings the praise of Yahweh (Pss 96:12; 98:8). The Gentiles are called to 'sing a new song to Yahweh' (Pss 96:1; 98:1). They are invited to join a worshipping community in the worship of the Creator God (Ps. 99:5). There is a strong sense of wonder in the Yahweh *mālāk* collection – wonder at creation, wonder regarding redemption, wonder with regard to acceptance by the God who reigns, wonder in response to the ideas of community belonging and the divine presence. The construct of reality presented in Psalms 93 – 100 is not purely cognitive. Through its rich anthropomorphisms and its vivid creational imagery this collection presents a vision of reality that is full of awe. In the presentation of the gospel's 'vision of reality', Christians must never allow that message to seem bland. It is a story of colour and vitality, life and energy. It is a dynamic construct of a God who triumphed over primordial chaos to bring order, beauty, justice, community and song. The poetic must speak in our apologetic, if a sceptical watching world is ever going to be captivated by the claims of Christ. Worship is an important act expressing our wonder. In seeking to communicate those claims we should do so as a worshipping community, captivated by a vision of reality that encompasses the whole universe and every nation.

5. THE SPIRIT AND THE RENEWAL OF CREATION: AN OLD TESTAMENT PERSPECTIVE

David G. Firth

Reflection on the place of the Spirit of God in relationship to creation in the OT has, not surprisingly, found as its primary focus the opening verses of Genesis. Of course, there remains considerable debate over how we should translate Genesis 1:2. On the whole I am persuaded that 'Spirit of God' is still the best option, though in doing so we still need to accept that there is a level at which the semantic range of any one instance of *rûaḥ* will exceed our ability to translate it.[1] As such, although there are points where *rûaḥ* clearly means either 'wind' or 'Spirit' (among other options), there are other times where both these senses are present.[2] But in terms of Genesis 1:2, a good case can be made for interpreting the *rûaḥ 'ĕlōhîm* as God's Spirit. As such, it is no surprise that reflection on the theme of the Spirit and creation has most frequently focused on the role of the Spirit in the act of creation. It is important to affirm this point, because only when we appreciate the role of the Spirit in creation as

---

1. See especially Robert L. Hubbard, 'The Spirit and Creation', in David G. Firth and Paul D. Wegner (eds.), *Presence, Power and Promise: The Role of the Spirit of God in the Old Testament* (Nottingham: Apollos, 2011), pp. 85–88. All translations in this chapter are my own.

2. Richard E. Averbeck, 'Breath, Wind, Spirit and the Holy Spirit in the Old Testament', in Firth and Wegner, *Presence*, pp. 34–35.

a foundational element within the OT can we then explore the role the OT gives to the Spirit in the sustenance of creation and, ultimately, to its renewal. The goal of this chapter, therefore, is to show that the OT affirms the continued role of the Spirit in the sustenance of creation and that this ultimately leads into a significant role in the renewal of creation. These elements are not distinct from one another. Rather, creation's renewal comes out of the Spirit's role at the point of creation and continuing role in sustaining it, though it should be noted that creation's renewal is linked to a wider restoration that is marked by justice. That is, the Spirit's role in the renewal of creation is not just associated with the 'biosphere' but must be linked also to all relationships so that all are seen within the framework of justice. In addition, it will be observed that there is a close relationship between the Spirit and Yahweh's word in these texts, in itself a reflection back on Genesis 1.

For the purposes of this chapter, attention is given only to texts that relate the divine *rûaḥ* to creation without explicit reference to salvation-historical themes. This has the obvious drawback of excluding a number of potentially important texts from the discussion.[3] But it also enables us to focus on the central theme of the relationship between God's *rûaḥ* and the creation without the risk of confusing this with issues associated with God's salvific purpose. Given the large number of potentially relevant texts, this chapter can offer only an initial OT perspective, though one that it can be argued is consistent with the wider picture. A second step would then be to examine those texts that link *rûaḥ*, creation and salvation in the light of the themes that can be seen in the texts examined here.

The Spirit and the sustenance of creation

We begin with three texts in the Psalms that may point to the Spirit's role in the sustenance of creation, though in two of these cases *rûaḥ* is routinely translated as something other than 'Spirit'. However, it will be seen that in both instances the sense of *rûaḥ* exceeds the sense of 'breath, wind' and moves into the semantic range of 'Spirit', even if the more basic sense remains. In both instances this occurs through the intertextual allusions established by the psalm to the opening verses of Genesis 1. As du Plooy notes, in some of these instances the reference to the *rûaḥ* is simply a poetic way of referring to

---

3. Among others, particular attention could be given to Isa. 11:1–9; 40:12–31; 42:1–9; 61:1–11; 63:7–14; Ezek. 36:16–38; Joel 3 (ET 2:28–32); Zech. 7:8–12.

God,[4] though the word's wider reference is not thereby lost. We will also note a close relationship between Yahweh's word and his *rûaḥ* as the means by which hope is provided. In our third example *rûaḥ* is more commonly translated as 'Spirit', though the element of 'breath' is not left behind. Further, this theme is always focused on praising Yahweh, though in each of the psalms we consider we shall note that the psalm does not assume that Yahweh's sustenance of the creation through his *rûaḥ* is necessarily experienced positively. The creation can be experienced as something that is threatening, but doxology, and specifically doxology that emerges from reflection on the work of Yahweh's *rûaḥ*, is a crucial means of engaging with this. What emerges from this is that, for the Psalms, one way that Yahweh's continued sustenance and renewal of creation is achieved is through his Spirit, and it is this that enables the psalms simultaneously to acknowledge the threat experienced from the creation and yet still to praise God.

Psalm 33:6

Psalm 33 is a hymn of praise to Yahweh that consists of three stanzas. As is typical of the *Gattung*, it opens with a plural summons to praise, inviting the worshipping community to express their joy in Yahweh (Ps. 33:1–3).[5] This is followed by a series of reasons why Yahweh is to be praised (Ps. 33:4–19), before the conclusion announces the community's trust in Yahweh, finally asking for the community's hope in Yahweh to be replicated by his *ḥesed* towards them (Ps. 33:20–22).[6] Indeed, although the psalm says a great deal about God, it is

---

4. R. du Plooy, 'Die Teologiese Gebruik van *rûaḥ* YHWH in die Ou Testament', PhD Thesis, Northwest University, 2004, p. 290, 'In sekere gevalle is "U Gees" 'n poëtiese manier om van die Here (U) te praat' (In certain instances 'your Spirit' is a poetic way to speak of the Lord [your]).

5. Konrad Schaefer, *Psalms* (Collegeville: Liturgical, 2001), p. 81, notes that the opening address of this psalm builds on the conclusion of Ps. 32. The blessedness described in that psalm thus finds a focus in this one.

6. Samuel Terrien, *The Psalms: Strophic Structure and Theological Commentary*, 2 vols. (Grand Rapids: Eerdmans, 2003), vol. 1, p. 297, points to the notable regularity of the structure of the psalm, where each strophe in the central section consists of two substrophes consisting of two bicola each. Rather than 'substrophes', it is better to follow P. J. Botha and J. H. Potgieter, '"The Word of Yahweh Is Right": Psalm 33 as a Torah-Psalm', *VE* 31 (2010), available at http://www.ve.org.za/index.php/VE/article/view/431/525 (accessed 21 June 2012), and speak only in terms of stanzas and strophes.

notable that only in the last line is God actually addressed, the people asking
for his *ḥesed* to be upon them. It is notable that as we progress through the
reasons why Yahweh is to be praised, the psalm progressively narrows the point
of focus from all creation (Ps. 33:4–7) down to the individual who trusts in
Yahweh's *ḥesed*.

The psalm's unity can also be observed in the number of key terms that occur
across the main sections of the text. For example, in the opening summons we
are told that praise befits the upright (*yāšār*, Ps. 33:1), while the first reason for
praising Yahweh is that his word is upright (*yāšār*, Ps. 33:4).[7] Similarly, Yahweh
is said to watch over those who hope (*yāḥal*) in his *ḥesed* (Ps. 33:18), while the
final prayer is to experience Yahweh's *ḥesed* as the people hope (*yāḥal*) in him
(Ps. 33:22). Finally, we can note that the claim is made that the earth is full of
Yahweh's *ḥesed* (Ps. 33:5), so that this theme both bookends the central section
and also leads into the final prayer.[8] This terminological interchange serves to
link the sections of the psalm, stressing that it is the upright who hope in Yahweh
and therefore offer him praise. We should note, however, that the closing note
of the central stanza is that Yahweh keeps his people from famine.[9] This may
suggest that the hymn emerges against a background of environmental struggle
in which famine is being faced, perhaps – given the associated references
pointing to the inability of royal and military power to save – a famine brought
about by human behaviour. In any case, themes associated with creation are
present at the beginning and end of the second stanza, providing a further
thematic link within the psalm. That some form of threat is experienced within
the creation is apparent from the final prayer for the people to experience
Yahweh's *ḥesed*.

---

7. John Goldingay, *Psalms*, 3 vols. (Grand Rapids: Baker Academic, 2006–8), vol. 1,
p. 466, thus suggests that Yahweh's word here should be understood as his promise,
as something that can be trusted.

8. See also Markus Witte, 'Das neue Lied – Beobachtungen zum Zeitverständnis von
Psalm 33', *ZAW* 114 (2002), pp. 523–525, on different framing patterns in the psalm,
though not all aspects of his proposed chiasm are convincing.

9. Mitchell Dahood, *Psalms I: 1–50* (Garden City: Doubleday, 1965), p. 203, treats
famine as 'the Hungry One', a personification of Death. But the introduction of
Canaanite deities at this point of the psalm is difficult to justify, as nothing earlier
in the psalm acknowledges the possibility of their existence. Moreover, although
the preposition '*b*' can mean 'from', it is much more common for it to mean 'in',
and the idea of 'keeping alive in famine' is more consistent with the rest of the
psalm.

More particularly for our purposes, we note that in verses 4–7 we have reasons for praise that focus on Yahweh's concern for justice and his role in creation, which is quite distinct from the other strophes in the second stanza that look more at human response to Yahweh.[10] As such, this strophe is marked out for special prominence through its placement at the head of the second stanza, its verbal links to the opening stanza and its thematic distinctiveness in comparison to the balance of the second stanza. Indeed, verse 4 thus becomes the pivot for the whole psalm as it first links back to the first stanza while preparing for the whole of the second stanza and then links to the third, especially the final prayer. The prominence given to these verses within the structure of the psalm also means that the theme of justice is particularly highlighted in describing Yahweh's works. Indeed, Yahweh's love of this is probably to be understood as characteristic[11] so that the subsequent finite verbs that describe his past actions are to be interpreted as particular expressions of this commitment on Yahweh's part.

Creation is thus the first example of Yahweh's commitment to justice, a commitment that is also seen in the fact that the earth is full of his *ḥesed*. The statement about creation in Psalm 33:6 then makes a quite direct reference to Genesis 1 by noting that the heavens were created by Yahweh's word, a reference to creation by divine fiat that typifies the chapter.[12] Verse 7 provides a further link to Genesis 1:2, by describing the waters as *těhômôt*, echoing the reference to the *těhôm* there. Hence, when we read that Yahweh made the hosts of the heavens by the *rûaḥ* of his mouth, we may legitimately note a further allusion to Genesis 1:2. That the *rûaḥ* comes from Yahweh's mouth leads naturally to the translation 'breath' that is typical of English versions,[13] but it also points

---

10. Botha and Potgieter, 'Word of Yahweh', prefer to see these verses as the conclusion of the opening section, since the subsequent reasons for praise focus on human response. Their basic observation is certainly correct, though it still seems better to see these verses as commencing the psalm's second section. However, the value of this observation is that it highlights the special function of these verses within this section.

11. Note the participle *'ōhēb* (v. 5).

12. In theory, the influence could be the other way round, but since Ps. 33 alludes to a number of other OT texts (e.g. v. 7 alludes to Exod. 15:8 and Josh. 3:13), it is more probable that Gen. 1 is part of the cluster of textual allusions it uses in building to the final prayer.

13. E.g. ESV.

to the larger semantic range of the word,[14] including, through its echoing of Genesis, the more particular sense of 'Spirit'. That is, even though 'breath' is an appropriate translation, *rûaḥ* here appears to mean more than just breath, confirming du Plooy's observation that sometimes it verges on being a poetic means of referring to God.

But these verses do not only allude to Genesis 1:2. We should note, for example, that in Genesis 7:11 it is the *tĕhôm* that opens up in the flood, and this is reversed only when Yahweh sends his *rûaḥ* to blow upon the flood (Gen. 8:1). By generating these allusions, the psalm points readers back to the wider context of Genesis where the *rûaḥ* is not only present in the creation itself but also points to Yahweh's continued involvement in the creation.

There are no further references to the *rûaḥ* in the psalm, but the echoes of Genesis (among other texts) are an important contribution to the psalm's rhetoric. Throughout, the psalm emphasizes Yahweh's presence within the created order as the one to be feared, who sustains his people, who observes all that is done. This is why hope is to be found in Yahweh alone, the one who is both creator and who continues to act in creation. If this psalm is summoning praise from within the context of a famine, then the allusion to the work of the *rûaḥ* is at least one way in which the psalm continues to encourage hope, providing the reason for the prayer with which the psalm closes.

Psalm 147:18

A related,[15] though less developed, reference to the *rûaḥ* is found in Psalm 147, in what is effectively an extended summons to praise Yahweh, especially summoning praise from Jerusalem.[16] In the post-exilic context of the close of

---

14. Hans-Joachim Kraus, *Psalms 1–59: A Commentary* (Minneapolis: Fortress, 1988), p. 376, sees it as synonymous with Yahweh's word, so that Yahweh's breath is a 'creative vital force'. But when seen in the light of the wider background from Gen. 1 we need to go one step further and note an association with the Spirit there.

15. On similarities between Pss 33 and 147:1–11, see Frank-Lothar Hossfeld and Erich Zenger, *Psalms 3* (Minneapolis: Fortress, 2011), pp. 621–622. But note especially the way vv. 10–11 here draw on Ps. 33:16–18.

16. As is well known, the LXX divides this into two psalms, with vv. 1–11 as LXX Ps. 146 and then vv. 12–20 as LXX Ps. 147, thus bringing the numeration of the LXX psalter back into line with MT (from which it had departed due to the earlier joining of MT Pss 9 – 10 to form a single psalm). Hossfeld and Zenger, *Psalms 3*, p. 620, consider Ps. 147 to be a diptych, but a stronger case can be made for the unity of the psalm as a whole, especially when we note the way that the creation themes develop

Book 5 of Psalms, this praise emerges in the context of the restoration of Jerusalem, quite possibly during the time of Nehemiah if the reference to rebuilding the city in verse 2 reflects events of that time. But even if we cannot be that specific,[17] it is still clear that the psalm offers praise against a background of struggle in which it is important to know that Yahweh protects and enables the weak. This is particularly evident in verses 3–6, which move from Yahweh's concern for the weak through a reflection on his power evident in creation and then back to his care for the humble. Such themes tend to be emphasized in times when people experience change or upheaval, and this psalm's concern with the outcasts of Israel gathered by Yahweh indicates that it emerges from a time of social challenge.

Throughout, the psalm juxtaposes Yahweh's care for Jerusalem with his sovereignty over creation. It is structured around three sets of imperatives in verses 1, 7 and 12. It is notable that the imperatives in the first two of these (halĕlû, v. 1; 'ĕnû and zamĕrû, v. 7) are plural, while in the third pair they (šabĕḥî and halĕlî, v. 12) are feminine singular as Jerusalem is directly addressed.[18] This focus on Jerusalem is nevertheless closely linked to the previous references to Yahweh's sustenance of the needy and of creation. It is possible that the perfect verbs in verse 13 might point to the situation that gave rise to the psalm as it reflects on Yahweh's activity in strengthening Jerusalem, but this is not entirely clear. What seems more certain, though, is that the strengthening of the city should be seen in parallel with Yahweh's power over creation as the mechanism by which he provides enduring security and peace for the city.

The psalm is also notable for the progression of themes associated with creation that run through it. In the first section it is Yahweh's sustaining power over creation as a whole that is stressed: he numbers and names the stars. What matters for this psalm is not that Yahweh created them but that they continue

---

through it in relation to previous acts of deliverance; similarly, J. Clinton McCann, 'Psalms', in *NIB*, vol. 5, p. 1267.

17. As Adrian Curtis, *Psalms* (London: Epworth, 2004), p. 262, points out, the participle *bônēh* more likely refers to Yahweh's continuing activity in building up Jerusalem, though perhaps for some readers the verse could trigger reflection on the period of Nehemiah.

18. Jacob Chinitz, 'Psalm 147', *JBQ* 27 (1999), pp. 115–117, offers a reconstructed order for the psalm, built around the three themes 'God in Nature', 'God's Morality' and 'God in Relation to Israel'. Although this helps to show the way in which the different themes occur across the psalm, it is better to recognize that these themes are integrated into the whole psalm rather than being separable elements.

to exist under his dominion. Nevertheless, the stars are distant, far from the immediate experience of the Jerusalem community. So in the second stanza the creational focus is on how Yahweh provides for animals and birds (vv. 8–9), while in the third stanza we come to the peace that Yahweh brings, one aspect of which is the provision of the wheat harvest. We thus move from that element of Yahweh's sustenance of creation that is most distant from human experience to that which is most specific to it.

Within this final section of the psalm we find the reference to Yahweh's *rûaḥ*, though as with Psalm 33 it is closely linked with Yahweh's word. References to Yahweh's word are particularly prominent here, as it is mentioned in both verse 15 (*'imrâ* and *dābār*) and verses 18–19 (both *dābār*). Indeed, Yahweh is said to be particularly active in distributing both his word and his power through creation, with the participle that commences each of verses 15–19 in some way related to the theme of distribution. This is structured on the following pattern:

a. Yahweh's word – verse 15
b. Elements of creation – verses 16–17
c. Yahweh's word and elements of creation – verse 18
d. Yahweh's word – verse 19

The climax of this pattern is the statement in verse 20 concerning the uniqueness of Israel's relationship with Yahweh. It is apparent from this structure that the reference to Yahweh's *rûaḥ* is less central in Psalm 147:18 than it is in Psalm 33:6. Nevertheless, the parallelism between Yahweh's word and the elements of creation in 147:18 does give *rûaḥ* a certain prominence. This is strengthened by the fact that the elements of creation in verses 16–17 are associated with winter, and are thus elements that are threatening to those who depend on local agricultural produce. This contrasts with verse 18 where we move to the elements of summer.[19] So, where the rhetorical question with which verse 17 ends suggests that none can stand before the cold sent by Yahweh, as we move into verse 18 we discover that when Yahweh sends his *rûaḥ*, creation is transformed into that which is life-giving and affirming. Here *rûaḥ* is most commonly translated as Yahweh's 'wind', though, as Allen has argued, 'breath' is a better translation since the *rûaḥ* clearly comes from Yahweh[20] (even if this breath is experienced as the warm wind that removes the elements of winter). But since *rûaḥ* is effectively a manifestation of Yahweh's presence, the sense of 'Spirit' also hovers in

---

19. Cf. Willem A. VanGemeren, 'Psalms', in *EBC*, vol. 5, p. 871.
20. Leslie C. Allen, *Psalms 101–150* (Waco: Word, 1983), p. 306.

the background. *Rûaḥ* here is more than a meteorological term, as it also conveys 'the power, presence and purpose of Israel's personal God'.[21] As with Psalm 33:6, *rûaḥ* and word together bring life, and it is this combination that sustains hope and praise in the midst of challenging circumstances.

Psalm 104:29–30

Psalm 104 represents a sustained reflection on themes associated with creation,[22] perceiving both Yahweh's work in sustaining the creation in general terms and also highlighting the specific role of the Spirit of Yahweh in bringing renewal (both *bārā'* and *ḥādaš*) to it. As with the psalms already considered, it is again a hymn, though this one begins by summoning the individual who speaks to bless Yahweh (*bārăkî napšî 'et yhwh*, vv. 1, 35c) and ends with a plural call to praise (*halĕlû yāh*, v. 35d).[23] Once again, there are close links with the text of Genesis, with the first seven stanzas all having a parallel with Genesis 1,[24] while the closing stanza (vv. 31–35) is preparation for the praise of Yahweh. Indeed,

---

21. McCann, 'Psalms', p. 1268.

22. Although connections with the Egyptian Great Amarna Hymn have been highlighted, it is notable that the recent study of Annette Krüger, 'Psalm 104 und der Große Amarnahymnus: Eine Neue Perspektive', in Erich Zenger (ed.), *The Composition of the Book of Psalms* (Leuven: Peeters, 2010), pp. 609–621, does not find any connections with the relevant portions of this psalm, so this issue is not pursued here.

23. Hossfeld and Zenger, *Psalms 3*, pp. 46–48, argue that vv. 1a, 35c–d are secondary framing elements because of the placement of the psalm to follow Ps. 103 and to prepare for the closing element of Book 4. Whether or not this is correct, John Walton, 'Psalms: A Cantata About the Davidic Covenant', *JETS* 34 (1991), pp. 21–31, also notes that Ps. 104 introduces Pss 104 – 106 as a 'series surveying the mighty and gracious deeds of God' (p. 29).

24. Following Terrien, *Psalms*, vol. 2, p. 710, who identifies the strophes as Sky (vv. 2–4), Earth (vv. 5–9), Water (vv. 10–13), Vegetation (vv. 14–18), Moon and Sun (vv. 19–23), The Great Sea (vv. 24–26), The Life Giver (vv. 27–30) and Praise of Yahweh (vv. 31–35). Terrien arranges these chiastically, with the pivot around strophes 4–5. It is also notable that this matches the eight creative acts of Gen. 1, though of course the order is different. Again, I would rather speak of stanzas. Although Terrien's chiasm does work, there are other structuring elements within the psalm, so too much stress should not be placed on the chiasm. Schaefer, *Psalms*, p. 257, perhaps goes too far the other way in claiming that '[w]hat results is not a logical composition, but the poet's impressionistic contemplation'.

the emphasis on creation is such that Goldingay can point to the complete lack of salvation or redemption language or any reference to Israel.[25] As with Psalm 33, this reflection on creation is ultimately directed to the prayer of the closing stanza, asking that Yahweh continue to rejoice in all aspects of his creation. But as we have seen in Psalms 33 and 147, it is again a creation that can at times be experienced as threatening.[26] So, although the psalm acknowledges that Yahweh has overcome the forces of chaos in creation (vv. 5–9) so that the earth continues to produce what is needed for the sustenance of all creation (vv. 10–18), it is also aware of prowling lions (vv. 21–23). There is a sense of danger in this, as there is in the description of the sea and the continued presence of Leviathan. These are aspects of creation that human beings would experience as threatening, even if the psalm acknowledges that all are under Yahweh's control. But it is because it brings these diverse elements together that the psalm can be both a celebration of the goodness of creation and a prayer that knows that creation can continue to be enjoyed only as Yahweh brings renewal to it.

Within this context it is notable that there is an abundance of *rûaḥ* language, and the psalmist draws on the breadth of the word's semantic range. These occurrences of *rûaḥ* are paired, so that, for example, in 104:3 Yahweh is described as the one who 'walks on the ends of the wind' (*hamĕhalēk 'al kanpê-rûaḥ*), while 104:4 affirms that he 'makes his messengers winds' (*'ōśeh mal'ākāyw rûḥôt*). In a section that is devoted to affirming Yahweh's greatness within creation, and especially the sky, it is natural that *rûaḥ* here should be associated with the wind, and indeed the combination of clouds (104:3) and flaming fire (104:4, probably lightning),[27] suggests that the language here is evocative of a storm, so that even the wildest elements of creation are under Yahweh's control; all are his messengers.[28]

The next pair of references occurs in verses 29–30, within a stanza that is concerned with the life of creatures that live on the earth (104:27–30), and that therefore matches the description of the earth in the second stanza (104:5–9) as a secure place in which to live. However, this section also has strong links

---

25. Goldingay, *Psalms*, vol. 3, p. 181. Much the same is true of Pss 33 and 147 too, though they seem to allude to some covenantal material.

26. Cf. Virgil Howard, 'Psalm 104', *Int* 46 (1992), p. 178.

27. Unless, with Mitchell Dahood, *Psalms III: 101–150* (Garden City: Doubleday, 1970), p. 35, we read 'flame and fire' as two separate nouns; but, since *ēš* can be a collective, this is unnecessary.

28. Note the repetition of *mal'ākāyw* from 103:20, providing a further link between these psalms.

back to the opening stanza, so it is important not to match one section of the psalm too precisely with another. However, that there are paired references to *rûaḥ* only in these two sections indicates that we should read them in the light of one another.

Where there is a broadly synonymous relationship between the two references to *rûaḥ* in verses 3–4, in this passage a strong contrast is drawn. In verses 27–28 the psalm describes the ways in which all creatures on earth are dependent upon Yahweh for their food. In effect, it is Yahweh's presence within creation that provides sustenance. Therefore, if for some reason Yahweh's presence is withdrawn (*tastîr pāneykā* – lit. 'you hide your face'), this causes dismay. Indeed, in an allusion to Genesis 2, the psalmist can declare that if Yahweh removes their breath (*rûaḥ*), then they die and return to the dust.[29] By contrast, when Yahweh sends his *rûaḥ* they are 'created' (*bārā'*) and – in an extension of this thought – Yahweh renews (*ḥādaš*) the ground (*'ădāmâ*). Thus, within the psalm overall, it can be claimed that all *rûaḥ* is under Yahweh's authority, and that in some way *rûaḥ* can be said to belong to Yahweh.

But what is the *rûaḥ* in this instance? Here, there is considerable variation among interpreters. So Kraus, for example, renders it as 'breath' in both verses 29 and 30,[30] and though he does not explain this, it seems implied that he regards the contrast between the two verses to be solely between Yahweh's 'taking' or 'sending' the *rûaḥ* so that in both instances 'breath' is appropriate. Such a reading might focus on 'breath' as something that brings continual renewal, though in fact Kraus makes explicit the links to Genesis 1 that are suggested by the vocabulary and sees *rûaḥ* as a creative power.[31] By contrast, Hossfeld and Zenger see an explicit reference to God's spirit, though they suggest that the *rûaḥ* that leaves the creatures is to be identified with God's creator Spirit, and it is this that is sent forth.[32] Although understanding *rûaḥ* in verse 30 as God's spirit seems probable, Goldingay's view, that the *rûaḥ* of the creatures is a pale reflection of the divine spirit, is preferable; though he too wants to see these as parallel references to the same spirit.[33]

Any attempt to make a close link between the divine *rûaḥ* and that of other creatures, however, suffers from the fact that although all creatures depend upon

---

29. The allusion to Gen. 2:7 is inexact in that Genesis refers to *nĕšāmâ*, not *rûaḥ*. Moreover, the Genesis text is discussing humans, not animals.

30. H.-J. Kraus, *Psalms 60–150* (Minneapolis: Augsburg, 1989), p. 296. See also ESV marg.

31. Kraus, *Psalms 60–150*, p. 297.

32. Hossfeld and Zenger, *Psalms 3*, pp. 56–57.

33. Goldingay, *Psalms*, vol. 3, p. 194.

Yahweh for their life and breath, Yahweh's *rûaḥ* can be said to act in ways otherwise directly attributed to Yahweh. Thus, although Yahweh is still the implied subject of the verb *bārā'*,[34] he acts here through his *rûaḥ*, so that the *rûaḥ* stands in Yahweh's place. At this point, therefore, to speak of too close a link between the two references is to miss the radically distinctive usage of *rûaḥ* in this context, and so 'Spirit' is surely the better translation. However, since there is undoubtedly some connection between God's *rûaḥ* and that of his creatures, we cannot lose sight of the fact that the element of 'breath' has not been completely removed.[35] Read in this way, the sending of the Spirit stands as a contrast to the removal of God's presence in verse 29, as a way of saying that God continues to be at work in creation. In particular, it then becomes apparent that it is through the Spirit, as a means of God's presence, that creation is renewed. This renewal is not here something that occurs eschatologically, but instead is an expression of continual renewal. Anderson's comment, in another context, is apposite: 'Creation is not just an event in the remote past but also includes the present cosmic order that the Creator sustains against continuing disruptions of the powers of chaos.'[36]

What our study of Psalms 33, 147 and 104 reveals is that this continued sustenance of the creation by Yahweh is specifically associated with his *rûaḥ*, and, though the way in which we best translate this moves between 'breath' and 'Spirit',[37] it is clear that the sense is always wider than any one equivalent in English. These psalms also link the *rûaḥ* with Yahweh's word and encourage praise in the face of challenging circumstances. In short, for the Psalms, the Spirit is not only a means by which God was present in creation, it is also a means by which God continues to be present and thus to sustain his creation.[38] This not only evokes praise – it continues to offer hope that God will ultimately overcome the challenging circumstances being faced. As McCann has observed, an environmental consciousness 'begins with praising God'.[39] These psalms

---

34. Though of course as a niphal there is no actual subject, but it seems to be a divine passive.

35. Howard, 'Psalm 104', thus prefers to speak of God's 'spirit-breath'.

36. Bernhard W. Anderson, *Contours of Old Testament Theology* (Minneapolis: Fortress, 1999), p. 212.

37. E.g. ESV.

38. This is partly why Michael A. Bullmore, 'The Four Most Important Biblical Passages for a Christian Environmentalism', *TrinJ* 19 (1998), pp. 143–149, affords pride of place to Ps. 104.

39. McCann, 'Psalms', p. 1100.

certainly all lead us to a greater consciousness of creation and thus of our responsibility for it through praise; but they also encourage us that the God who spoke and whose Spirit was active in creation continues to be active in sustaining the creation.

The Spirit and the renewal of creation

Whereas the psalms we have considered so far use *rûaḥ* more broadly than just to refer to God's 'Spirit', the final two texts we shall consider seem to use the word in a narrower sense. Thus most translations render *rûaḥ* in these texts as 'Spirit', and, though the notion of 'breath' is not completely absent, it here represents only a minor element of the *rûaḥ*. These texts also take on an eschatological hue, though we shall see that they never lose contact with the current state of creation. As such, where eschatological elements are included, they represent an extension of the work of the Spirit of God from the sustaining role we have already noted. Both of our relevant texts here come from the book of Isaiah.

Isaiah 32:15–20

The exact divisions of this passage are disputed, and in particular the relationship between verses 9–14 and 15–20. However, although most commentators see 32:1–8 as a distinct unit, it is worth noting that both verses 1–8 and verses 15–20 focus on the theme of justice and its implications. In 32:1–8 this is through a righteous king, whereas in 32:15–20 this occurs when the Spirit is 'poured out upon us from on high' (Isa. 32:15). Hence, although the various oracles within the chapter may have originated in different settings,[40] it seems that there is evidence within the chapter to suggest that we are to read them in the light of one another.[41] However, the woe oracle (*hôy*) at 33:1 clearly introduces a new set of oracles, though again themes associated with justice are prominent.[42] For our purposes, it is not necessary to identify the means by

---

40. On this point there is no agreement as to date. For a concise summary, see Gene M. Tucker, 'Isaiah', in *NIB*, vol. 6, p. 264.

41. Similarly, Walter Brueggemann, *Isaiah 1–39* (Louisville: Westminster John Knox, 1998), p. 253.

42. It is notable that each of chs. 28, 29, 30 and 31 also begins with *hôy*. The opening *hēn* of 32:1 is not dissimilar orthographically, but of course offers a significant alternative.

which the various oracles in chapter 32 came together, but we can note that there is reason to read 32:15 – 20 in the light of what precedes it, while still acknowledging that this interrelationship of texts is a redactional achievement. We should also observe that the idea of the *rûaḥ* being poured out from above means that the word seems to be used without reference to wind or breath, and so 'Spirit' seems to be the primary sense here.

In 32:9–14 the prophet addresses a group of women, warning them against their complacency. They are warned that their current agricultural bounty will end as the various harvests fail so that the land will return to wilderness. It is against this backdrop of a creation that is struggling that there is the sudden 'until' (*'ad*) of 32:15, which introduces a marked contrast.[43] Although this contrast is stark, there are clear points of contact between the two passages, as key words occur across them, even if they are used with rather different senses.[44] More importantly, there is a clear change in focus that is generated by the pouring out of the Spirit, a change that is essentially one of reversal. Where the situation described by 32:9–14 is one of creation returning to chaos and insecurity, 32:15–20 describes a creation that is secure and productive. The most obvious evidence for this is found in the two occurrences of *šālôm* (32:17–18), though in fact this passage uses a range of words to emphasize the security of the people as a result of the presence of the Spirit. This ultimately extends to all the creation, so that where 32:14 speaks of the city as a place overrun by wild animals, 32:20 can envision the blessedness (*'ašrê*) of those who let ox and donkey wander freely.

Closely linked to the blessedness and fruitfulness of creation is the theme of justice, and this in turn brings us back to the reference to the king in 32:1–8.[45] It is clear from a number of passages in Isaiah that justice is something expected of the king, but also in more eschatological settings in Isaiah, the king and justice are particularly associated with the Spirit. This is most obviously the case in Isaiah 11:1–9, which links justice from the king with a reordered creation, a combination also evident in 28:6. As such, it is possible to read Isaiah 32 as

---

43. I understand the niphal *yē'āreh* as a divine passive, so that it is not just 'a spirit' that is poured out (so NRSV), but Yahweh's Spirit.

44. Wonsuk Ma, *Until the Spirit Comes: The Spirit of God in the Book of Isaiah* (Sheffield: Sheffield Academic Press, 1999), p. 79, points to *ša'ănanôt* (vv. 9, 18) and the root *bāṭaḥ* (vv. 11, 18). One can add that references to the city (*'îr*) occur in both vv. 14 and 19, though the sense of v. 19 is unclear.

45. R. E. Clements, *Isaiah 1–39* (Grand Rapids: Eerdmans, 1980), p. 263, fittingly observes that 'prosperity without justice is a worthless acquisition'.

referring to the king and his responsibility, perhaps in verses 1–8 looking ahead, as some have argued, to a future anointed king (messiah).[46] However, although these associations are important for how we read this passage, we should note that there are no references here to any human figure as the central focus. Rather, the Spirit is poured out more generally 'upon us'.[47] That is, although the book of Isaiah clearly sees a special relationship between the king, justice and the Spirit, this is not something that is unique to the king. Rather, the restoration of creation described here is a matter of God's own initiative, and this is something that he offers to all his people through the Spirit. Thus, although a king who is empowered by Yahweh's Spirit is a vital element in creating a context for justice, the fact that this passage expresses this without reference to a king is an effective means of declaring that the source of justice and a restored creation is ultimately to be found in Yahweh through his Spirit and not through the king alone.

Reference to the Spirit here thus evokes a range of Isaianic texts, but it also looks beyond them to point to the pre-eminent role of the Spirit in restoring creation, with this restoration itself as the first step in the establishment of justice. In this instance, it is only after the pouring out of the Spirit from on high has taken place and creation is restored that justice is brought about.

Isaiah 34:9–17

In many ways this final text from Isaiah is a polar opposite to what we find in chapter 32. Where that chapter looks to the establishment of justice, and in particular the work of the Spirit in establishing that justice through the restoration of creation, here we encounter an expression of Yahweh's judgment where the land becomes uninhabitable, though again Yahweh's Spirit is present. Complicating matters in this instance is the relationship of this passage to 35:1–10, though there does seem to be good reason to regard them as a

---

46. So Brevard S. Childs, *Isaiah*, OTL (Louisville: Westminster John Knox, 2001), p. 241, though he believes the messianic dimension is achieved redactionally. Christopher R. Seitz, *Isaiah 1–39* (Louisville: Westminster John Knox, 1993), pp. 228–233, goes further, arguing that the king in 32:1–8 is Hezekiah, and that the land restoration brought about by the Spirit refers to events after 701 BC. This background is possible, but the text still seems to look forward eschatologically, so even if this is the historical context that triggered the passage, it still looks beyond the historical moment.

47. Cf. Thomas L. Leclerc, *Yahweh Is Exalted in Justice: Solidarity and Conflict in Isaiah* (Minneapolis: Fortress, 2001), p. 84.

diptych.[48] If so, then the restored wilderness in 35:1–2 now stands as a deliberate contrast to the destruction of the created order that we see in 34:9–17.

The passage itself is directed against Edom, a nation not covered by the
oracles against the nations in chapters 13–23. However, it seems that Edom
here is representative of those nations opposed to Yahweh,[49] with her judgment
symbolic of Yahweh's greater authority over all the nations. But what is described
for Edom is devastating, as the orderliness of creation itself is wound back –
though in fact what is lost is the area of human habitation through spreading
desertification.[50] Hence, although what is described is clearly intended to reflect
a longer-term desolation of Edom from the perspective of humans – and this
stands in marked contrast to the security of human experience relative to animals
in 35:1–10 – it is not an experience that excludes animals. So, although the
animals that gather are apparently[51] those that are capable of living in a more
extreme environment, their presence there is understood as evidence of
Yahweh's provision for them.

Particular evidence for this can be seen in 34:16–17. Although the exact
reference there to the 'scroll of Yahweh' (*sēper yhwh*) is uncertain, it is apparently
something that could be identified since it was to be searched. But the claim of
this scroll is that the various animals mentioned are all present because Yahweh
has decreed their presence, and that what his mouth has ordered (*ṣāwâ*) his Spirit
has gathered (*qābaṣ*). In this case the Spirit is understood as the means by which
Yahweh has acted within creation to bring about his purpose for it, and that
which is therefore ordained by Yahweh for the animals in 34:17 is effectively
brought about by his Spirit. In this instance it is clear that the sense of *rûaḥ* has
little reference to wind or breath and in effect stands in place of Yahweh. In
addition, we note again the clear association between Yahweh's word and

---

48. So, Childs, *Isaiah*, p. 253.

49. Edom's role as a representative is a widespread interpretation. E.g. Ma, *Until the
Spirit Comes*, p. 75. Ma (p. 76) also notes the strong connections between 32:9–14
and 34:9–15.

50. Cf. Hilary Marlow, 'Justice for Whom? Social and Environmental Ethics and
the Hebrew Prophets', in Katharine Dell (ed.), *Ethical and Unethical in the Old
Testament: God and Humans in Dialogue* (Edinburgh: T. & T. Clark, 2010),
pp. 103–121 (110–111).

51. We should, of course, acknowledge that the identification of many of these
creatures is uncertain. However, the point does not depend upon a specific
identification, as the passage assumes that the animals are able to prosper in
this otherwise forbidding landscape.

Yahweh's Spirit in relation to the creation. And although this time Yahweh has made the land uninhabitable for humans, the role of the Spirit is to carry out Yahweh's word so that animals continue to experience Yahweh's provision. Where the work of the Spirit had been to bring about justice for humans in 32:15–20, here the Spirit has made provision for the animals, because these too continue to be the object of Yahweh's care while nations that oppose Yahweh are overthrown.

Conclusion

We must be careful not to claim too much from a relatively small range of texts, especially as the association between Yahweh's Spirit and creation without explicit association with salvation-historical themes occurs only in Genesis, Psalms and Isaiah. In all likelihood all three psalms allude to Genesis 1, though such allusions are less likely in the two passages we noted in Isaiah, so for the purposes of this chapter we are dealing with a relatively narrow section of the canon. However, we can observe that for these traditions at least there is a strong association between the Spirit and the creation, and that for all of them the Spirit is understood as providing continued hope for all the created order. In doing so, the three psalms all offer hope that even challenging situations within creation can be faced because of the involvement of the Spirit, an involvement that is associated with Yahweh's word. It is notable that all three do this through doxology. We do not know why this approach was chosen, but perhaps it is because praising God for what he has and continues to do within creation in turn encourages us to take responsibility for it. But even if this guess is wide of the mark, it is still the case that Yahweh's continued involvement in the creation is a reason to praise God while also leading to prayer for his continued involvement. This involvement insists not only that Yahweh continues to sustain and renew his creation, but that he does so through his *rûaḥ*, which as we have seen incorporates the sense of both breath and Spirit.

These themes are developed further in the texts we noted from Isaiah where the Spirit is both the means for initiating a renewal of creation as a vital step in the establishment of justice and also in providing for animals in a context where humans are excluded. That the *rûaḥ* in both these passages is a source of life suggests that the motif of breath has not been left entirely behind, but in both instances the work of the *rûaḥ* so closely matches that which Yahweh does that it is more appropriate to think here in terms of the Spirit. For these five texts, then, it is vital to think of the sustenance and renewal of creation in the light of the Spirit of God and in association with the word of God. Creation is not something that has necessarily ended in the past but rather is a continued sphere of Yahweh's work, and thus is precisely where we might expect to find his Spirit bringing about renewal and justice.

6. DESTRUCTION OR TRANSFORMATION? EARTH'S FUTURE IN BIBLICAL PERSPECTIVE

Paul Williamson

Introduction

A decade ago, in a tongue-in-cheek parody, Keith Dyer compiled a fundamentalist version of the Earth Bible's ecojustice principles.[1] His 'six Biblicist Eschatological principles' were as follows:[2]

1. *The principle of imminent cataclysm* – Earth is headed for disaster (sooner rather than later).
2. *The principle of disconnectedness* – we humans do not have to share or feel responsible for Earth's fate (salvation is for humans, not Earth).
3. *The principle of inevitability* – there's nothing we (or Earth) can do about it.
4. *The principle of transcendence* – what really matters is the next world . . .
5. *The principle of sovereignty* – God is in ultimate (even direct) control of all this.
6. *The principle of self-interest* – God will rapture 'believers' out of this mess in the nick of time.

---

1. The ecojustice principles are listed at the beginning of each volume in the Earth Bible series.
2. K. D. Dyer, 'When Is the End Not the End? The Fate of Earth in Biblical Eschatology (Mark 13)', in N. C. Habel and V. Balabinski (eds.), *The Earth Story in the New Testament*, Earth Bible 5 (London: Sheffield Academic Press, 2002), pp. 44–56 (45).

Such a negative view of creation is based largely on what Dyer dubbed, 'texts of cosmic terror':[3] biblical depictions of global or cosmic catastrophe that, *prima facie*, imply radical discontinuity between this world and the next. The difficulty, however, is that (1) one set of biblical texts has been foregrounded, while another has been muted; and (2) a literal meaning has been assumed, even where texts arguably employ hyperbole or figurative language.

Undoubtedly a more eco-friendly reading of the Bible is possible if the situation is reversed (i.e. if we foreground texts stressing continuity and read any language of cosmic destruction metaphorically). However, tempting as this may be in the twenty-first century, the problem is that this may simply be replacing one form of distortion with another.

So what is the biblical perspective on the future of our planet? Indeed, given the diversity already alluded to, can we really speak of a single perspective? If there are diverse viewpoints (or at least different emphases), how should we adjudicate between such? On what grounds might it be appropriate to give a relative weighting to one tradition over the other? Indeed, is this even necessary? Is it possible to reconcile the biblical traditions, or is this achievable only by flattening out their distinctive emphases through some form of harmonization?

This chapter addresses such questions by examining the future of our planet from the perspective of biblical theology. To begin with, we shall briefly consider the earth's place in the Bible's metanarrative;[4] then we shall survey the biblical material that seems most relevant to the cosmological issues being addressed.

The earth's place in the biblical metanarrative

Earth's significance in the biblical metanarrative is immediately obvious. It is an important focus of God's original creation; and it is also an important focus of God's new creation. As numerous scholars have rightly observed,[5] God's

---

3. Ibid., p. 44.

4. Such an approach gives Scripture (rather than e.g. ecojustice principles) its proper 'generative and normative role in the ongoing articulation and reformulation of Christian doctrine' (D. G. Horrell, *The Bible and the Environment: Towards a Critical Ecological Biblical Theology* [London: Equinox, 2010], p. 121).

5. See J. R. Middleton, 'A New Heaven and a New Earth: The Case for a Holistic Reading of the Biblical Story of Redemption', *JCTR* 11 (2006), pp. 73–97; cf. also H. A. Snyder (with J. Scandrett), *Creation Means Salvation Healed. The Ecology of Sin and Grace: Overcoming the Divorce Between Earth and Heaven* (Eugene: Cascade, 2011). Even

creative and redemptive goal for humanity is not some kind of ethereal existence 'somewhere in outer space', but an embodied state in a physical place where God rules and righteousness dwells. As Ladd observes, 'The earth is the divinely ordained scene of human existence.'[6] And so, both at the beginning and end of the biblical story, the earth has a very prominent place.

In between these two poles there is considerable focus on both the physical space we inhabit and the impact of human sin upon our environment. This is especially clear in the early chapters of Genesis. As a consequence of human sin, the ground becomes cursed (Gen. 3:17–18; 5:29; cf. 4:12), and by Noah's day violence had so marred the earth that God had to destroy it.[7] Subsequently, we see the same thing with respect to the Promised Land, which essentially functions as a microcosm of the planet.[8] Israel's unfaithfulness and rebellion resulted in drought and ecological disaster. Along similar lines, the sins of the nations also had repercussions for the lands they inhabited. Human sin affects not only us, and our relationship to God; it also affects the earth, and our relationship to the environment – as reflected today in the impact of human behaviour on climate change.[9]

Since the earth has been adversely affected by human sin, it seems reasonable to anticipate that 'the earth must also share in God's final redemption'.[10] Thus Hoekema insists that '[t]he total work of Christ is nothing less than to redeem this entire creation from the effects of sin . . . God will not be satisfied until the entire universe has been purged of all the results of man's fall.'[11] This is fore-shadowed in God's re-creation of the earth after the flood, and in the prophetic expectations of rejuvenation of the land after the exile (e.g. Isa. 35:1–10;

---

strong advocates of discontinuity do not dispute that the final state will involve an earthly existence for humanity. Cf. E. Adams, *The Stars Will Fall from Heaven: Cosmic Catastrophe in the New Testament and Its World*, LNTS 347 (London: T. & T. Clark, 2007).

6. G. E. Ladd, *The Presence of the Future* (Grand Rapids: Eerdmans, 1974), p. 59.

7. The same Hebrew verb is used of the earth's 'corruption', the 'corrupting' behaviour of all flesh, and God's intent to 'destroy' both them and the earth. This is therefore the first instance of God's 'destroying those who destroy the earth' (Rev. 11:18).

8. For more on this, see P. S. Johnston and P. Walker (eds.), *The Land of Promise: Biblical, Theological and Contemporary Perspectives* (Leicester: Apollos, 2000).

9. For more on the latter, see R. S. White (ed.), *Creation in Crisis: Christian Perspectives on Sustainability* (London: SPCK, 2009).

10. Ladd, *Presence of the Future*, p. 60.

11. A. A. Hoekema, *The Bible and the Future* (Grand Rapids: Eerdmans, 1979), p. 275. This is obviously the major thesis in Snyder, *Salvation Means Creation Healed*.

Jer. 33:10–13; Ezek. 36:1–15). And such an expectation evidently underpins texts like Romans 8:21, where creation itself is said to await liberation 'from its bondage to decay'.[12]

But what form will such 'liberation' take? Will the new world be just the old one with a facelift – a wonderfully transformed version of the present edifice? Or should we expect something more radical than that? Will the old world be completely demolished, and replaced with an entirely new construction?[13] Or is there a *via media* that better fits the biblical testimony?

The analogy with the Genesis flood (cf. 2 Pet. 3) implies that some demolition work will be involved.[14] While the world before and after the flood is obviously the same physical reality, the flood itself is depicted as a work of de-creation. The earth was returned in some measure to its primordial state, as part of the process of being cleansed and renewed.

Another biblical analogy, the final redemption of our bodies, suggests both continuity and discontinuity, as reflected in the resurrection body of Jesus. The bodily scars and his ability to eat physical food clearly testify to the former, whereas the extraordinary ability to pass through grave clothes and walls highlights the latter. So if both continuity and discontinuity are involved in the redemption of our bodies, it would follow that it might be likewise for the liberation of our planet. Not surprisingly, the relevant biblical texts bear this out.

An analysis of the relevant biblical texts[15]

The Torah
Earth's future prospects are first raised in the immediate aftermath of the flood

---

12. Unless stated otherwise, all Scripture translations in this chapter are from the NIV.

13. So R. L. Overstreet, 'A Study of 2 Peter 3:10–13', *BSac* 137 (1980), pp. 354–371; D. J. Macleod, 'The Seventh "Last Thing": The New Heaven and the New Earth (Rev. 21:1–8)', *BSac* 157 (2000), pp. 439–451.

14. For debate over the extent of Peter's analogy, see J. Dennis, 'Cosmology in the Petrine Literature and Jude', in J. T. Pennington and S. M. McDonough (eds.), *Cosmology and New Testament Theology*, LNTS 355 (London: T. & T. Clark, 2008), pp. 157–177 (173–175).

15. This analysis is generally limited to texts that (1) refer to the earth and/or the heavens (including the sun, moon and stars) and (2) make a statement about their durability or otherwise.

(Gen. 8:22). This divine deliberation clearly forms the basis of the covenantal promise that follows (cf. Gen. 9:11; cf. 9:15), which involves not just Noah and his family, but also 'all living creatures of every kind' (Gen. 9:15) and 'all generations to come' (Gen. 9:12). Therefore God's assurance seems to be both all-encompassing and 'everlasting' (Gen. 9:16; cf. Isa. 24:5; 54:9).[16] But what, exactly does 'everlasting' signify here?[17] The immediate context suggests 'as long as the earth endures' (Gen. 8:22). While that entire clause appears only here, the key phrase within it (lit. 'all the days of . . .') is used quite frequently, and always denotes a fixed period of time (usually someone's lifespan). Since it is used in the latter sense in each of its other twelve occurrences in Genesis, one could reasonably infer that it has a similar connotation here also. Thus understood, the phrase implies that the earth has a *fixed* as opposed to an *unlimited* lifespan.[18] Nevertheless, in the present context the emphasis is clearly not on earth's mortality, but on the reliability and enduring nature of God's creation 'decrees' (cf. Jer. 31:36).

In a similar vein, Deuteronomy 11:21 holds out the prospect of Israel's tenure of the land being prolonged as long as 'the heavens are above the earth'. Again, the context demands the idea of longevity and perpetuity – something that the physical cosmos evidently exemplifies. As with Genesis 8:22, the key phrase used here ('as the days that . . .') may arguably denote a fixed period of existence (cf. Lev. 12:2; 15:25; 25:50).[19] Once again, however, to foreground this idea would seem at odds with the thought of perpetuity being expressed in the text. In other words, although we may infer from both these texts (Gen. 8:22 and Deut. 11:21) that the present cosmos will not last for ever, the emphasis is on its stability and endurance, not its mortality and impermanence.

The Prophets

While the Former Prophets occasionally use the language of cosmic upheaval, this does not concern the future of the planet. The Song of Deborah uses such language (Judg. 5:4–5; cf. 5:20) to describe a thunderstorm that facilitated Barak's

---

16. While the allusion in Isa. 24:5 is disputable, the permanence of the Noahic covenant is clearly underlined in Isa. 54:9.

17. The Hebrew word *'ôlām* basically denotes 'a long time'.

18. Adams (*Stars Will Fall*, p. 28) categorically maintains that 'Applied here to the earth, the formulation indicates its mortality. The earth has an allotted period of existence like every other created thing.'

19. Ibid., p. 33.

victory over Sisera. Likewise, 2 Samuel 22:8–16 employs such graphic images metaphorically, depicting God's intervention on David's behalf (cf. 2 Sam. 22:1). Such a figurative use of cosmic imagery also seems to be reflected in the Latter Prophets.

In several passages Isaiah depicts God's judgment in grandiose terms – involving cosmic disturbance or catastrophe. The immediate context of some of these passages focuses on the judgment of particular nations (e.g. Babylon in Isa. 13, and Edom in Isa. 34). However, the cosmic upheaval described seems to be more closely associated with *universal* judgment, with which these oracles are introduced. Indeed, according to Raabe,[20] this literary convention in prophetic texts (i.e. the move from the universal to the national, or vice versa) is used to show that the judgment of any specific nation is a particularization of universal judgment. Adams uses this to counter the argument that catastrophic imagery is simply a metaphor for local sociopolitical upheaval (i.e. it is conventional OT language for 'earth-shattering' events).[21] While Adams recognizes that the images could still be *metaphorical* for human judgment, albeit on a larger scale, he claims that 'it would be more natural to read them as picturing the calamitous, nature-wrenching form that the coming judgment is expected to take'.[22] Whether this interpretation is natural or otherwise, it is certainly important to approach this material with epistemological humility, rather than simply pre-judging what we think it can or cannot mean.[23]

In Isaiah 13 Babylon's fate is linked to the Day of Yahweh,[24] a day on which the divinely appointed light-bearers will be darkened (Isa. 13:10), and both heaven and earth will quake violently (Isa. 13:13). Rather than suggesting that celestial bodies will be changed, Isaiah may simply be describing the physical effects of cloud and smoke – motifs elsewhere associated with the Day of Yahweh.[25] Moreover, while the cosmic shaking may allude to physical phenomena (e.g. earthquake, thunderstorm), it may well be hyperbole – as with the similar depiction

---

20. P. Raabe, 'The Particularizing of Universal Judgment in Prophetic Discourse', *CBQ* 64 (2002), pp. 652–674.

21. Adams, *Stars Will Fall*, pp. 42–44.

22. Ibid., p. 44. Adams, however, is more cautious than this statement suggests; cf. his following paragraph.

23. Cf. D. B. Sandy, *Plowshares & Pruning Hooks: Rethinking the Language of Biblical Prophecy and Apocalyptic* (Downers Grove: InterVarsity Press, 2002), pp. 163–164.

24. Cf. Isa. 13:6, 9, 13b.

25. See Joel 2:2, 30–31; Zeph. 1:15. Also cf. Ezek. 32:7.

of God's intervention in 2 Samuel 22 (cf. vv. 9–12).[26] The use of these motifs may therefore simply convey the magnitude of God's judgment, which, in Babylon's case at least, took the form of military conquest (cf. Isa. 13:17–18).

In Isaiah 24 the scene is apparently one of global catastrophe stemming from sinful human behaviour – people have broken 'the everlasting covenant' (Isa. 24:5).[27] Human rebellion has once more jeopardized earth's future, prompting God to decimate the earth (i.e. to initiate a further reversal of creation). The latter is graphically depicted in verses 19–20. One could infer from these verses that earth's anticipated demise will be terminal, but the wider context seems to anticipate restoration after such catastrophe.[28] It would appear, therefore, that even if this destructive imagery does allude to physical, global catastrophe, it is not intended in either a literal or absolute sense.[29]

Some measure of cosmic catastrophe also seems to be envisaged in Isaiah 34. Here again the immediate context is Yahweh's judgment of all nations (Isa. 34:2), of which Edom is representative (Isa. 34:5–17).[30] While some have interpreted the graphic imagery of 34:4 in terms of eschatological cataclysm,[31] the language on either side of this verse (i.e. mountains *dissolving* in blood, and Yahweh's *sword drinking its fill* in the heavens[32]) is clearly figurative. A figurative

---

26. Note especially the mention of Yahweh's heaven-splitting descent in the context of cosmic shaking (2 Sam. 22:10); cf. Isa. 64:1 (MT 63:19).

27. While the connotation of *'ereṣ* is potentially ambiguous (i.e. land or earth), prompting some to argue in favour of 'land' (of Judah) here, the parallel use of 'world' (Hebr. *tēbēl*) in v. 4 suggests otherwise, as does the universalistic tenor of the passage as a whole.

28. Cf. the references to Euphrates, Egypt and Jerusalem in Isa. 27:12–13. Admittedly, however, it may have been difficult to envisage the new cosmic reality other than in terms of the existing one. Cf. Adams, *Stars Will Fall*, pp. 12–13.

29. The description of sun and moon in Isa. 24:23 is clearly figurative. Rather than implying a diminishing of their light (cf. Isa. 13:10), the point here is probably that God's glory will so outshine them that they pale to insignificance (cf. Isa. 60:19–20).

30. Edom probably symbolizes all the rebellious nations here at the climax of this extended section on the nations that began in ch. 13, which would explain why such an oracle is located here and not among the other judgment oracles in Isa. 13 – 23.

31. E.g. E. J. Young, *The Book of Isaiah*, 2 vols. (Grand Rapids: Eerdmans, 1969), vol. 2, p. 431; B. G. Webb, *The Message of Isaiah: On Eagles' Wings*, BST (Leicester: Inter-Varsity Press, 1996), p. 142.

32. Even if the variant reading of 1QIsaᵃ ('My sword has appeared in the heavens') is adopted, the point stands.

interpretation of rotting or falling stars, as well as rolled-up or shrinking skies, may thus seem more appropriate: for example, the text could be depicting the manifest defeat of pagan deities, represented by the stars (Deut. 4:19; cf. 2 Kgs 17:16; 21:3, 5; 23:4–5; Jer. 8:2; 19:13),[33] or the destruction of actual celestial powers or heavenly forces that stand behind the armies of the nations (Isa. 24:21; cf. Dan. 10:13, 20–21).[34] Either way, the imagery has more to do with the nations' vulnerability than with cosmic destruction. Admittedly, the subsequent description of Edom's judgment does allude to the cataclysmic destruction of Sodom and Gomorrah (cf. Isa. 34:9). Moreover, Edom's desolation is pointedly described in terms of earth's primordial state (Isa. 34:11; cf. Gen. 1:2). But the fact that desert creatures can survive these circumstances (Isa. 34:11–17; cf. 13:21–22) cautions against taking any of this material too literally.[35]

However, as well as using these depictions of cosmic disaster, Isaiah also sets the permanence of Yahweh's salvation or steadfast love over against the transience of creation (Isa. 51:6; cf. 54:10). While both texts are primarily making a theological point, they seem to reflect a cosmological premise: heaven and earth – ancient symbols of permanence and stability – *may* not last for ever.[36]

Arguably this should be understood in the light of the book's ultimate hope of a new or renewed creation (Isa. 65:17), which will endure for ever (66:22). Isaiah envisages a virtual return to the conditions that pertained in Eden.[37]

---

33. J. N. Oswalt, *The Book of Isaiah, Chapters 1–39*, NICOT (Grand Rapids: Eerdmans, 1986), p. 609.

34. J. Blenkinsopp, *Isaiah 1–39*, AB (New York: Doubleday, 2000), pp. 356, 452; J. Goldingay, *Isaiah*, NIBC (Peabody: Hendrickson, 2001), p. 194.

35. Nevertheless, since other OT texts countenance at least the possibility of creation's eventual demise (see below), due caution should be exercised lest a metaphorical interpretation inadvertently empties a text of its literal significance (so Mark B. Stephens, *Annihilation or Renewal? The Meaning and Function of New Creation in the Book of Revelation*, WUNT 307 [Tübingen: Mohr Siebeck, 2011], pp. 41–42).

36. Despite being an assertion ('for . . . will') in some English translations, a concessive reading ('though . . . should'; see REB) of Isa. 51:6 is more appropriate, making this a hypothetical possibility rather than an absolute certainty.

37. 'The dominant feature of Isa 65:17–25 is its utopian perspective, marked by an "*Endzeit wird Urzeit*" motif (i.e. an eschatological reversion to primeval conditions), with Zion becoming like Eden' (R. L. Schultz, 'Intertextuality, Canon, and "Undecidability": Understanding Isaiah's "New Heavens and New Earth"', *BBR* 20.1 [2010], pp. 19–38 [33]).

In some ways Isaiah's vision surpasses the similar utopia anticipated in Ezekiel (cf. Ezek. 36:33–38; cf. 34:25–31; 47:1–12). However, while clearly highlighting the radical newness of this better future, 'the piling up of diverse descriptions . . . suggests that these are not to be taken too literally'.[38] Even so, it is doubtful if this utopia should be understood simply in sociopolitical terms.[39] As suggested by the use of the verb 'create' in conjunction with 'heaven and earth' (cf. Gen. 1:1), what is depicted here, albeit in embryonic form,[40] is new creation, God's definitive solution to Israel's past and present troubles.[41] While this new creation is arguably portrayed in terms of transformation and renewal,[42] this is not necessarily incompatible with the alternative model (i.e. destruction and replacement).[43] Even so, as Adams acknowledges,[44] there is no hint of any such cosmic destruction in these final

38. Schultz, 'Intertextuality', p. 34.

39. *Pace* Watts (*Isaiah 34–66*, WBC 25 [Waco: Word, 1987], p. 354), 'earth' should not be translated 'land' here (in conjunction with 'heavens' it signifies the entire planet) and thus this promise does not simply envisage a new sociopolitical situation. Cf. J. W. de Gruchy, 'The New Heaven and the New Earth: An Exposition of Isaiah 65:17–25', *JTSA* 105 (1999), pp. 65–74 (71).

40. As Schultz observes, 'Isaiah's "new earth" looks like a "new improved" version, but it cannot be "as good as it gets" if death and, consequently, sorrow, have not yet ceased' ('Intertextuality', p. 36). However, while John's vision of the new earth goes well beyond Isaiah's in this respect (cf. Rev. 21:4), the kernel of this future utopia is decidedly formed in Isaiah.

41. As such, it is also difficult to conceive how this new-creation language could simply be an oblique reference to Jerusalem and its temple mythology. Cf. C. H. T. Fletcher-Lewis, 'The Destruction of the Temple and the Relativization of the Old Covenant: Mark 13:31 and Matthew 5:18', in K. E. Brower and M. W. Elliott (eds.), *'The Reader Must Understand': Eschatology in Bible and Theology* (Leicester: Apollos, 1997), pp. 145–169 (156–162).

42. Cf. Isa. 65:8–10, 18–25. See also the concise discussion in Stephens, *Annihilation or Renewal?*, pp. 27–29.

43. The difference between these two concepts is less polarized when some measure of continuity *and* discontinuity is acknowledged. This is clearly not the case, however, if recreation is envisaged as *ex nihilo* – but even Adams does not adopt such an extreme position.

44. E. Adams, 'Does Awaiting "New Heaven and New Earth" Mean Abandoning the Environment?', *ExpTim* 121 (2010), pp. 168–175 (169).

chapters.[45] For that, one must go back to Isaiah 51:6 – yet, as noted above, there too the future of the present cosmos is left somewhat uncertain.

Much less uncertainty is reflected in Jeremiah. While the book contains a rather gloomy passage using de-creation language to describe Yahweh's judgment of Judah (Jer. 4:23–28), this is clearly not a prophecy concerning the end of the world, and thus cannot be taken to represent Jeremiah's cosmological outlook. This is more clearly reflected in chapters 31 and 33, where Israel's future is underwritten by an appeal to creation and the enduring nature of its divinely decreed structures (cf. Jer. 31:35–36; 33:20). Jeremiah's perspective on earth's future, therefore, seems entirely positive.

Of the remaining prophets, the most significant material is found in Joel and Haggai.[46] The cosmological imagery associated with Joel's Day of Yahweh (Joel 2:10, 30–31; 3:15–16) is analogous to that of Isaiah 13:10, and thus may have similar connotations, namely the kind of seismic or atmospheric activity associated with theophany.[47]

Haggai also anticipates a cataclysmic shake-up of the heavens and the earth (Hag. 2:6, 21), although for him: (1) this is imminent ('in a little while'); (2) it has a positive goal (a kind of divine shake-down of the nations, unleashing their wealth for temple restoration); and (3) it involves sociopolitical change (Hag. 2:22–23). However, none of these events is 'eschatological' in the narrow sense (i.e. relating to the end of the world).[48]

The Writings

Here the relevant texts are largely confined to the Psalms, and the dominant perspective aligns with that of Jeremiah; permanence and stability are

---

45. The 'former things' that will not be remembered (Isa. 65:17) refers either to God's previous acts of salvation (cf. Isa. 43:18; so Adams, 'Does Awaiting?', p. 169) or to Israel's former troubles (cf. 65:16; so Stephens, *Annihilation or Renewal?*, p. 237). Either way, it has no connotation of cosmic destruction.

46. Other texts employing cosmic imagery include Ezek. 32:7–8; 38:19–22; Mic. 1:4; Nah. 1:4–5; Hab. 3; Zeph. 1:2–3. However, none of these necessarily envisages global geophysical disaster; rather, the focus is more on earth's inhabitants than on the cosmos.

47. While Peter understands Joel's 'wonders' to have been fulfilled in some sense in the first century (cf. Acts 2:14–36), this does not exclude further fulfilment, as suggested by allusions to Joel's imagery in 2 Pet. 3 and Revelation.

48. Even Adams acknowledges that Haggai's shaking of the cosmos 'is not a world-ending catastrophe' (*Stars Will Fall*, p. 48).

emphasized, rather than instability or transience. Indeed, the latter ideas are reflected only in Psalms 46 and 102. The former emphasizes God's faithfulness and dependability – even in the midst of the most chaotic situation imaginable. The psalmist envisages a destabilizing of creation that threatens to reduce it to its primordial state (Ps. 46:2–3), a hypothetical scenario that shows that the stability of the cosmos was not thought of in absolute terms.[49] This is further reflected in Psalm 102:25–27, where once again the contrast between God and the cosmos emphasizes divine stability (Ps. 102:27). To illustrate the point, the psalmist states that the present cosmos 'will perish . . . wear out like a garment [and] . . . be discarded'.[50] However, the yiqtol verbs here could arguably be expressing a jussive and modal idea rather than an indicative: that is, 'they *may* perish . . . they *may* wear out . . . you *could* change them'.[51] Even so, these two psalms represent a distinctive note in the psalter.

The permanence and stability of the cosmos is affirmed in numerous psalms. In several it is simply asserted, without further comment, as a self-evident truth (e.g. Pss 93:1; 96:10; cf. 1 Chr. 16:30). The same thought is expressed slightly differently in Psalm 104:5, which develops the idea by referring to the flood and God's subsequent covenant (Ps. 104:6–9). Psalm 148:6 likewise claims that God set the cosmos in place 'for ever and ever – he issued a decree that will never pass away', apparently echoing the language of Jeremiah (Jer. 31:35–36; 33:25; cf. 5:24). In other psalms the cosmos is used as a symbol of endurance and permanence (cf. Pss 72:5–7, 17; 89:29, 36–37). Still other psalms apply the simile of the earth's immovability to Yahweh's sanctuary and/or Mount Zion (Pss 78:69; 125:1–2), or to Yahweh's word (Ps. 119:89–90). While obviously not the primary focus, all these texts thus bear eloquent testimony to the enduring nature of the cosmos.

Elsewhere in the Writings there is at least one more text that conveys this

---

49. As Adams puts it, 'The psalmist does not say that the earth *must* degenerate, but its dissolution is viewed as . . . a genuine geophysical possibility' (*Stars Will Fall*, p. 29 [his italics]).

50. What is envisaged here is 'the end of the whole created scheme' (D. Kidner, *Psalms 1–72*, TOTC [Downers Grove: InterVarsity Press, 1973], p. 175).

51. So also J. Goldingay, *Psalms*, vol. 3: *Psalms 90–150* (Grand Rapids: Baker, 2008), p. 160. L. Allen is a little more cautious. While his translation similarly allows for uncertainty, he comments, citing Isa. 51:6, 'Unlike material things, Yahweh alone is immortal and immune from decay' (*Psalms 101–150*, WBC [Dallas: Word, 2002], p. 23).

idea of cosmological stability.[52] The immediate context makes it obvious that, rather than expressing a firm belief in either, Job 14:12 is dismissing the prospect of human resurrection by the *inconceivable* idea that the moon should cease to exist. In the ancient world, the cosmos was the most stable and permanent thing imaginable. There can be little doubt, therefore, that the dominant perspective in the Writings is very positive.[53]

Overall, therefore, the testimony of the OT is mixed. Some texts imply that the earth has a limited lifespan and suggest that it will/may not endure for ever. However, unless the highly figurative language of some prophetic texts is taken literally, there is much more emphasis, overall, on earth's immovability and permanence. While the emphasis is not quite the same, a similar twofold perspective is apparently reflected in the NT.

The Gospels and Acts[54]

In the Sermon on the Mount, Jesus declares that 'the meek . . . will inherit the earth' (Matt. 5:5). While plainly a citation of Psalm 37:11, here in Matthew the focus is on our eschatological inheritance; hence it is probably the 'new earth' that is primarily in view.[55] Nevertheless, without any such qualification, a considerable measure of continuity between the present earth and the new earth is arguably implicit. This is also true of those petitions in the Lord's Prayer 'hallowed be your name, your kingdom come, your will be done, *on earth as it is in heaven*' (Matt. 6:9–10). This is essentially a prayer that the kingdom will come in all its fullness. However, to restrict the focus entirely to the new earth would seem at odds with the NT concept of inaugurated eschatology.

---

52. Eccl. 1:4 is probably irrelevant; the statement is probably more about earth being the only constant in an endless sea of change (i.e. earth is *relatively* enduring) than a claim that it is everlasting; so C. L. Seow, *Ecclesiastes*, AB (New York: Doubleday, 1997), p. 106.

53. Given the predominant emphasis in the last section of the OT canon, the underlying 'development in Old Testament cosmological thinking' suggested by Adams (*Stars Will Fall*, p. 33) seems unlikely.

54. In keeping with the OT discussion, different sections of the NT will be considered in their *canonical* arrangement.

55. Admittedly, it is also possible to read this blessing simply in terms of Jesus' redefining Abraham's heirs in a spiritual (as opposed to an ethnic) sense. Even so, as these heirs extend beyond Israel's borders, so too (implicitly) must the promised land (cf. Rom. 4:13).

In the same context Jesus uses the idea of cosmic endurance to highlight the continuing validity of the Law: 'until heaven and earth disappear, not the smallest letter . . . will by any means disappear from the Law until everything is accomplished' (Matt. 5:18). If the first clause is understood at face value, Jesus appears to be suggesting that the Law continues in force until the eschaton. If, however, such cosmic catastrophe is inconceivable (cf. Luke 16:17), this saying apparently suggests that the Law remains authoritative for ever. Obviously both these suggestions would make sense only if Jesus were referring to truth enshrined within the Law, rather than every stipulation it contains.[56] Fletcher-Lewis resolves this conundrum by insisting that here, as in Mark 13:31, Jesus is not referring to the physical cosmos at all; rather, he is alluding to the end of the Jerusalem temple and the related Torah constitution.[57] However, the non-figurative use of 'heaven' and 'earth' in the immediate and wider context (Matt. 5:5, 34–35; cf. 11:25) seems to undermine this interpretation, which leans heavily on a metaphorical use of this terminology.[58] In any case, it is difficult to decide whether Matthew 5:18 constitutes testimony to the future demise of heaven and earth, or (like the Lucan parallel) views such a prospect as inconceivable.[59]

For some, the latter concept also holds good for the similar saying used in the Olivet Discourse. Here, however, the claim that 'heaven and earth will pass away' (Mark 13:31; cf. Matt. 24:35; Luke 21:33) appears unequivocal. Thus Adams sees it as 'an unambiguous affirmation of the ultimate cessation of the created order'.[60] Likewise, for Sim, 'A more clear expression of the end of the present cosmic order would be difficult to find.'[61] This is obviously disputed by those who conclude that it is idiomatic language expressing the opposite

---

56. Many stipulations of the Law were clearly set aside by both Jesus and the apostles.

57. Fletcher-Lewis, 'Destruction of the Temple', p. 146.

58. Arguably, the same is true in the case of Mark 13:31 (cf. 13:27). Fletcher-Lewis (ibid., p. 167) detects the presence of temple symbolism in Matt. 5:13–14, although this seems even less plausible.

59. Adams (*Stars Will Fall*, p. 178, n. 221) maintains that 'the formulation of [Luke] 16.17 does not indicate that cosmic dissolution is totally impossible'. However, *contra* Adams, the use of the same formulation in Luke 18:25 hardly supports this conclusion – the whole point of Jesus' simile is that it is impossible to conceive of a camel passing through the eye of a needle.

60. Adams, *Stars Will Fall*, p. 163.

61. D. Sim, 'The Meaning of *Palingenesia* in Matthew 19:28', *JSNT* 50 (1993), pp. 3–12 (8).

of what it apparently affirms.[62] However, none of the metaphorical interpretations seems immediately obvious. Moreover, the following statement about
'that day or hour' (Mark 13:32; Matt. 24:36) – and the related exhortations to
vigilance – suggest that the focus has shifted from first-century events to the
eschaton. The transition point between 'all these things' (Mark 13:30; i.e. events
culminating in the temple's destruction) and 'that day or hour' (Mark 13:32) is
arguably this statement about heaven and earth.[63] If this is granted, the cosmic
imagery in verses 24–25 must be understood figuratively.[64] Alternatively, if the
transition point is signalled by the opening words of verse 24, the cosmic
imagery can be interpreted as theophanic phenomena associated with the Day
of the Lord.[65]

But whatever the association, if any, between the cosmic imagery and the
passing away of heaven and earth, attention seems to have shifted by verse 31
to climactic eschatological events. Thus understood, the Olivet Discourse anticipates (among other things) the end of the world as we know it. Even so, a
woodenly literal interpretation of the language that leaves no room for the
renewal of the present creation is surely wrong-headed in view of Matthew
19:28 and Acts 3:21 – texts that arguably attest to its rejuvenation.

The Pauline Epistles
The Pauline epistles reflect a generally positive outlook. Not surprisingly,
Romans 8 has attracted much attention.[66] In the midst of a discussion of the

---

62. Cf. N. T. Wright, *Jesus and the Victory of God*, COQG 2 (London: SPCK, 1996),
    pp. 364–365; R. T. France, *The Gospel of Mark*, NIGTC (Grand Rapids: Eerdmans;
    Carlisle: Paternoster, 2002), p. 540. For a critique, see Adams, *Stars Will Fall*,
    pp. 161–163.

63. So Dyer, 'When Is the End?', p. 54. This resolves the conundrum presented by
    Jesus' insistence that 'this generation will certainly not pass away until all these
    things have happened' (Mark 13:30 and parallels); 'all these things' refers only to
    what Jesus has spoken of prior to this verse (i.e. events that unfolded in the first
    century).

64. Since this is apparently how the OT material drawn together here was originally
    intended, such an interpretation seems appropriate.

65. Such a reading does not necessarily insist on interpreting the cosmic imagery in
    a woodenly literal manner: cf. Adams, *Stars Will Fall*, p. 160.

66. As Stephens observes, 'This passage represents the clearest reference to
    cosmic eschatology within the entire Pauline corpus' (*Annihilation or Renewal?*,
    p. 118).

certain hope that awaits believers, Paul focuses in verses 19–23 on creation itself.[67] This present creation, we are told, 'was subjected to frustration [*mataiotēs*]' (v. 20), quite possibly because of 'its bondage to decay [*phthora*]' (v. 21).[68] In any case, it was 'subjected . . . *in hope* that the creation itself will be liberated from its bondage to decay and brought into the freedom and glory of the children of God' (vv. 20–21). Both here and in the verses that immediately follow, Paul links hope for humanity with hope for creation. Both have a future, one that is inextricably related, and both 'groan' for such to materialize (vv. 22–23). Thus, whatever the exegetical uncertainties of this text, it seems clear that, for Paul, Christian hope encompasses not just humanity, but all creation.[69]

A similar inference can be drawn from the Christological hymn in Colossians 1:15–20. According to this text, Christ is 'the firstborn over all creation'; the one through whom and for whom 'all things were created'; the one in whom 'all things hold together'; and the one through whom 'God was pleased . . . to reconcile to himself *all things*'. It is clear from the immediate context (cf. vv. 15–18) that *ta panta* refers to all created things, thus in some sense the entire creation is encompassed in Christ's work of reconciliation. What this denotes, however, is not universal salvation, but rather the restoration of the peace (*šalôm*) that was evident in God's original creation and which the OT prophets anticipated for the new creation.[70]

Such an eschatological renewal of creation is at least implicit in 1 Corinthians 15 and is arguably foreshadowed in Paul's explicit references to 'new

---

67. As Jonathan Moo observes, there is now a broad consensus that *ktisis* refers here to the entire non-human creation ('Continuity, Discontinuity, and Hope: The Contribution of New Testament Eschatology to a Distinctively Christian Environmental Ethos', *TynB* 61.1 [2010], pp. 21–44 (26); cf. also Stephens, *Annihilation or Renewal?*, p. 120, n. 13).

68. Both phrases are enigmatic, but seem to allude to the consequences of human sin.

69. As Stephens (*Annihilation or Renewal?*, pp. 123–124) concludes, 'this passage clearly and unambiguously testifies to material continuity between present and future . . . the core motif of being "freed" from bondage/slavery can only make sense if there is some degree of material continuity between the present and the eschatological future'.

70. D. J. Moo, 'Nature in the New Creation: New Testament Eschatology and the Environment', *JETS* 49.4 (2006), pp. 449–488 (472). In some cases (e.g. the spiritual beings alluded to in Col. 1:20) this is achieved by vanquishing rather than saving them.

creation'.[71] Romans 4:13 also appears relevant: the promise that Abraham would 'inherit the world' (*kosmos*, my tr.) extends the territorial promise in line with the analogous extension of Abraham's heirs to include Gentiles.

A less positive note is apparently sounded in 1 Corinthians 7:31. Adams infers from this that 'Paul . . . does not take a consistent position on the fate of the created order. His formulation . . . strongly suggests a scheme of cosmic destruction followed by re-creation.'[72] However, here Paul is surely not referring primarily to the physical world per se, but to human society, especially human society aligned against God. In any case, it is doubtful that Paul had no firm opinion on how the cosmic future would unfold.[73] While the temptation to flatten contrasting ideas through harmonization must be resisted,[74] it seems unlikely that Paul just plainly contradicts himself on this issue. Rather, Paul probably did not consider these ideas to be polar opposites: the fact that 'this world in its present form is passing away' does not preclude creation's anticipated 'liberation from decay'.

The General Epistles

Of the general epistles, two stand out in particular: Hebrews and 2 Peter.[75] The citation of Psalm 102:25–27 in Hebrews 1:11–12 leaves little room for

---

71. For 1 Cor. 15, see J. White, 'Paul's Cosmology: The Witness of Romans, 1 and 2 Corinthians, and Galatians', in Pennington and McDonough, *Cosmology and New Testament Theology*, pp. 90–106 (102–106). For Paul's 'new creation' language, see D. J. Moo, 'Creation and New Creation; Transforming Christian Perspectives', in R. S. White, *Creation in Crisis*, pp. 241–254.

72. Adams, *Stars Will Fall*, p. 256, n. 4.

73. Adams (ibid., p. 257) concedes that there is not necessarily a 'uniform biblical eschatology' in either testament. However, it is arguably a better reflection of Adams's own conclusions to acknowledge 'distinct emphases' than to admit 'disparate viewpoints'.

74. So Adams (ibid.), and positively endorsed by Horrell (*Bible and the Environment*, p. 113). While also sounding this cautionary note, J. A. Moo ('Continuity, Discontinuity and Hope', pp. 25–26) is nevertheless reluctant to acknowledge irreconcilable differences between the 'different portraits of creation's future'.

75. Also worth noting is 1 Pet. 1:4 (which could imply that the present world is perishing). While 1 John 2:17 may appear to add its voice to the biblical testimony that 'the world . . . is passing away', here a cosmological connotation of 'the world' is not intended (cf. 1 Cor. 7:31).

uncertainty about creation's fate.[76] As elsewhere, the main point of the comparison (cf. 1:11b, 12b) is theological – the permanence of the Son. But this point is made by a comparison that clearly assumes such permanence *does not* apply to the cosmos.

This again comes to the forefront in chapter 12, where the point is supported by citing Haggai 2:6. As noted previously, the cosmic shaking Haggai envisaged was certainly not eschatological in the narrow sense; Haggai anticipated a shaking that would impact the economy much more than the environment. However, for the author of Hebrews, this cosmic shaking would constitute the final intervention of God, resulting in the removal of created things (Heb. 12:27).[77] What such removal entails is not spelt out,[78] but it clearly includes both earth and heaven – and thus, in some measure, implies the end of creation as we know it.[79]

For most interpreters, the same is true of 2 Peter 3. Despite attempts to interpret this passage in a more eco-friendly way, most concede that this is exegetically challenging, to say the least.[80] The text unambiguously relates to the promise of the Lord's return and associated eschatological events (cf. 2 Pet. 3:3, 9–10, 12–13). And these include a judgment that will encompass the entire

---

76. As Adams (*Stars Will Fall*, p. 184) notes, the same verb for 'growing old/wearing out' is later used of the Mosaic covenant, which was destined to perish (Heb. 8:13).

77. While *metathesis* may mean 'change' or 'removal', most interpreters favour the latter (cf. K. L. Schenck, *Cosmology and Eschatology in Hebrews: The Settings of the Sacrifice*, SNTSMS 143 [Cambridge: Cambridge University Press, 2007], p. 126, n. 35).

78. Adams infers an act of de-creation, whereby heaven and earth 'will be reduced to their pre-created, *material* condition' (*Stars Will Fall*, p. 191 [italics his]). Others (e.g. C. R. Koester, *Hebrews*, AB 36 [New York: Doubleday, 2001], pp. 547–548) allow for at least some degree of transformation also being involved. There are no explicit references to new creation, prompting Schenck (*Cosmology*, pp. 130–32) to conclude that the writer envisages cosmic annihilation and non-replacement. However, there are several allusions to 'new creation', most notably Heb. 12:22 and 13:14. For others, see Adams, *Stars Will Fall*, pp. 197–198.

79. For a concise discussion and critique of alternative conclusions, see Adams, *Stars Will Fall*, pp. 192–194.

80. For a concise summary of the major arguments and a critique, see E. Adams, 'Retrieving the Earth from the Conflagration: 2 Peter 3.5–13 and the Environment', in D. G. Horrell, Christopher Southgate and Francesca Stavrakopoulou (eds.), *Ecological Hermeneutics: Biblical, Historical and Theological Perspectives* (London: T. & T. Clark, 2010), pp. 108–120 (110–115).

cosmos (2 Pet. 3:7, 10, 12) and precipitate a new creation (2 Pet. 3:13). However, does Peter actually envisage a literal destruction of the cosmos? The main focus is on the coming judgment of earth's sinful inhabitants (cf. 2 Pet. 3:7). Thus for some this is a metaphorical description of a purging process from which the new (i.e. transformed) creation will emerge.[81] But does this necessarily exclude some measure of actual destruction (de-creation), as arguably implied by the language of the heavens 'passing away' and the 'elements melting in the heat' (both my tr.)? The precise meaning of 'elements' (*stoicheia*) is key. Discerning an underlying Stoic cosmology, Adams sees the reference to water, fire, earth and air – the four constituent elements of the world. While the extent of the Stoic influence is debatable,[82] this interpretation is certainly in keeping with first-century usage and would also explain the otherwise anomalous absence of 'the earth' in verse 12 (cf. 2 Pet. 3:7). Others, however, contend that the 'elements' refer here to the 'heavenly bodies' that,[83] along with the outer heavens, are stripped away so that the earth and its inhabitants are exposed to the testing fire of divine judgment (cf. 1 Cor. 3:13).[84] This makes sense of the sequence of events in verse 10 (heavens . . . heavenly bodies . . . earth), and the enigmatic reference to the earth and everything that is done on it being 'found' or 'laid bare'.[85] It also ties in better with the primary focus of the anticipated judgment and its objective, namely godless humanity and the eradication of human evil. However, while this interpretation may arguably leave the earth more or less

---

81. While the concept of cosmic conflagration is not developed in the OT (see P. W. van der Horst, *Hellenism – Judaism – Christianity: Essays on Their Interaction* [Leuven: Peeters, 1998], pp. 277–279), the following texts all employ the image of fiery judgment: Deut. 32:22; Ps. 97:3; Isa. 66:15–16; Ezek. 38:22; Zeph. 1:18; 3:8; Mal. 4:1.

82. Significant differences between Stoic cosmology and the perspective in 2 Peter, as well as the terminology employed, undermine the idea of a Stoic influence to some extent. Cf. J. A. Moo, 'Continuity, Discontinuity and Hope', pp. 32–33; Dennis, 'Cosmology', pp. 175–177.

83. Such a connotation of *stoicheia* is well attested from the middle of the second century, although it is less certain before that (Adams, *Stars Will Fall*, p. 223).

84. Cf. J. A. Moo, 'Continuity, Discontinuity and Hope', pp. 33–34.

85. Most commentators now accept *heurethēsetai* (it will be found) as the original reading. Textual variants include 'it will be *burned up*', 'it will *disappear*', 'it will *not* be found' and 'it will be found *dissolved*' – all of which presuppose the context requires the concept of destruction (R. Bauckham, *Jude, 2 Peter*, WBC 50 [Waco: Word, 1983], p. 317).

intact,[86] it seems to do so at the expense of the rest of the universe. Moreover, depending on the nature and extent of the 'conflagration' envisaged, the difference between this position and destructive de-creation may be rather semantic.[87]

Revelation

Echoing the language of Isaiah and Joel, Revelation 6:12–17 anticipates catastrophic cosmic upheaval that exposes everyone on earth, whatever their social or political status, to the wrath of the Lamb. In many respects the picture is similar to that in 2 Peter 3, especially regarding the removal of that which might otherwise shield earth's inhabitants from exposure to divine judgment. Thus understood, the description of stars falling to the earth (6:13) and 'every mountain and island . . . removed from its place' (6:14) could simply be a metaphorical depiction of destructive judgment,[88] rather than a more literal description of actual cosmological events.

The same is evidently true a couple of chapters later. With the opening of the seventh seal (8:1), more cosmic catastrophe and ecological disaster is unleashed.[89] But the language is clearly metaphorical: Revelation 8 – 9 is not a description of the end of the physical universe, but a highly symbolic depiction of divine judgment. Such judgment is also the focus in Revelation 20:11, which again highlights the comprehensiveness of God's judgment, from which nothing and no one can escape.[90]

However, while these other texts may be more about judgment than 'the end of the world', there can be little doubt that this is precisely what John alludes to in Revelation 21:1. Here what other texts have anticipated has apparently transpired:[91] the present cosmos – or, perhaps more accurately, the present

---

86. However, this is not necessarily so; cf. Stephens, *Annihilation or Renewal?*, p. 135, n. 91.

87. Significantly, Adams resists any idea of creation's obliteration and new creation *ex nihilo*, and his emphasis on material continuity between what he envisages as being 'destroyed' and the new creation leads Moo to conclude that 'his conclusions at this point are not far from my own' ('Continuity, Discontinuity and Hope', p. 36).

88. For fallen stars being instrumental in judgment, see Rev. 9:1.

89. Clearly these apocalyptic depictions reflect a recursive rather than a linear design.

90. G. Z. Heide, 'What Is New About the New Heaven and the New Earth? A Theology of Creation from Revelation 21 and 2 Peter 3', *JETS* 40.1 (1997), pp. 37–56 (41–42).

91. Cf. Matt. 5:18; 24:31; Luke 16:17; 21:33; 2 Cor. 5:17; 2 Pet. 3:10. While a slightly different (but closely related) verb is used, the connotation seems identical.

form of the cosmos – has 'passed away'.[92] And the sea – associated with death and symbolizing that which was tumultuous and threatening – has been removed.[93] But, unless we press John's language literally, the book does not actually depict the end of the old cosmos and the beginning of the new, leaving considerable room for continuity.[94] Such continuity is further implied in some of the book's more positive images (e.g. Rev. 4:3;[95] 5:10). Thus Revelation seems much more positive about earth's future than initial exposure to its imagery might suggest.

Conclusion

So where does this leave us with respect to earth's future? Well, as we have seen, the scriptural testimony is certainly not univocal; at least two different emphases can be discerned – one that stresses stability, permanence and continuity; another that emphasizes vulnerability, transience and discontinuity. This diversity, as we have seen, is reflected not only across the testaments, but within individual books and corpora. It is unlikely, therefore, that biblical authors or editors considered these diverse ideas irreconcilable or mutually exclusive. On the contrary, it seems that the idea of earth's transience and the idea of earth's permanence can both be upheld – so long as neither is understood in an absolute or unqualified sense. In other words, while the present world will one day 'pass away', whatever this entails, it certainly does not mean that our planet will be annihilated or cease to exist. Rather, there will be significant material continuity

---

92. *Pace* Heide ('What Is New', p. 43), this does not seem to be just phenomenological language. Rather, *aperchomai* is used to describe the cessation of a state or condition (cf. 9:12; 11:14; 21:4), as is *parerchomai* in the texts listed above.

93. For a concise explanation of the symbolic significance of the sea in Revelation, see Stephens, *Annihilation or Renewal?*, pp. 236–237.

94. As Stephens (*Annihilation or Renewal?*, pp. 230, 235–237) observes, unlike 2 Pet. 3, there is no explicit reference to heaven and earth being incinerated (cf. Rev. 20:14); moreover, unlike the sea, death, mourning, crying or pain (Rev. 21:1; cf. 21:4), they are not said to be 'no more'.

95. Stephens (*Annihilation or Renewal?*, p. 176) judiciously comments, 'If one were to only use the ensuing events . . . as evidence for God's purposes towards the earth, one could reasonably conclude that God intends to destroy the earth with no thought of preservation. But the presence of the rainbow signals a note of caution that such a negative perspective towards the future of the earth is inappropriate.'

between the present cosmos and the new creation. How much of the present creation will survive is a matter of speculation. But however much (or little) this may be, the new earth for which we hope is not a new world, but a world made new. This may not be much of an incentive to 'save the planet' – ultimately, this is really something only God can (and will) do. Nevertheless, the fact that this planet is also our eschatological home means that we, of all people, have a vested interest in its long-term well-being and survival. In any case, it is a human responsibility, and thus all the more a Christian responsibility, to care for and look after God's good creation. And this will surely remain so, for as long as earth endures.

7. NEW TESTAMENT HOPE AND A CHRISTIAN ENVIRONMENTAL ETHOS

Jonathan Moo

Introduction

In 1989 the Tyndale Lecture in Ethics was delivered by the Oxford economist Donald Hay.[1] The title of his lecture, 'Christians in the Global Greenhouse?', suggests that Hay was prescient in identifying the significance of what has come to be considered one of the greatest challenges facing life on earth.[2] Only the question mark at the end of his title would be less appropriate if he were delivering the lecture today. Every single year since his lecture has been significantly above the long-term average in global temperature, with 2010 the warmest year

---

1. This chapter is a lightly revised version of an article previously published as 'Continuity, Discontinuity and Hope: The Contribution of New Testament Eschatology to a Distinctively Christian Environmental Ethos', *TynB* 61 (2010), pp. 21–44, and is reprinted here by permission. It was originally delivered as the 2009 Tyndale Lecture in Ethics and Social Theology, in Cambridge on 9 July 2009. Some of the arguments made in this chapter have recently been expanded in Jonathan A. Moo and Robert S. White, *Hope in an Age of Despair: The Gospel and the Future of Life of Earth* (Nottingham: Inter-Varsity Press, 2013).

2. Hay's lecture was published as Donald Hay, 'Christians in the Global Greenhouse?', *TynB* 41 (1990), pp. 109–127.

globally yet recorded. Even the coldest year of the twenty-first century so far, the La Niña year of 2008, was warmer than 1989 – and indeed 2008 still ended up being warmer than every year of the previous century, save 1997 and 1998.[3] The Inter-governmental Panel on Climate Change (IPCC), which released its first report the year after Hay's lecture, is now able to claim, in its fourth assessment, in 2007, that the 'warming of the climate system' is 'unequivocal' and moreover that it is 'very likely' that anthropogenic greenhouse gas emissions are the primary cause. Early signs are that the fifth assessment, due in 2013–14, will reaffirm this conclusion, but with an even higher level of certainty.[4]

Debate in the scientific community has progressed from questions about whether the climate is warming and whether greenhouse gas emissions are a significant contributor to this warming to questions about the precise magnitude of future temperature increases to be expected, what the wider effects might be and what can be done about it. The science has continued to move forward; but little of substance has yet changed on the political front. Despite plenty of rhetoric, greenhouse gas emissions have continued to increase globally year on year. It is little wonder that some keen observers have begun to despair, suggesting that it is already too late to do anything to prevent catastrophic climate change. University lecture series in climate change mitigation are giving way to lectures on climate change adaptation. Western governments are being forced to consider seriously just how they will deal with challenges ranging from rising sea levels to the hundreds of millions of environmental refugees that global warming is likely to create in the coming decades.

And if there are signs of gloom among global-warming activists, there are even greater reasons for despair among those who labour to address more traditional environmental problems. Global warming may indeed be the most pressing and potentially catastrophic challenge facing us, but the unprecedented explosion in human population that has occurred over the last century, combined with our ever-growing rates of consumption, have many more mundane and much more predictable effects on land, water and fellow creatures. There is not

---

3. For up-to-date data and analysis of the global temperature record, see the website run by the University of East Anglia's Climatic Research Unit at http://www.cru.uea.ac.uk (accessed 17 June 2013) and NASA's Goddard Institute for Space Studies at http://data.giss.nasa.gov (accessed 17 June 2013).

4. The IPCC reports are available free to download at http://www.ipcc.ch (accessed 17 June 2013). According to a leaked version of the IPCC's fifth assessment, due officially to be released in late 2013/early 2014, it is now 'virtually certain' that human factors are the primary cause of recent warming.

space to detail any of this here, but – for an easily accessible place to start – readers might consult the sober (and sobering) assessment provided in the United Nations Global Environment Outlook.[5] This report, incidentally, treats the effects of environmental degradation only from the standpoint of human life and well-being. Debates about whether the earth and its creatures have independent value and merit consideration in their own right tend to fall by the wayside when the threats to humankind itself are so great.[6]

What does any of this have to do with Christian faith? Some early suggestions that Christianity and the world view it engenders is actually responsible for the global environmental crisis have been largely refuted on historical grounds or at least have given way to more nuanced accounts. But the church today, especially in its evangelical expressions, still seems uneasy and uncertain about just what role it ought to play. There are those who argue strongly that Christians ought to jump on the bandwagon of environmentalists or global-warming activists; and there are others who argue just as strongly that environmentalism represents a threat to economic growth and traditional values and so Christians should oppose attempts to mitigate climate change or to implement costly environmental programmes. Popular among many evangelicals is the apparently more innocuous notion that Christians ought to get on with proclaiming the gospel and let the rest of the world sort out such earthly problems. A large body of literature has unsurprisingly grown up to explore each of these and many other approaches, with most of those who bother to write about it naturally calling for greater Christian involvement in caring for the earth (although the United States has remained a robust market for contrarian perspectives).

Meanwhile, it has to be said that until recently the handful of biblical scholars who have bothered to ask whether Scripture provides any resources for thinking about these questions have often ended up carrying on their conversations within self-contained ghettos of the like-minded. A retreat to exclusively

---

5. The most recent version of this report, the fifth, was released in 2012 and is available as a free download at http://www.unep.org/ geo (accessed 17 June 2013). Robert White and I have also recently attempted to summarize the 'state of the planet' in Moo and White, *Hope in Age of Despair*, pp. 22–88.

6. J. Baird Callicott has nonetheless made a convincing case for why the question of nature's intrinsic value still demands to be answered even when purely anthropocentric approaches to environmental ethics converge with those based on some notion of nature's intrinsic value; see J. Baird Callicott, *Beyond the Land Ethic: More Essays in Environmental Philosophy* (Albany: State University of New York, 1999), pp. 241–246.

hermeneutical questions and a turn to reader-response criticism has left many fellow researchers (and certainly most ordinary Christians) bemused and in any case largely free to ignore the fruits of their work. The lack of a strong connection between exegesis and Christian environmental ethics has also at times been perpetuated by sharp academic divides between theology, ethics and biblical studies, even if the genuinely difficult hermeneutical problem of whether and how Scripture can be used to address contemporary issues refuses to go away. In any case, there are still too few bridges between exegesis and environmental ethics; and would-be bridge builders are perhaps put off by the knowledge that on the one side they are likely to be attacked by biblical scholars who find their constructions anachronistic and lacking adequate exegetical foundations and that on the other side they are likely to be met by environmental ethicists who are not interested in the sort of incoming traffic that such bridges encourage.

I obviously cannot hope to address all of these issues in this chapter, and so I shall proceed from the assumption that the mission of the Christian church does necessarily include concern with such earthly problems as environmental degradation, unsustainable resource use, ecosystem integrity, and the plight of the poor and of future generations. Moreover, although I take it for granted that the Christian Scriptures, and the NT in particular, have little or nothing to say directly about so-called environmental issues, I am convinced that if Scripture has much to tell us about who we are, who God is and how we ought to live in the world, it has tremendous potential to shape us into the sorts of people from whom particular responses to even a new challenge like the global environmental crisis will be expected and indeed required.

But rather than merely arguing that we ought to take science seriously and to care more wisely for the earth, I want to consider what can be *distinctive* about a Christian environmental ethos. There is no reason why Christians should not make common cause with those of other faiths or none to work for a more just and sustainable world, but I want to suggest that as Christians our motivation, our purpose and our hope will necessarily be different from those of our co-belligerents who do not profess biblical faith; and there will be times when these differences will also lead to differences in method and approach. I intend to argue that it is especially the eschatological perspective of the NT that can provide a distinctive lens for understanding the created world and the Christian's role within it.

My emphasis on NT eschatology is not meant to imply that it is only here that the biblical tradition has something to contribute to a Christian environmental ethos. Stephen Williams has reminded us that love must always remain at the centre of Christian social and environmental action – and indeed, at the centre of any discussion about eschatology.[7] Whatever the future holds, we are called to love and care for the world as we encounter it. Nonetheless, the NT's theology of creation is inescapably eschatological, and the wideness of biblical hope can provide both a strong impetus as well as the necessary context for the exercise of Christian love and charity.

This chapter seeks, then, to develop somewhat further than is often done the exegetical basis for a distinctively Christian perspective of the future that has important implications for how we understand our task in and for the created world. I propose that the diverse ways in which the NT portrays the future of the earth, taken together, provide an indispensable resource for the development of a Christian environmental ethos. I argue that this resource is not rendered more valuable by well-intentioned attempts to collapse the different emphases that emerge from, say 2 Peter 3 and Romans 8, into one version or the other. Nonetheless, I also argue that the contradiction that is often felt to exist between these different portraits of creation's future is not so acute that we cannot identify vital strands of continuity between them; and, most importantly, that the ecological ethos that emerges from serious reflection on the implications of these visions is as radical as it is consistent with the OT prophets in their stern calls for righteousness and justice to be realized on earth. Thus part of my argument rests on the observation that when the biblical (by which I mean the OT) and Jewish contours of the NT's theology of creation and new creation are taken seriously, the significance of the Hebrew Bible's concern for the land can find fresh ways of being expressed within a contemporary ethos of care for the earth. In what follows, I shall focus on just a few key texts, moving from Romans 8 to 2 Peter 3 and finally to Revelation 21 – 22.

Romans 8

Romans 8:18–25 is a popular text with Christian environmentalists. The passage is used uncritically at times and perhaps too often is cited in isolation from what the rest of the NT has to say about creation and eschatology,[8] but for all that, it

---

7. Stephen Williams, 'Thirty Years of Hope: A Generation of Writing on Eschatology', in K. E. Brower and M. W. Elliott (eds.), *'The Reader Must Understand': Eschatology in Bible and Theology* (Leicester: Apollos, 1997), pp. 243–258.

8. See the assessment of different interpretative approaches in Cherryl Hunt, David G. Horrell and Christopher Southgate, 'An Environmental Mantra? Ecological Interest

does provide a vital foundation in the construction of a biblically rooted environmental ethos. Here Paul's story of human redemption in Christ is seen in its full cosmic context; here we have confirmation, if it were needed, that Paul's gospel has not left behind the groaning earth whose restoration the OT prophets assumed would accompany the liberation and transformation of God's people.

Nearly all commentators on Romans 8 now accept that *ktisis* refers in this passage to 'creation' and especially to the non-human creation.[9] In verse 21 the 'creation itself' is linked with but distinguished from the 'children of God', with whom it looks forward to sharing in the glorious freedom to come. In the present age, however, creation is said to be subjected to futility. James Dunn helpfully unpacks Paul's rather compressed thought at this point: 'God subjected all things to Adam, and that included subjecting creation to fallen Adam, to share in his fallenness.'[10] That *creation* is subjected to futility in being subjected to humankind is something of an ironic reversal of the usual biblical pattern in which *human beings* become subject to futility by worshipping created things instead of the Creator. The background for Paul's thought here probably includes the prophetic motif of the earth's suffering and mourning under human evil and injustice, especially as this is developed in Isaiah 24. If this is the case, then creation's subjection and groaning denotes for Paul not only the immediate result of Adam's rebellion and the curse pronounced in Genesis 3 but also the ongoing effects of this state of affairs as they continue to be played out in the relationship between God, his rebellious human creatures and the earth itself.[11] The groaning of creation is something that continues, Paul says, even into the present time.

It is difficult for today's ecologically aware reader not to equate this picture of creation's groaning with modern scenes of environmental ruin. Paul did not of course envision the sorts of threats to life on earth that we now face, but that does not mean that such a link is as anachronistic as it first appears. For it is precisely in the link that Paul perceives between humankind and the rest of creation that today's global environmental crises are explicable within a Christian

---

in Romans 8:19–23 and a Modest Proposal for Its Narrative Interpretation', *JTS* 59 (2008), pp. 546–579.

9. See especially the concise case for this made by C. E. B. Cranfield, *A Critical and Exegetical Commentary on the Epistle to the Romans*, vol. 1, ICC (Edinburgh: T. & T. Clark, 1975), pp. 411–412; more recently the consensus has been upheld by Robert Jewett, *Romans*, Hermeneia (Minneapolis: Fortress, 2007), pp. 511–512.

10. James D. G. Dunn, *Romans*, vol. 1, WBC (Dallas: Word, 1988), p. 471.

11. Jonathan A. Moo, 'Romans 8.19–22 and Isaiah's Cosmic Covenant', *NTS* 54 (2008), pp. 74–89.

world view. When this biblical perspective is taken seriously, it should hardly be a surprise to find that human greed and injustice – and sometimes just plain ignorance – is capable of leading to such frightening consequences for the earth as we have begun to witness in our time. But Paul's purpose in Romans 8 is not simply to make the negative point that creation has found itself subjected to futility in being subjected to humankind. Paul's intent is rather to assure readers that this is not the end of the story, for them or for the earth. Creation itself groans with them in their suffering as they eagerly anticipate the realization of the hope to be revealed as to who they truly are: children of God and co-heirs with Christ. In verse 23 Paul makes it clear that this coming revelation of the children of God will be brought about in the 'redemption' of their 'bodies', in the resurrection. Creation's future is thus bound up with the future of God's children, and this future consists in resurrection and the liberation of creation itself.

Romans 8 in fact lends support for the idea that the resurrection of the body is an appropriate NT model for envisioning the material restoration of all of creation. This would suggest that what Paul says elsewhere about glorifying God with the physical body, for example in 1 Corinthians 6:12–20, may be of some relevance for considering how God may be glorified by living rightly within creation – in ways that respect its integrity, value and God's ultimate purposes for it. As Paul says of the body, the earth does not finally belong to us; and its future too has been bought at a price, since in Paul's conception creation cannot attain its *telos* unless and until those human creatures to whom its fate is linked become who they are intended to be in Christ. Colossians 1:20, where God through Christ 'was pleased to reconcile to himself all things, whether on earth or in heaven, by making peace through the blood of the cross', is perhaps more explicit in presenting Christ's atoning work as having cosmic significance in and of itself; but in Romans 8 the ramifications of God's redemption in Christ are no less significant for the entire creation, even if they are here portrayed as in some sense mediated through those human creatures whose adoption as God's children Christ has secured.

The full revelation of God's children must await the resurrection, but for Paul the new creation has already in some sense broken into the old. As he says in 2 Corinthians, 'If anyone is in Christ, there is new creation!' (5:18). The children of God are – even within Romans 8 – thus declared by Paul in verse 16 already to be God's children now, the Spirit testifying to their identity as children of God and co-heirs with Christ. As often for Paul, the ethical imperative that necessarily follows is that God's children begin to live now as who they truly are and as they one day will be fully revealed to be. And if God's children do begin to live as who they are, it is surely appropriate to expect that the non-human creation ought also to begin to experience something of its future liberation from its subjection to futility and ruin. Reconciliation with God through Christ must mean humankind's reconciliation with the earth too. There is support here for Jürgen Moltmann's claim that 'there is no fellowship with Christ without fellowship with the earth. Love for Christ and hope for him embrace love and hope for the earth'.[12]

There is much more that could be said, but, by way of summary, I would suggest that the importance of Romans 8 for formulating a Christian environmental ethic lies in the first instance in the continuity that Paul assumes exists between the present creation and the new creation to come. Whatever elements of discontinuity there may also be, it can be nothing other than the same creation that is now groaning that will one day be released from its present subjection to futility and come to share in the glorious freedom of the children of God. According to Paul, the resurrection of the body is accompanied by – and perhaps is rightly seen as a model for – the renewal of creation itself. The ethical implications of this for living in right relationship with the rest of creation are not of course developed by Paul, but I would suggest that they emerge quite powerfully all the same.

Romans 8 also indicates that for Paul – as for other biblical writers – the whole of creation's fate is mysteriously bound up with the fate of one of its creatures – humankind. In our own day, such an idea might seem naive, aware as we are of the billions of years that the earth existed before human beings and the billions of years that it would seem to be able to go on without us. But ironically we are also far more aware today than at any other time of humankind's potential radically to alter the earth and to affect its life; so, in one sense, it should be clearer than ever that the future of the world – at least as we know it – has become bound up with our future, for good or for ill. But more fundamentally, of course, what Scripture suggests about creation's future is something beyond any mere extrapolation of present conditions. The ultimate future lies in the hands of the one who calls into being that which is not; according to the NT, individual and cosmic futility are finally reversed only in resurrection and new creation. The call for those who are in Christ is to live as beachheads of that new creation in the present age, to engage in what Dietrich Bonhoeffer calls 'truly responsible' action that reflects care for the penultimate in the light of God's ultimate future.[13]

---

12. Jürgen Moltmann, *The Coming of God: Christian Eschatology*, tr. M. Kohl (Minneapolis: Fortress, 2004), p. 279.

13. I am indebted at this point to the way in which Bonhoeffer's language relating to ethics and eschatology has been developed and applied by Neil Messer, *Selfish Genes and Christian Ethics: Theological and Ethical Reflections on Evolutionary Biology* (London: SCM, 2007), pp. 207–211, esp. 211.

2 Peter 3

If Romans 8 is the most popular text with Christian environmentalists, 2 Peter 3 is perhaps the least. At the November 2008 meeting of the Society of Biblical Literature's Ecological Hermeneutics group, Barbara Rossing went so far as to claim that there is nothing redeemable in this passage.[14] According to Rossing (and many other contemporary interpreters), 2 Peter 3 cannot be reconciled with what other portions of the NT teach about the earth, and it has nothing helpful to say to Christians today. My argument in this chapter is quite different. I shall first argue at some length that the eschatological picture painted so vividly in 2 Peter 3 is not in any necessary conflict with that of Romans 8, for example, and that the emphasis in 2 Peter on discontinuity between the present world and the world to come does not in fact entail the sort of world-denying 'pie in the sky' mentality it is so often assumed to encourage. But I also want to suggest that this passage's undoubted emphasis on judgment and discontinuity is a theme that must in any case be taken seriously. To ignore it is to risk missing what is a potentially distinctive and important component of a Christian environmental ethos.[15]

It is generally assumed that 2 Peter 3 unequivocally portrays the complete dissolution of the present cosmos and its replacement with a new heaven and a new earth. Edward Adams, to take a recent example, concludes at the end of what is a thoughtful and thorough study that '[t]he writer has expressed the conviction that the existing created order will come to a violent end as emphatically as he could.'[16] I shall call attention to some features of the passage that might support a more cautious assessment, but there can be no doubt that the emphasis here is on the radical discontinuity envisioned between the present age and the age to come. The author of 2 Peter is in fact addressing those who claim that things will carry on as they always have;

---

14. Barbara Rossing, 'Apocalyptic Discourses, Global Warming, and Empire: Is This the End of the World?' (Paper presented at the 2008 Annual Meeting of the SBL, Boston, 24 Nov. 2008.)

15. In this section on 2 Pet. 3 I have partly reproduced and expanded material that appears in Jonathan A. Moo, 'Environmental Unsustainability and a Biblical Vision of the Earth's Future', in Robert S. White (ed.), *Creation in Crisis: Christian Perspectives on Sustainability* (London: SPCK, 2009), pp. 255–270, here 261–269.

16. Edward Adams, *The Stars Will Fall from Heaven: Cosmic Catastrophe in the New Testament and Its World*, LNTS 347 (London: T. & T. Clark, 2007), p. 234.

and he uses powerful imagery to refute them, making the point that not only has God judged the world in the past but that he will do so again in the future.

The events associated with the 'day of the Lord' are described with three short clauses in verse 10:

the heavens will pass away with a loud noise,
and the elements will be dissolved with fire,
and the earth and everything that is done on it will be disclosed.[17]

As is well known, older translations of the final phrase have the earth and the works on it being 'burned up' rather than 'found' or 'disclosed' as in the NRSV cited here and in most other modern translations. The difference is due to a number of textual variants in the verse, but nearly all present-day commentators accept what is the best supported, though more difficult reading, *heurethēsetai* (will be found), not only because of the powerful manuscript evidence[18] but precisely because all of the other variants can be explained as attempts to clarify

---

17. Unless stated otherwise, all translations in this chapter are from the NRSV.

18. The range of readings and their manuscript support is presented most clearly in *Novum Testamentum Graecum: Editio Critica Maior*, but – in a rather astonishing move – whereas the NA27 text reads *heurethēsetai*, the editors of *ECM* (and hence the NA28) now opt for *ouch heurethēsetai*. This is not on the basis of any fresh manuscript evidence (indeed, there is no Greek evidence for this reading whatsoever; it finds support only in the Syriac Philoxeniana and in the Sahidic), but evidently the change has been made because the editors have decided to treat all of the readings that attest to the idea of destruction, burning or removal as mutually supportive rather than as reflecting – as Richard Bauckham and others have convincingly argued (see below) – different scribal attempts to correct what may have been a difficult (but not impossible) original reading, *heurethēsetai* (attested by Sinaiticus [01], Vaticanus [03], 018, 025, 323, 424Z, 1175, 1241, 1448, 1739T, 1852, 1881 and some Syriac MSS). Bauckham's explanation is a more economical one than either of the alternative explanations that would seem to be required by the reading of *ECM*, that is (1) that a rather conventional way of describing judgment, *ouch heurethēsetai*, has occasioned such a wide diversity of glosses and alternative readings, or (2) that the negative particle was lost at a very early stage and yet was somehow preserved (only?) in the manuscript(s) available to the Syriac and Sahidic translators.

this rather unusual way of describing the final judgment.[19] The possible significance of this terminology will be taken up shortly. First, however, it is necessary to consider the meaning of another difficult term in this verse and the wider background for 2 Peter's language and ideas.

The referent of the 'elements' (*stoicheia*), which are said to be destroyed by 'fire' or 'burning' in verse 10 and to 'melt with fire' in verse 12, remains a subject of much debate. Adams is a strong advocate of the view that the author of 2 Peter draws heavily on Stoic cosmology to refute the arguments of his opponents, and, if Adams is right, *stoicheia* should almost certainly be interpreted as referring to the four constituent elements of the world – water, fire, earth and air. This, as Adams points out, is how the term was regularly used and understood in Stoicism as well as in the wider Greek-speaking world.[20] According to Adams, the 'elements' are then essentially equivalent to the 'earth'; the point of verse 10 is that the heavens and the earth will be destroyed by fire and, in the process, the earth and the works on it will be 'found' in the sense of being judged.[21] This idea is hinted at already in verse 7, where the 'present heavens and earth' are said to be 'reserved for fire, being kept for the day of judgment and destruction of the ungodly' (NIV).

Adams's argument has much to recommend it, and it seems indisputable that many of the first readers of 2 Peter would hear echoes of competing versions of contemporary cosmological 'science', perhaps especially as advanced by

19. See Richard Bauckham, *Jude, 2 Peter*, WBC 50 (Waco: Word, 1983), pp. 303, 316–321; Al Wolters, 'Worldview and Textual Criticism in 2 Peter 3:10', *WTJ* 49 (1987), pp. 405–413, esp. 405–408; Eric Fuchs and Pierre Reymond, *La deuxième épitre de Saint Pierre / L'épitre de Saint Jude*, CNT 2.13b, 2nd ed. (Geneva: Labor et Fides, 1988), p. 117; Henning Paulsen, *Der Zweite Petrusbrief und der Judasbrief*, KEK 12.2 (Göttingen: Vandenhoeck & Ruprecht, 1992), p. 168; Jerome H. Neyrey, *2 Peter, Jude*, AB 37c (New York: Doubleday, 1993), pp. 243–244; Anton Vögtle, *Der Judasbrief / Der 2. Petrusbrief*, EKK 22 (Neukirchen-Vluyn: Neukirchener, 1994), pp. 234–238; Daniel J. Harrington, *Jude and 2 Peter*, SP 15 (Collegeville: Liturgical, 2003), p. 289 (although Harrington finds it necessary to translate the last clause as a question – 'will they be found?'); Peter H. Davids, *The Letters of 2 Peter and Jude*, PNTC (Grand Rapids: Eerdmans, 2006), pp. 286–287; Gene L. Green, *Jude and 2 Peter*, BECNT (Grand Rapids: Baker Academic, 2008), p. 331.

20. Adams, *Stars Will Fall*, pp. 222–224. Cf. Gerhard Delling, '*stoicheō, systoicheō, stoicheion*', *TDNT*, vol. 7, pp. 666–687; Neyrey, *2 Peter*, p. 243.

21. This argument has also been advanced recently by Green, *Jude and 2 Peter*, p. 330.

Stoics and Epicureans.[22] Despite the similarities, however, even Adams is forced to concede that there are important differences between Stoic conceptions of the world's end and that which is given in 2 Peter 3. One obvious difference is that 2 Peter does not envision an infinite cycle of destruction and regeneration, but rather one final and climactic 'day of the Lord'. Moreover, whereas the cause of the world's fiery end in Stoic thought is envisioned as an essentially physical process, the cosmic catastrophe of 2 Peter 3 results solely from the Creator's prerogative in judgment. It is also telling that the author of 2 Peter does not use the precise terminology we might expect if he intended to call attention to Stoic support for his own view. Why not use the language of *ekpyrōsis* (conflagration) or *palingenesia* (renewal, regeneration), for example? While the author of 2 Peter may well have been happy to enlist some Stoic ideas to support his case, the evidence is less compelling than Adams suggests for Stoicism being the primary influence on the way the world's final judgment is here portrayed. The basic impetus and overall shape of 2 Peter's argument seems in the end to remain much nearer to biblical and Jewish apocalyptic thought.[23]

There is in fact an alternative interpretation of *stoicheia* that takes more seriously the potential OT and Jewish background of 2 Peter and that may better account both for the unusual use of 'will be found' in verse 10 and for the progression in this verse from 'heavens' to 'elements' to 'earth'. By the second century, *stoicheia* is indisputably used in some instances with the meaning 'heavenly bodies', referring to the stars, sun and moon;[24] and it is also possible that these material elements of the heavens could be associated with spiritual forces, as may be the case in Paul's use of *stoicheia* (Gal. 4:3, 9; cf. Col. 2:8, 20). The text of 2 Peter would be the first extant example of an author using *stoicheia*

---

22. Adams, *Stars Will Fall*, pp. 206–209, rejects the common association of the world view of the 'scoffers' with Epicureanism, instead linking their thought to the more general Aristotelian belief in cosmic indestructibility. Adams's arguments against a connection with Epicureanism could equally apply to the close connection he claims to find between 2 Peter and Stoicism, where the differences are possibly even more acute.

23. This has recently been argued by John Dennis, 'Cosmology in the Petrine Literature and Jude', in J. T. Pennington and S. M. McDonough (eds.), *Cosmology and New Testament Theology*, LNTS 355 (London: T. & T. Clark, 2008), pp. 157–177, esp. 175–177, who nevertheless is more favourable towards other aspects of Adams's reading.

24. Regularly cited in this regard are Theophilus of Antioch, *Autol.* 1.4; Justin, *2 Apol.* 5.2; *Dial.* 23.2.

for 'heavenly bodies', but this meaning for 3:10, 12 has nevertheless managed to garner some substantial scholarly support.[25] This is primarily because it fits the context so well. On this scenario, the picture presented in verse 10 is something like this: the outer heavens are torn away, the intermediary heavenly bodies are dissolved with fire, and then the earth and all the deeds of human beings are laid bare before God, being 'found' before him, with nothing to separate them from the testing fire of his judgment.

Support for such an interpretation can be adduced from the parallel between the way in which the elements are described as 'melting with fire' in 2 Peter 3:12 and the description of God's judgment in Isaiah 34:4, where one Greek translation reads, 'all the powers of the heavens will melt'. This version of Isaiah 34:4 is in fact echoed in 2 *Clement* 16.3, a text that combines Isaiah 34:4 with Malachi 4:1 (3:19 LXX), where the 'day of the Lord' is said to come 'like a burning oven'. According to 2 *Clement*, the end result of this fiery judgment is that 'the secret and open works of men will appear'. As several commentators have observed, this traditional description of God's judgment does not sound far removed from the rather more unusual way of expressing what may be the same idea in 2 Peter 3:10, where it is said that 'the earth and the works on it will be found'.

Whatever the precise relationship between 2 Peter and 2 *Clement*, the latter text reveals the potential for an early Christian writer to envision the final judgment along the lines of the fiery judgment of Malachi 4:1 and to link this with the melting of the heavens (or the powers of the heavens) in Isaiah 34:4 (LXX).[26] This observation strengthens the possibility that *stoicheia* in 2 Peter 3 similarly refers to the 'powers of heaven' and not to the melting or destruction of the four components of the earth itself.[27]

---

25. E.g. Bauckham, *Jude, 2 Peter*, pp. 315–316; Paulsen, *Zweite Petrusbrief*, pp. 166–168; Vögtle, *Judasbrief / 2. Petrusbrief*, p. 234; Steven J. Kraftchick, *Jude / 2 Peter*, ANTC (Nashville: Abingdon, 2002), p. 163; Davids, *2 Peter and Jude*, pp. 284–287.

26. Bauckham, *Jude, 2 Peter*, pp. 304–305, suggests that 2 Peter and 2 *Clement* here both rely on a common source.

27. It also calls into question Adams's argument against any possible Jewish or biblical background for the imagery used in 2 Pet. 3. While Adams may be right to point out that 'cosmic conflagration' is not a common motif in the OT or early Judaism, his discounting of the many instances where fire is associated with theophanies or localized judgments (and texts such as Mal. 4:1 or Isa. 66:15–16, where it could be argued there is a more universal scope) as possible sources for such an idea begins to sound like special pleading, especially given his own readiness to see connections with Stoic thought.

Putting all of this together yields a somewhat different interpretation of 2 Peter 3:10 than the popular one to which I alluded earlier. We are left with the cataclysmic fire of God's judgment, but its function in the context is primarily to lay the earth bare before God, to reveal it as it is and to leave human beings and their works without any place to hide. A similar theme could be argued to lie behind Paul's caution that a Christian worker 'build' carefully on the 'foundation' of Christ: 'the work of each builder will become visible, for the Day will disclose it, because it will be revealed with fire, and the fire will test what sort of work each has done' (1 Cor. 3:13). In a somewhat different application of the same imagery, 1 Peter 1:7 encourages Christians to rejoice in their hope even in the midst of trials so that 'the genuineness of your faith – being more precious than gold that, though perishable, is tested by fire – may be found to result in praise and glory and honour when Jesus Christ is revealed'. Al Wolters is perhaps the strongest advocate for interpreting 2 Peter 3 along these lines, suggesting that the fire here is a purifying fire that destroys human evil but leaves everything else intact or renewed; he goes so far as to suggest that, rather than picturing the end of this creation, 'the text of 2 Pet 3:10 . . . stresses instead the permanence of the created earth, despite the coming judgement'.[28]

Wolters undoubtedly presses his argument too far, but it is striking that nowhere in 2 Peter 3 is the end of the earth unambiguously described. In 2 Peter 3:7 the author does claim that 'the present heavens and earth have been reserved for fire, being kept until the day of judgement and destruction of the godless'; but though both heaven and earth are 'reserved for fire', the purpose of this fire is expressly stated to be for the 'judgement and destruction of the godless' – in other words to do away with *human* evil. In 2 Peter 3:12 it is again only the heavens and the elements that are said to be burned with fire prior to the appearance of the new creation. More challenging might be 3:11, where the author's ethical admonitions are rooted in the fact that 'all these things are to be dissolved in this way'. The referent of 'all these things' would seem in the context to include the heavens, the elements and the earth of the previous verse.[29] Nonetheless, Peter Davids points out that if 3:10 is taken 'at face value as expressing the vision of the future that our author wishes to communicate, then "all these things" [in v. 11] are [limited to] the heavens and the elements (heavenly bodies)'; whatever effects such a judgment might also have on the

---

28. Wolters, 'Worldview and Textual Criticism', p. 413.

29. Thus Bauckham, *Jude, 2 Peter*, p. 324, claims that though the dissolution of the earth is not described in v. 10, the author must, based on v. 11, assume that it too is destroyed.

earth, the author's focus remains on 'the positive vision of the future and what it means for the present'.[30]

Wolter, Davids and others have helpfully exposed some potentially deliberate ambiguities in the way 2 Peter 3 portrays the future 'day of the Lord' and its effects on the earth, ambiguities that may call into question Adams's claim that the author has described the violent end of the present creation 'as emphatically as he could'. There is, at the least, some reason to be cautious in our assessment of just what the author intends to describe. Above all, we must finally attend to the *implications* that the author derives from his eschatological expectations. But before we turn to these implications, it is worth pausing to consider just what the significance might be if the author of 2 Peter 3 does intend to describe the ultimate destruction of the present earth; what, in any case, would 'destruction' mean in such a context?

Adams points out that even when early Jewish and Christian texts do describe a cosmic catastrophe, the absolute destruction of the world into non-existence is never what is in view. The parallel used by the author of 2 Peter himself is instructive; he compares the future judgment by fire with the past destruction of the *cosmos* by the flood (3:6). This may sound like an intensification of the effects of the Noahic flood described in Genesis, but it is most unlikely that 2 Peter envisions the world that emerged after the flood as anything other than one that was in 'material continuity' with what had existed before. Even the Stoic cycle of cosmic conflagration and regeneration was seen as essentially a purifying and renewing process. Adams himself therefore concludes that 'the destructive process' described in 2 Peter 3 'is part of the process of renewal and renovation (conceived along the lines of the Stoic *ekpyrōsis*), which leads to a new heaven and new earth which stand in material continuity with the present heavens and earth'.[31] Thus, while I am not persuaded by the degree of importance that Adams assigns to the Stoic background for 2 Peter 3, his conclusions at this point are not far from my own.

It should be evident by this stage that on my reading there is no need to posit any irreconcilable differences between the eschatological conception of Romans 8 and that of 2 Peter 3. Nonetheless, the emphasis in 2 Peter on God's cosmic judgment and on the radical rupture with the past that it entails does represent a challenge to any notion that the new creation emerges slowly in the course of history or through mere human effort. The substantial continuity that Paul assumes in Romans 8, and that I have argued the author of 2 Peter at least allows

---

30. Davids, *2 Peter and Jude*, p. 288.

31. Adams, *Stars Will Fall*, p. 259.

for in 2 Peter 3, emerges only because of the faithfulness of the God who does not abandon his purposes for his people and his creation even through the discontinuity of death and judgment. And I would argue that for the Christian striving to live as a child of God and to care for a groaning earth, 2 Peter's focus on divine initiative and divine agency can be nothing other than a profound encouragement in an age of environmental despair. As Allen Verhey has said of eschatological hope in general, it frees us from 'the crushing burden of messianic pretensions', from assuming that in the end it is all up to us.[32]

Yet 2 Peter 3 provides a strong warning against complacency. For the author of 2 Peter expects his readers not only to await but, according to verse 12, even to hasten – to 'speed on' – the coming day of God. The author of 2 Peter explains that the way the day of the Lord is hastened is through 'holy ways of living and godly acts', as the Lord's followers 'strive to be found by him at peace' (v. 14). Steven Kraftchick points out that the plurals in the Greek text, the 'holy ways of living and godly acts', 'underscore that many kinds of godliness characterize the Christian life'.[33] Presumably this includes cultivating the virtues listed in 2 Peter 1:5–8, where readers are called on to

> support your faith with goodness, and goodness with knowledge, and knowledge with self-control, and self-control with endurance, and endurance with godliness, and godliness with mutual affection, and mutual affection with love.

But it must also include the very many practical things that constitute 'godly acts', concrete examples of goodness, self-control and love that find expression in different ways in different times and places. And it is precisely here that I would suggest that our scientific knowledge about the present state of the earth, the plight of its people and creatures, and its probable future if things carry on as before enters in to supply the context and material with which Christian love and hope must do their work.

It is intriguing that when Jesus talks about the coming of the Son of Man 'like a thief' – the saying echoed in 2 Peter 3:10 – Jesus immediately follows this prediction with a parable about a servant whose master has put him in charge of his household. The servant cannot know when his master will arrive, but, in keeping with what has been entrusted to him, the 'faithful and prudent manager' will endeavour 'to be found' working diligently in expectation of the master's

---

32. Allen Verhey, *Reading the Bible in the Strange World of Medicine* (Grand Rapids: Eerdmans, 2003), p. 140, quoted in Messer, *Selfish Genes*, p. 210.

33. Kraftchick, *Jude / 2 Peter*, p. 166.

return (Matt. 24:45–51; Luke 12:42–48). Whether or not 'stewardship', at least as it is popularly understood, is quite adequate for capturing the full biblical teaching on humankind's responsibilities within creation,[34] Jesus' formulation of a stewardship ethic in the context of awaiting the return of the master raises for today's readers the question of what it might mean to be wise stewards in caring for what has been entrusted to us. What does it mean to lead 'lives of holiness and godliness', to care for the earth and to love our neighbours in a world of staggering inequalities, in countries built upon profligate use and abuse of the planet's resources, and in societies addicted to unsustainable practices that endanger the earth's life, alter its atmosphere and threaten all who live at the margins? Jesus' stern challenge at the end of his parable in Luke must surely resonate with us in the Western world today: 'From everyone to whom much has been given, much will be required; and from the one to whom much has been entrusted, even more will be demanded' (Luke 12:48).

Before leaving 2 Peter, we must finally consider this passage's compact description of the new creation itself. The language of 'a new heavens and a new earth' is of course borrowed ultimately from Isaiah 65 and 66. But the remarkable personification here of righteousness 'making its home' in the new creation echoes most closely the language of Isaiah 32. In Isaiah 32 there is a vision of God's desolating judgment upon human habitation in the land, which is followed by reference to a time when 'a spirit from on high is poured out on us' and the wilderness becomes a 'fruitful field', a fruitful place where 'righteousness' will 'abide' (vv. 15–16). 'The effect of righteousness', verse 17 goes on to say, 'will be peace'. In the same way, of course, 2 Peter 3:14 encourages readers, as they await the day of the Lord and the new heaven and new earth, to 'be found by him at peace'. The hope for the future held out by 2 Peter, then, does not sound far from the ecological vision of Isaiah 32, where the wilderness, cleared of human injustice, is renewed by God's spirit as a fruitful field where righteousness dwells and peace is found.

Revelation 21 – 22

The most expansive picture of Christian hope, where the language of Isaiah, Ezekiel and Jewish apocalypticism finds its fullest NT expression, is found

---

34. See the wide variety of essays assessing the stewardship model in R. J. Berry (ed.), *Environmental Stewardship: Critical Perspectives – Past and Present* (London: T. & T. Clark, 2006).

of course in the book of Revelation and in its portrait of the new heaven and new earth. There is also a brief glimpse near the beginning of this book of what the author would consider to be the plight of creation without redemption, of a world without Christ and without hope. This is the moment in the heavenly throne room when the one sitting on the throne is seen holding a sealed scroll in his hand, a scroll that in the context of the narrative must represent the unfolding of God's purposes for the world. No one can be found 'in heaven or on earth or under the earth' who can 'open the scroll' or even 'look into it' (Rev. 5:3). The seer John reports that he 'wept and wept' until, hearing that the lion of Judah has conquered and is worthy to open the scroll, he turns to see the lamb standing as though slain in the centre of the throne. The praise of the Creator with which chapter 4 concluded is now echoed by praise for the Redeemer; and the result for those who have been purchased by the blood of the lamb is that they are made for our God 'a kingdom and priests', and 'they will reign on earth' (5:10).

Revelation 11:15 describes this redemption in terms of the kingdom of the world becoming the kingdom of God and his Messiah. The continuity between the two ages envisioned here is particularly striking in the Greek text, which reads simply *Egeneto hē basileia tou kosmou tou kyriou hēmōn kai tou Christou autou.* As Poul Guttesen has argued, the compressed syntax suggests that it is the same entity, the same kingdom that finds itself reorientated around a new centre of authority, from that of the world to that of the Lord and of his Messiah.[35] This new reign is said to extend 'for ever and ever'; and it is clearly only in the context of this reign of God and his Messiah that the earthly reign of those purchased by the blood of the lamb described in 5:10 becomes possible; and so their reign too can be said to last 'for ever and ever' (22:5). As in chapter 5, the response to all of this can be nothing other than worship, and the prerequisite of this worship is the laying down before the throne of all other claims to power and authority. In the description of the final judgment within the hymn that follows, then, a striking contrast is drawn between, on the one hand, the rewarding of God's servants, prophets, saints – those who fear his name, both small and great – and, on the other hand, the destruction of those who destroy the earth (11:18).

---

35. Poul F. Guttesen, *Leaning into the Future: The Kingdom of God in the Theology of Jürgen Moltmann and in the Book of Revelation*, Princeton Theological Monograph Series (Eugene, Oreg.: Pickwick, 2009), pp. 128–130.

According to Revelation, fear, reverence and the worship of God stand over and against the destruction of his earth.[36] To honour God as Creator and Lord, to heed the call of what John calls elsewhere the 'eternal gospel' (14:6–8), requires in the first instance the acknowledgment that no mere human being can bear the title of lord or god; as mere creatures, awe and worship is what is demanded. It is only in reverencing God the Creator and Redeemer that human beings join in the worship of all of creation that resounds in the heavenly throne room. In worship, human beings find their appropriate place alongside the rest of creation within the economy of God's kingdom; and it is only in this that they become able to rule in his earth, and to rule in a way that does not lead to the earth's destruction.

The future of earth, however, is finally something given by God. This future is described with vivid imagery in chapters 21–22 of Revelation, and there is a strong emphasis here on all of creation reaching the *telos* for which it is intended. Thus, to pick one theme among many, there are echoes of the early chapters of Genesis, echoes that call attention not only to creation's restoration but also to its transformation, to its being taken beyond what it was in the beginning to become something genuinely new. If waters and darkness were there from the start of the first creation, according to Genesis 1:2, the sea and night have no more place in the new (Rev. 21:1; 22:5); and the results of the tragedy of Genesis 3 – death, sorrow, mourning, pain and curse (Rev. 21:4; 22:3) – are thus not only absent from the new creation but even the potential for them ever to pose a threat again is permanently removed.[37] Yet the new creation is not *ex nihilo*,[38] for it is a making of 'all things' new, a restoration of life and a healing of the nations, with space even for the glory of the kings of the earth to be

---

36. Most commentators assume without argument that 'earth' in this verse is merely equivalent to people (or God's people) here. See e.g. David E. Aune, *Revelation 6–16*, WBC 52b (Nashville: Nelson, 1998), p. 645; G. K. Beale, *The Book of Revelation: A Commentary on the Greek Text*, NIGTC (Grand Rapids: Eerdmans, 1999), pp. 615–616. But this would be an unusual use of 'earth'. Its plain meaning should be retained, even if for John the destruction of the earth occurs indirectly as a result of the corruption, idolatry and violence of those who live in it.

37. For a more fully developed argument of this point, see Jonathan Moo, 'The Sea That Is No More: Rev 21.1 and the Function of Sea Imagery in the Apocalypse of John', *NovT* 51 (2009), pp. 148–167.

38. Adams, *Stars Will Fall*, p. 238, claims that for a first-century writer this notion was not even a genuine option in any case.

brought in through the ever open gates of the New Jerusalem (21:24–25). If John has hesitated earlier in his book to repeat Isaiah's claim that the whole earth is full of God's glory (Rev. 4:8; cf. Isa. 6:3),[39] the coming of the one 'who is and was and is to come' means that in this new heaven and new earth God is indeed fully present with his people and his glory can truly be said to suffuse all things (21:3, 22–24).

These images of hope and judgment in Revelation, as with those in Romans 8 and 2 Peter 3, may seem like fantasies that have little bearing on life in the here and now; but I suggest that – for those 'with eyes to see' – they have the potential to serve as a powerful source of encouragement and motivation for even those today who seek to go about the humble task of living rightly in creation and caring for the earth. In the context of Revelation, the images serve above all to challenge complacency and to encourage perseverance among John's readers, whose putative situations seem, based on the messages to the seven churches, to range from reasonably comfortable accommodation with the surrounding culture to experiences of persecution of one kind or another. For all of those tempted to revere false gods, to give in to the pressure to conform and to compromise their faith, John challenges them to fear and worship only the Creator and Judge of the world, the one who 'made heaven and earth, the sea and the springs of water' (14:7). For those who are tempted to give up their faithful witness, John encourages them that the victory has already been won and that, no matter how desperate things may appear in the present, God's good purposes for his people and his creation cannot fail.

In our own context, it can actually seem rather fashionable for a Christian to be concerned about the environment. But it remains worryingly unfashionable and strongly countercultural actually to contemplate doing anything much about it; and I suspect that many of us will become profoundly weary, if we are not already, of caring about or trying to address a crisis that seems from within our limited perspective to unfold in extreme slow motion, a crisis that has effects usually felt most acutely by communities far away from us, and a crisis that – when fully grasped and understood – easily breeds despair due to its scale, complexity and apparent intractability. Faithfulness and perseverance are virtues of which we shall have great need; and John and other NT writers have much to teach Christians about how they may be cultivated.

---

39. See the brief discussion of Rev. 4:8 and its use of Isa. 6:3 in Richard Bauckham, *The Theology of the Book of Revelation* (Cambridge: Cambridge University Press, 1993), pp. 46–47.

Assessment

The sort of hope we have been tracing fundamentally reorientates the life of the believer, and it does so in ways that are surprisingly crucial for a Christian environmental ethos. In the first instance, it drives out the sort of fear that often lies behind our acquisitiveness and grasping materialism and that prevents us from contemplating radical changes in our individual lives and in our wider societies. In Luke's Gospel it is no coincidence that just before Jesus talks of the Son of Man coming unexpectedly like a thief, he speaks against greed and anxiety, against the sort of greed that causes a rich fool to store up wealth for himself while failing to be rich towards God and against the sort of anxiety that prevents generous, self-sacrificial giving. 'Do not be afraid, little flock,' Jesus says, 'for it is your Father's good pleasure to give you the kingdom. Sell your possessions, and give alms' (Luke 12:32–33).

As in 2 Peter's call for pursuing godly acts that hasten in the new creation, biblical hope also encourages an ongoing and persistent commitment to personal virtue through all circumstances, even when things look bleak or when the actions of all of those around us would seem to render the actions of one individual ineffective. In the hope for a future that is at once given by God and yet demands radically new life now, Christians are left without the excuse that unless and until our neighbours change we might as well not change ourselves since it seems to make no difference in the big scale of things. In the context of biblical hope, it is precisely in the big scale of things that individual actions do make a difference; and for Christians to deny the value of the small and apparently insignificant is to deny the possibility of grace, the possibility that God in his faithfulness can honour even our feeble efforts; and it is finally to reject our identity as children of God in Christ.

NT hope does not merely encourage personal piety, however. The content of biblical hope reveals the value within God's purposes of the creation itself, a creation that praises the Creator simply by being itself and yet whose fate is linked to ours and for whose care in the present age we bear much responsibility. Household stewards, as Jesus' parables remind us, require wisdom to manage well, to discern aright the master's will, and to care and provide for those alongside whom they work; likewise, wisdom of all kinds is necessary for those who seek to care appropriately for the earth, wisdom to perceive the value that it has for its owner, wisdom to discern the master's purposes for it, and wisdom to learn one's own limits in caring for and living within it. And alongside such wisdom must be humility; if God is the owner and master and it is him who is to be revered, it must be only in fear and trembling that the flawed creatures who have been given such responsibility seek to exercise it.

For Christians today, this humility must also derive in part from a profound awareness of how we are embedded in and complicit with systems and ways of living that we now recognize as unsustainable and that are contributing to the plight of the poor and of the rest of creation. Christian creation care will not be guilt-driven but nor can it be arrogant, for it proceeds from an awareness of our own limitations and trusts not in ourselves but in the God who by his grace provides the results.

Finally, if NT hope makes strong demands upon those who would seek to live in its light, there is also a promise of joy even in the present for those who await and work for the new creation. If it is in some sense this same creation that is carried over into the new, that finds God's purposes for it realized at the resurrection and restoration of all things, there must be – as Moltmann reminds us – something of the promise of the new creation within the old.[40] This is consonant with our own experience too; however shot through it is with grief and suffering, human life consists also in profound glimpses of joy – perhaps especially in encounters with the world outside ourselves, with creation in all of its otherness, beauty and awesomeness. If Francis Schaeffer was right when he observed that the death of joy in nature is the beginning of the death of nature itself,[41] we should be encouraged to reacquaint ourselves with the natural world, to learn more intimately about the creation within which we are embedded, and to honour its Creator in our delight in what he has made, in our worship of him, and in our attentiveness to creation's health and well-being. Bonhoeffer went so far as to suggest that we must love this world if we are rightly to anticipate the next.[42] But the ultimate source of our joy in this age – as in the next – comes from the Creator himself. This is the claim of Peter in Acts 3:19–21, who like the other NT writers we have examined, holds together the promise of the present and the future for those who turn to God:

---

40. Moltmann, *Coming of God*, p. 279.

41. Francis Schaeffer, *Pollution and the Death of Man* (Wheaton: Crossway, 1970), p. 10.

42. See Dietrich Bonhoeffer, *Letters and Papers from Prison*, ed. E. Bethge (London: SCM, 1953), p. 157 (letter dated 5 Dec. 1943). It must be admitted that Bonhoeffer's point is slightly different from mine: 'It is only when one loves life and the earth so much that without them everything seems to be over that one may believe in the resurrection and a new world; it is only when one submits to God's law that one may speak of grace; and it is only when God's wrath and vengeance are hanging as grim realities over the heads of one's enemies that something of what it means to love and forgive them can touch our hearts.'

Repent therefore, and turn to God so that your sins may be wiped out, so that times of refreshing may come from the presence of the Lord, and that he may send the Messiah appointed for you, that is, Jesus, who must remain in heaven until the time of universal restoration that God announced long ago through his holy prophets.

Here is motivation for faithful Christian witness and care for the earth; in repenting and in turning to God with all of the ramifications that follow, there is the promise not only of the future restoration of all things but of anticipatory moments of refreshing and relief. As Christians labour to speed on the day of the Lord for which they and all of creation yearn, as they seek to live transformed lives that are in keeping with a world where righteousness is at home, there is hope for glimpses of that glorious future and even instantiations of it in the present as God's will begins to be done on earth, as it is in heaven.

© Jonathan Moo, 2014

8. PARADISE BY THE DESOLATION TRAIL: DE-CREATION AND THE NEW TESTAMENT

Sean McDonough

Tourists hungry for sun, sand and tropical greenery might be forgiven for bypassing one of the attractions of the Big Island of Hawaii, the aptly named Desolation Trail. But there it lies, in the midst of Hawai'i Volcanoes National Park, a one-mile trek through an ashen landscape covered by the cinder outfall of the 1959 eruption of Kilauea Iki. In the same way, green-minded theologians venturing into the NT understandably focus their attention on those passages that affirm the goodness of the created order: the restorative miracles of Jesus, the liberation of creation in Romans, the lilies in the field and the Eye on the sparrow.

But it is impossible to ignore the trail of desolation that runs through the NT corpus. The pyrotechnics of Jesus' apocalyptic discourse and the book of Revelation are only the most striking examples of the dismantling of the created order. The shockwaves of the future cataclysm may be felt in subtler ways throughout the canon: the world is regularly depicted as transient and fragile. Jacques Ellul has termed this 'de-creation'.[1] Rather than downplaying this evidently central aspect of NT theology, those interested in the environment should meet it head on.

---

1. Commenting on the trumpet plagues of Revelation, Ellul writes, 'In these verses we find ourselves both in the presence of a recollection of the "plagues of Egypt", which all the commentators have noticed . . . and also, which has been rarely seen, a sort of "de-creation", a putting in question by going back, of the works of the third day (the vegetation and the waters), of the fourth day (the lights), of the fifth day

Before we begin our brief survey of de-creation in the NT, we must note two important points. First, while we shall focus on the dismantling of the environment, we cannot ignore altogether the microcosmic sufferings of human beings. This is not simply because people are a part of creation: in the biblical drama, the fate of the earth is entwined with that of humanity. Secondly, we should not put up an artificial wall between de-creation in the Old Testament and the New, as if the early church were only governed by beliefs that sooner or later made their way in explicit form into the NT canon. The OT was the Bible of the early church, and thus texts concerning the dissolution of the world would always have been in play. It is only the constraint of space that focuses our discussion on the NT proper.

De-creation in the Gospels

We may begin with that most unusual of Jesus' recorded miracles, the cursing of the fig tree (Mark 11:12–14 // Matt. 21:18–22). In every other instance Jesus' mighty works involve either a restoration of the created order (most notably the healings) or a positive demonstration of his sovereignty over the natural world (e.g. feeding of the five thousand, walking on the water). Only here does de-creation raise its head.[2]

While the withering of the tree may be an isolated incident, its roots go deep into the theology of the Gospels. The sign itself of course points towards the looming destruction of the temple. It thus leads us straight towards Jesus' apocalyptic discourse, with its earthquakes and famines and darkened sky. Questions have been raised as to whether the dis-ordering of creation envisioned in the discourse refers to the ultimate end of all things, or whether it employs hyperbolic language to presage the catastrophe about to envelop Jerusalem and the temple.[3] It may well be doing both: Jews and Christians in the Second Temple period would probably have read the OT prophets as a

---

(the fish)' (Jacques Ellul, *Apocalypse: The Book of Revelation*, tr. George W. Schreiner [New York: Seabury, 1977], p. 74).

2. One may cite the deaths of Ananias and Sapphira in Acts 5 as an analogous phenomenon.

3. For a recent evocation of this ongoing debate, see Dale Allison's critique of N. T. Wright, 'Jesus & the Victory of Apocalyptic', in Carey C. Newman (ed.), *Jesus and the Restoration of Israel: A Critical Assessment of N. T. Wright's Jesus and the Victory of God* (Downers Grove: InterVarsity Press, 1999), pp. 126–141.

mélange of predictions involving both near term and eschatological fulfilments (see e.g. Isa. 7). Why might not the gospel writers, and indeed Jesus himself, have taken this as a model for their own prophetic discourse? Even if one is inclined to think the discourse refers specifically to the temple devastation, we should remember that the temple was itself regarded as a kind of microcosm.[4] Thus any attack on it was a blow at the very nexus of earthly and heavenly life.[5]

We should not imagine, however, that de-creation enters into Jesus' ministry only at the very end. To anticipate the language of Hebrews, the introduction of the unshakeable new creation is necessarily accompanied by the shaking of the old. This is most evident in Jesus' words on discipleship and his disposition towards the Mosaic Law. His injunction to 'hate one's mother and father' would be viewed as a serious fracturing of the social order in any culture, and in the context of Israel represents one more instance of his ambiguous relationship with traditional views of the Law. This disruption of Israel's corporate traditions is of a piece with the more dramatic cosmic catastrophes of the apocalyptic discourse. Israel's Law, from family relationships to Sabbath to the purity code, was grounded in the creation account.[6] In the ancient world there was an intimate link between the cosmic order and the social order. Pull at one thread, and you threaten the fabric of the whole.

This comprehensive de-creation of the old world order may be traced most clearly in Matthew, though analogous material may be found in all the Gospels. The Gospel begins with the words *Biblos geneseōs Iēsou Christou*. Someone with very little Greek might be tempted to translate it, 'The Book of Genesis of Jesus Christ',[7] and in fact that is arguably at least one aspect of what Matthew wants us to think. The phrase itself goes back to the genealogy from Adam in Genesis 5, with the implication that Jesus represents a radical new beginning for humanity. Jesus then recapitulates the history of Israel in his little exodus from Egypt, his passing through the Jordan, and his forty-day temptation in the wilderness – or rather rewrites that history, since for Matthew he will succeed in exhibiting the faithfulness to God that Israel largely failed to show in the OT.

---

4. For a thorough exploration of the connections between the temple and the cosmos, see G. K. Beale, *The Temple and the Church's Mission* (Leicester: Apollos; Downers Grove: InterVarsity Press, 2004).

5. See Jon Levenson, *Creation and the Persistence of Evil: The Jewish Drama of Divine Omnipotence* (Princeton: Princeton University Press, 1994), pp. 87–88.

6. Jacob Milgrom, *Leviticus: The Book of Ritual and Ethics* (Minneapolis: Fortress, 2004), p. 13.

7. All translations in this chapter are my own.

But the beginning of the new means in some sense the end of the old; not peace, but a sword. This is transparent, at least with respect to the Law of Moses, in the sayings, 'You have heard it said . . . but I say to you' in the Sermon on the Mount. This dramatic re-visioning of the Law (which makes sense only under the assumption that the eschatological renewal of Ezek. 34 and Jer. 31 is underway) was clearly seen by many of Jesus' contemporaries as a dismantling of the multitudinous sacred traditions of Israel. Depending on what one makes of the date of the traditions in Bereshith Rabbah 1, it might even have been seen as a serious assault on the integrity of creation itself: 'The Torah was to God, when he created the world, what the plan is to an architect when he erects a building.'

But the dismantling of Torah tradition and the dismantling of creation appear even more strikingly in what appears to be an unstinting affirmation of the Law: 'Truly I say to you, until heaven and earth pass away, not an iota or a serif will pass away, until all things come to pass' (Matt. 5:17). Why do we have the unwieldy device of the two 'until' clauses in one sentence? I believe that there are two clauses because there are two layers of meaning here. On the one hand, the verse affirms that the Law *as re-visioned by Jesus and centred on the love command* is binding until 'heaven and earth disappear'; that is, to the very end of the age. On the other hand, the Mosaic Law as such and in detail remains valid only 'until all things come to pass' in the death and resurrection of Jesus.

We can see both poles of the statement in play in the incident of the grain plucking on the Sabbath (Matt. 12). There is nothing to suggest that the disciples were in fact breaking the Sabbath simply by grabbing a few heads of corn. The letter of the law is arguably being kept. Yet it is telling that Jesus does not enter into a quantitative analysis of how much activity constitutes 'work'. Instead, he highlights his messianic authority with an illustration from the life of David and declares that 'the Son of Man is Lord of the Sabbath' – a two-edged sword by which he declares the centrality of the love command (human need trumps ritual observance) and asserts the primacy of his own interpretation of the law over and against Pharisaic tradition (I, the Son of Man, will tell you what constitutes proper Sabbath observance). The complete re-visioning of the Law consequent upon his death has not yet broken upon the Pharisees, but here we may see it rumbling beneath their feet.

What rumbles in Matthew 12 explodes in Matthew 27 and 28. Matthew's depiction of the death of Christ (heavily indebted to Ezek. 37[8]) is a pageant

---

8. See Donald Senior, 'The Death of Jesus and the Resurrection of the Holy Ones (Mt. 27:51–53)', *CBQ* 38 (1976), pp. 312–329.

of OT end-of-the-world imagery: darkness in the land, ravaging of the temple, shaking of the earth, and the righteous raised from their tombs. It is hard not to see here the proleptic shaking of the old world order. The (presumably eschatological) earthquake recurs at the resurrection of Christ in 28:2. The old world order has in a meaningful sense fallen in the death of Christ; all the necessary things have come to pass to permit a radical re-evaluation of what constitutes Torah obedience for the people of God in the new age.

De-creation in the Gospels, then, does not consist of a few awkwardly inserted texts concerning cosmic conflagration. It is a purposeful and pervasive aspect of Jesus' ministry as interpreted by the evangelists. Jesus' death may shatter the very rocks of the earth and darken the heavenly bodies, but he has already in his life dissolved the traditional bonds of kinship, nation and cult that are equally a part of the old world order. We speak readily enough of Jesus making a way for people to enter the kingdom of God; it is equally true that the world as currently constituted must itself make way for the kingdom to enter.

De-creation in the Epistles

The Pauline and General Epistles (with a few significant exceptions) do not feature much in the way of graphic depictions of world deformation. This is not surprising, since they are focused on the local problems besetting the burgeoning messianic gatherings around the Mediterranean. We do find in them, however, a pervasive sense of the transitory nature of the present world order. 'The form of this world is passing away', Paul writes in 1 Corinthians 7:31, and so he enjoins the Corinthians to hold loosely to the created ordinances of marriage and community life. James 5 likewise informs its readers that 'the Lord is near', and will bring with him an eschatological rain (*sic*; cf. 5:7, 18) of terror for the wicked. Examples could be multiplied.[9] The lens does occasionally widen to encompass what we now call the environment, with Romans 8 and 2 Peter 3 being the most notable examples. Jonathan Moo has dealt with these passages in detail in the present volume (chapter 7), so I offer here a brief summary treatment of these two key texts, followed by a separate treatment of the book of Hebrews.

Romans 8 gives us a glimpse of the cosmic implications of the Messiah's work. The focus remains on the people of God: thus 8:19, 'The eager expectation

---

9. See e.g. 2 Cor. 5:1–5; Gal. 6:14; Phil. 3:18–20; Col. 3:1–4; 1 Thess. 4:13 – 5:11; 1 Tim. 6:17–19; 1 Pet. 1:1–21.

of the creation awaits the revelation of the children of God.' That revelation means liberation for the creation, though Paul only drops hints as to how those two things coinhere.

The most important hints lie within Paul's assertion that 'the creation has been subjected to futility' (Gk. *tē . . . mataiotēti hē ktisis hypetagē*; Rom. 8:20). The verb for subjected, *hypotassō*, is an important one for Paul. A comparison with 1 Corinthians 15 is in order, not least because God's order, his *taxis*, is at the rhetorical heart of the passage in Corinthians. The root appears in various forms seven times in the central section of the chapter, verses 20–28. Paul's use of *hypotassō* here goes back to Psalm 8: 'you have subjected all things under his feet', which is then brought into juxtaposition with the touchstone messianic Psalm 110 by *gezera shawa*: 'until he puts all his enemies *under his feet*'. The Messiah fulfils the primal command to subject the earth to God.

This alone does not ensure that Paul is alluding to the creation narrative in Romans 8:20. But such an allusion is strongly suggested by the second key word in the phrase, 'subjected to *futility*'. Again, a comparison with 1 Corinthians 15 is instructive. Futility – in the various lexical guises of *eikē, mataios* and *kenos* – is a pervasive theme and forms an *inclusio* for 1 Corinthians 15 as a whole. A belief in the resurrection is not in vain (*eikē*, v. 2) and thus there is no emptiness in present-day Christian labour (*ouk . . . kenos*, v. 58). The force of Romans 8:20, by contrast, is precisely that the present creation is subjected to this futility. Reading Romans 8 with the aid of 1 Corinthians 15, we may see that the creation finds itself in a nightmarish inversion of Psalm 8. While it ought to be flourishing under the benevolent stewardship of humans, it is instead thwarted at every turn as a consequence of their rebellion. Because 'the disposition of the flesh . . . does not submit (*hypotassō*) to the law of God' (Rom. 8:7), the creation must be submitted to futility. Well may it groan in anguish (Rom. 8:22).

The specifics of this groaning remain somewhat obscure. The most natural candidate for the anguish of creation would be the curse on the ground in Genesis 3:17. But the curse there is at least as much directed towards humanity as it is to the land per se: the intractability of the ground leads to toil for humanity. We might turn, then, to the following chapter of Genesis where the ground becomes the unhappy receptacle of the blood of righteous Abel. Alternatively, Paul could have in mind passages like Isaiah 24, where the woes of the earth are directly attributable to human sin: 'The earth is polluted underneath its inhabitants, because they have transgressed the law, they have changed the statute, they have broken the eternal covenant' (Isa. 24:5).

Whatever Paul's source may be, it is evident that the restoration of creation is somehow consequent upon the restoration of humanity to a proper standing before God. At the very least he affirms that the present travails of the world are not God's final word: the groanings are a way station on the road to the complete redemption of the cosmos.

2 Peter 3 has long been a thorn in the side of Christians concerned with the creation. Even with the adoption of the reading 'the earth and its works *will be disclosed*' in verse 10, the text presents a pretty thoroughgoing destruction of the world order: 'The Day of the Lord will come as a thief, in which the heavens will pass away with a whir, and the elements will be destroyed as they burn, and the earth and its works will be disclosed . . .'. Has 2 Peter exchanged the life-affirming inheritance of his Jewish forebears for a world-denying philosophy, happily fiddling while the world burns?

Hardly. As Moo demonstrates, the author of 2 Peter has pulled his eschatology neither out of thin air nor from some handbook of Stoic physics: his account of the end is very much rooted in OT texts.[10] I would argue that it in fact constitutes, like much else in the NT, a kind of commentary on the latter chapters of Isaiah. The overt citation of Isaiah 65:17 ('the new heavens and new earth') in 2 Peter 3:13 is matched by probable allusions to the *melting* of the mountains in Isaiah 63:19 (64:1 LXX) and the melting of the elements in 2 Peter 3:12,[11] and the fiery judgment of God in Isaiah 66:15–16 or 2 Peter 3:10, 12. No doubt other OT passages contributed to the text in 2 Peter, not least the similarly apocalyptic Isaiah 34;[12] but it scarcely seems a coincidence that the precise language of Isaiah 63 – 66 should appear in such close juxtaposition to a direct quotation from Isaiah 65. Whatever 2 Peter is affirming, it is doing so in close continuity with the legacy of the Hebrew Bible.

As for what it is affirming, we have already seen that it involves a radical makeover of the current state of affairs. But if his description of the world's travails is more conflagratory than Romans 8, the two passages end up in the same place: the new heavens and new earth in which righteousness dwells. This is critical for properly assessing the imagery of world destruction in 2 Peter. If the author deemed materiality as such a bad or inconsequential thing, it would make little sense for him to hold forth the prospect of *more* materiality, even if it is somehow renewed. The problem is rather the current

---

10. See above, Moo, 'New Testament Hope', pp. 154–162.

11. Where the MT uses only the language of shaking (*zālal*) in Isa. 63:19 [64:1], the LXX adds the same verb 2 Peter does, *tēkō*: 'if you open the heaven, the mountains will receive a shaking from you, and *they will melt*, as wax *melts* from fire, and those who oppose you will be burned up . . .' (my tr. and italics).

12. See Moo, 'New Testament Hope', p. 158.

absence of righteousness, which brings us into the same domain of thought as Romans 8: the fate of humanity and the fate of the earth are intertwined. The eschatological fire of God serves to burn through the idolatrous conceits of humanity and reveals things for what they really are. Such a revelation may also have a purgative effect – not so much *tout comprendre c'est tout pardonner* (to understand all is to forgive all) as the unmasking of pretence as the first step to rehabilitation.[13]

We conclude this section with the book of Hebrews, which contains one of the most theologically sophisticated meditations on the meaning of de-creation for Christian faith. The epistle admittedly focuses on the superiority of the New Covenant to the Old, with a concomitant emphasis on matters of temple cult. But this argument is embedded within a very nuanced understanding of the relationship between the present, earthly, realm and the coming, heavenly, one.[14] While the author of Hebrews (AH) undoubtedly privileges heavenly and future realities over present, earthly, ones, he nonetheless works within the customary early Christian eschatology: God created the world through Christ, but the present order of things will give way to the glorious new world order of resurrection life. The AH has a variety of images at hand to describe the coming kingdom: it is real, well ordered ('straightened out', in the language of Heb. 9:10), heavenly, eternal, perfect and unshakeable.

The present world order is in sum *provisional* in the eyes of the AH, and thus its disassembly is a natural consequence of its place in God's plan. It is the good creation of God through Christ, but it remains *shakeable*. The AH takes the words of Haggai 2:6, 21, 'Yet once more will I shake not only the earth but also the heaven', as a reference to the eschatological shaking of the 'things that have been made' (*pepoiēmenōn*), the things 'of this creation'. This is in contrast to the unshakeable realities of God's kingdom, which endure for ever (Heb. 12:26–29).[15] The destruction of the 'things that have been made' should not be

---

13. Cf. ibid., p. 159: 'We are left with the cataclysmic fire of God's judgment, but its function in the context is primarily to lay the earth bare before God, to reveal it as it is and to leave human beings and their works without any place to hide.'

14. For an overview, see Jon Laansma, 'The Cosmology of Hebrews', in Jonathan Pennington and Sean McDonough (eds.), *Cosmology and New Testament Theology* (London: T. & T. Clark/Continuum, 2008), pp. 125–143.

15. Having just left our discussion of 2 Peter, the reader will not be surprised to find in this eschatological context God designated as a 'consuming fire' (v. 29).

taken as a critique of God's creative activity as such. The critique of 'madeness' here is driven by Hebrews' governing contrast between the earthly sanctuary and the heavenly one. In both 9:11 and 9:24 the heavenly sanctuary is said to be 'not handmade' (*ou cheiropoiētos*; note the *poi-* root), with 'handmade' being tantamount to 'man-made'.[16] Furthermore, in 1:2, the AH pointedly avoids using the typical formula that 'all things' were made through Christ, and says instead that 'through him he made the *ages (tous aiōnas)*'. This plural form should be taken, I believe, as a reference to the creation of the present age, and the creation of the age to come.[17] The created nature of the world to come is supported most clearly by Hebrews 11:10: Abraham looks forward to the city 'whose designer and maker is God'. As in the rest of the NT, the present world is not cast aside in favour of an immaterial, uncreated reality; rather, it must make way for a new and better creation.

De-creation in Revelation

The eschatological shaking-up spoken of Hebrews finds its most vivid expression in the book of Revelation. De-creation pervades the book. War, famine and death ride forth in chapter 6 to open the spectacle, followed in short order by rolled-up skies, falling stars, poisoned seas, and a host of other calamities. The boundaries separating world and underworld are breached by a variety of malevolent beings; and the sense of unnatural incursion is heightened by the monstrous combination of locust, lion and scorpion in the warriors from the pit who emerge after the fifth trumpet sounds (Rev. 9). Disorder appears to

16. Note that the designation 'not made with hands' (*acheiropoiētos*) is also used with respect to a heavenly tent/temple in Mark 14:58 and 2 Cor. 5:1 (2 Corinthians is directly referencing the resurrection body, but the sanctuary terms *oikia* and *skēnē* are employed); cf. Acts 7:48 and 17:24, where God is said not to dwell in handmade temples. See e.g. F. F. Bruce, *The Epistle to the Hebrews*, rev., NICNT (Grand Rapids: Eerdmans, 1990), pp. 212–213. The AH was also no doubt well aware that in the LXX *cheiropoiētos* is consistently used for idols fabricated by human beings. He is not therefore stating that the temple is tantamount to an idol; but the ominous OT overtones of 'man-made' do suggest that the temple as a human fabrication is unable to bear the full weight of the eschatological glory of God.

17. See further Sean McDonough, *Christ as Creator* (Oxford: Oxford University Press, 2010), pp. 201–214.

reign. What God put together in six days is increasingly ripped apart in six seals, six trumpets and six bowls.[18]

The presence of these numbered, and thus ordered, 'de-creation weeks' shows that events are not careening out of control in the Apocalypse. The unravelling of the world is quite purposeful, and constitutes the necessary preparation for the re-creation of all things by God. All is under the eye of the One seated on the throne, who is quite deliberately introduced in chapter 4 as maker of heaven and earth. Richard Bauckham has argued that the rainbow around the throne signals the faithfulness of God to the creation, particularly against the backdrop of the flood narrative. The ultimate end of all things echoes the time of Noah, when God sets about to 'destroy the destroyers of the earth' (Rev. 11:18).[19] As the narrative of chapters 12–14 comes to a climax, the first angel proclaims the 'everlasting gospel': 'Fear God, and give him glory, because the hour of his judgment has come, and *worship the one who made the heaven and the earth and sea and springs of water*' (14:7). As in the previous texts we have studied, the shaking up of the current world order is designed to make way for a new and better one. From one angle, this can be seen as something tantamount to *creatio ex nihilo*: the New Jerusalem descends from heaven as the utterly gracious gift of God. Yet on closer inspection, there are equally strong elements of continuity between the new and the old: to take the simplest example, the New Jerusalem is founded upon the works of the patriarchs and apostles *in history*; the heavenly city is in certain respects consequent upon the work of the people of God on earth.

This complex calculus for the appearance of the eschatological city holds equally true for the unravelling of creation that precedes it. John regularly introduces catastrophes by saying, 'it was given' (*edothē*) for some event to happen.[20] This is usually taken as a simple divine passive, a circumlocution for 'God made it happen'. But John is fully capable of making God the subject of sentences (1:1; 7:17; 11:17; etc.). Why does he avoid doing so in these cases?

---

18. I recognize that there are seven seals, bowls and trumpets. But the 'work' of de-creation is primarily done during the first six units in the sequence. There is then a pause in which people are shown the way out of consummate final judgment (the sealing of the saints in ch. 7; the measuring of the temple in ch. 10; and the exhortation to keep awake in 16:15). The seventh unit then represents a 'sabbath' of ultimate judgment in which God's rule is established for good.

19. Richard Bauckham, *The Theology of the Book of Revelation* (Cambridge: Cambridge University Press, 1993), pp. 51–53.

20. See e.g. Rev. 6:2–11; 9:1, 5.

It seems to me that the passive voice invites a necessary ambiguity as to the question of responsibility for the destruction unleashed on the earth. God may be in charge of it all, but this does not preclude maleficent agents from doing awful things (witness again the locust-demons of the fifth seal); nor does it preclude God himself allowing creation and humanity to endure the consequences of humanity's self-destructive behaviour (e.g. if we take the poisoned-water imagery as at least partly fulfilled by the devastating ecological consequences of pollution).

The importance of personal agents and de-creation emerges with particular clarity in chapters 12–20. Here we find a showdown between the reality of the God Who Is and the pretensions of the Dragon, with the earth in some respects caught in the crossfire. The will of the Dragon finds political expression in the two beasts; the three together form the Satanic trinity. It finds civilizational expression in the great city Babylon, the counterfeit of God's city, the New Jerusalem. The treasures of the good creation have been hoarded into the lair of the Dragon. Babylon's idolatry and worldwide economic empire make it a hideous simulacrum of what God envisioned for the cosmos in the beginning. As in 2 Peter, then, the target of God's wrath is not so much the sea or the sky, but rather the entire satanic enterprise that has infiltrated the world. The creation, which has heretofore served in its beautiful ordering as the means through which life is sustained for humanity, now in its dismantling becomes the agent of death for the unrepentant wicked.

Nor is the reader meant to envisage a divine sovereignty exercised as sheer caprice. Perhaps the most salient note for de-creation in the whole book is the mention in 4:5 that 'from the throne there go forth lightnings and sounds and thunders . . .'. These elements, drawn from the Sinai theophany, form the base for the descriptions of consummate judgment in the rest of the book.[21] The theology embedded in this series of images is profound: God's judgment, which includes the de-creation of the present world, is not an arbitrary infliction of woes drawn out of some judgment jar lying in a heavenly storehouse. It is rather at heart the inevitable shattering of a world too frail to bear the revelation of a God who is constitutionally glorious, who in some sense *is*, or at least is experienced as, lightnings, sounds and thunders. God is the life of the world, and therefore must appear for the world to live. But before that can happen, the world itself must be renewed to endure the weight of his glory.

---

21. Bauckham, *Book of Revelation*, pp. 41–43.

Insight for the present

We can see from this survey that the Desolation Trail wends it way through the entirety of the NT corpus; it is the inescapable path to Paradise. And God's dismantling of the present world is unsparing: everything from the stars in the heavens to the elements of earth is subject to shaking. How might this help ground our thinking on 'the environment'?

Surely not by way of callous disregard for the earth. Any account we give of the desolation of the world must be balanced by the NT's affirmation of God's creation. The lilies of the field remain lovely, and good order is meant to be kept in the Christian community. As the Pastoral Epistles in particular make clear, work is to be done well, families are meant to flourish, food is to be enjoyed with thanksgiving to the God who provided it. Even on the precipice of absolute destruction, people are enjoined to worship God precisely as the one 'who made the heaven and the earth and the sea and the springs of water' (Rev. 14:7). Furthermore, the promise for the faithful is not a disembodied existence in an ephemeral heaven, but full-bodied resurrection life in the new heavens and new earth.

But it remains the case that, if nothing else, the NT consistently depicts the present creation as *transient*. Is there a theological rationale for the removal of the creation from the stage of history . . . the removal of the creation *as* the stage of history? Most Christians will affirm the method to the made-ness of the world – the ordering of creation is a self-evident good. Is there a method to the apparent madness of de-creation?

The texts adduced above give at least four reasons for answering these questions in the affirmative. They are (with unabashed alliteration): Pedagogy, Progress, Purgation and Preparation for Liberation. While these musings are not intended to address directly what constitutes a viable ecological ethic in the present, they may stimulate thinking about the theological foundation for such an ethic.

Pedagogy

It may be trite to say, 'we learn through suffering'; it is also true. The dissolution of our bodily microcosm forces us to reckon with the brevity of life: 'You return man to the dust . . . so teach us to number our days, so that we may get a wise heart' (Ps. 90:3, 12). The NT applies that same lesson with respect to the macrocosm: 'Since all these things are to be destroyed in this way, what sort of people ought you to be in holy behaviour and godlines . . .?' (2 Pet. 3:11). Our lust for autonomy leads us to imagine that the world is a self-sustaining, eternal entity. The eschatological shaking of the world to its foundations will evaporate that fantasy.

Consummate de-creation unveils the general truth that Irenaeus applies specifically to the death of the individual. Commenting on 1 Corinthians 15, Irenaeus asks why we must die before entering resurrection life. He answers:

> in order that we may never become puffed up, as if we had life from ourselves, and exalted against God, our minds becoming ungrateful; but learning by experience that we possess eternal duration from the excelling power of this Being, not from our own nature, we may neither undervalue that glory which surrounds God as He is, nor be ignorant of our own nature, but that we may know what God can effect, and what benefits man receives, and thus never wander from the true comprehension of things as they are, that is, both with regard to God and with regard to man. And might it not be the case, perhaps, as I have already observed, that for this purpose God permitted our resolution into the common dust of mortality, that we, being instructed by every mode, may be accurate in all things for the future, being ignorant neither of God nor of ourselves?[22]

Perhaps in suffering the loss of this world we think of as 'ours', we get a taste of the infinite self-giving of God in creation and redemption.

Progress

At one level the NT depicts the now world as a necessary step towards the perfection of the new world. Colin Gunton aptly spoke of God's creation *project*: the inaugural six days of creation in certain respects only set the stage for the drama of the complete exercise of God's dominion over the world through his human vicegerents. The fact that the project went off the rails almost immediately does not take away from the fact that God intended the world to move forward, not simply to stay where it was. Thus to recognize the provisionality of the present age is no shame to it, anymore than the transience of infancy is a shame to the adult.

Perhaps the easiest way to see this is in the physical body of the Messiah Jesus. The fact that he is 'born of Mary' can only be an affirmation of the essential goodness of what God has made. It is this body that is raised to eternal glory. Yet it must be raised: what has been made by God in the now must be raised eternal in the new.

Such a view sits particularly well with NT texts that posit a strong connection between the now world and the new world. Paul affirms the meaningfulness of the present body and its deeds in 1 Corinthians 6, arguing that believers ought

---

22. Irenaeus, *Against Heresies* 5.2, *The Ante-Nicene Fathers*, vol. 1, ed. Philip Schaff.

to abstain from sexual immorality because 'God raised the Lord and he will raise us up also by his power' (1 Cor. 6:14). Even in 1 Corinthians 15, where the discontinuity of the resurrection body is stressed, and where Adam's earthly body is compromised by corruptibility, an argument can be made that the body of the first Adam is the necessary precursor to the 'spiritual' body of Christ and resurrected believers. Paul is no doubt aware that Adam 'becomes a living being' (1 Cor. 15:45; Gen. 2:7) before the fall; and our earthly body corresponds to the seed sown in the agricultural analogy of verses 36–38. Corn may be better than seed; but there is no corn with no seed. We may return to the example adduced above concerning the New Jerusalem. It does descend out of heaven as the gift of God in Revelation 21. But there is also undoubted continuity with the present order of things: the apostles and patriarchs who form the foundation of the city, the nations who walk into the city bringing their glory with them . . . even the very name of the place is an inheritance from its earthly forebear. It is the resting place at the end of the pilgrim city's progress.

Purgation

But the world is of course not simply the proverbial 'work in progress'. As often as not it appears to be a work *in regress*. The world falls apart not only as a kind of natural progression, but equally as a necessary purgation. De-creation is part of the cleansing process of the earth. We can isolate at least three aspects of purgation here.

The first is the removal of malefactors. The final judgment upon the wicked is not simply the assignment of individuals to heaven or hell. The fate of the world is entwined with that of humanity; it is not for nothing that the evildoers of the Apocalypse are termed 'the destroyers of the earth'. If the greatest blessing for humanity is to live at peace with God in a well-ordered world, the corresponding curse is to have that order collapse at the behest of a God who has become your adversary. This punitive dimension of de-creation is most evident in the book of Revelation. As with Egypt of old, the oppression of God's people by the 'earth dwellers' calls forth devastating judgment from God. This judgment consists precisely in the dis-ordering of the world around them. The note of ecological catastrophe as divine judgment is sounded most clearly, and most grimly, at the pouring out of the second and third bowls of wrath in Revelation 16:3–4. The waters turn to blood, and the angel of the waters declares (v. 5), 'You are righteous, the One who is and who was, the holy one, in that you judged these people, for they poured out the blood of the saints and prophets, and you have given them blood to drink. They are worthy!'

Such a vision of divine retribution will not be greeted with warm enthusiasm by many in the modern West. Ironically, though, it is just here that Revelation finds meaningful points of connection with some modern ecological discourse. Those who warn about the perils of climate change routinely put forward doomsday scenarios directly tied to human transgressions: if our relentless fuel consumption leads to a wasted planet incapable of sustaining life, we shall only be getting what we deserve. This is not a precise analogue to the overtly theological concerns that drive the NT writers; but it may be enough to invite people to reconsider the viability of thinking of ecological catastrophe in terms of divine retribution.

The second two aspects of purgation both address the defilement itself, but from two different angles. The world has been so profoundly touched for ill by humanity that it stands in a state of impurity. We have already noted Isaiah 24, where responsibility for the agonies of the tortured earth is placed squarely on its covenant-breaking inhabitants. It is no accident that even today we speak so readily of the environment's 'pollution', a word redolent of ritual defilement. The ravishing of the world cannot be reckoned as 'things taking their course'. It is a sad thing to read in Genesis that man should return to the dust whence he came; but that the earth should harbour the blood of the innocent slain like Abel is an unbearable defilement.

From one perspective the desecration of the earth is so profound that it seems the creation itself must be purged from God's presence. 'Flesh and blood cannot inherit the kingdom of God,' Paul says of people in 1 Corinthians 15, not least because that flesh has been made corruptible by the bad company we keep.[23] We find the cosmic equivalent again in Revelation: 'And I saw a great white throne, and one seated upon it, and earth and heaven fled from his face, and there was no place found for them' (20:11). The disappearance of the defiled old world makes room for the pure new creation: 'And I saw a new heaven and new earth, for the first heaven and the first earth had passed away, and there was no longer any sea' (21:1).

But the NT also suggests that the creation is purged *from* its impurity by the fires of judgment, and not only in the sense that evil personal agents are removed from the scene. Numerous writers use the language of purification in their discussions of 2 Peter 3.[24] The purgative effects of fire are a commonplace in

---

23. Note the connection between *phtheirousin* in 1 Cor. 15:33 and *phthor-* in 15:42, 50; Paul seems to imply that the corruptibility of the flesh is not simply a stage on the path of perfection, a part of Adamic earthiness. It is instead the result of moral failing. It is perhaps not a coincidence that the same 'corruption' root plays a significant role in Isa. 24 (LXX); see 24:1, 3–4.

24. See Moo, 'New Testament Hope', pp. 159–162.

the NT (though usually with reference to the cleansing of a given community), so there is much to commend this reading of 2 Peter.

Even the dissolution of the created order can be read in a positive, purgative way. Reducing things to their primal state allows for their re-emergence as something new. If I may be permitted another OT text:

> I looked on the earth, and lo, it was waste and void;
> and to the heavens, and they had no light. I looked on the mountains, and lo,
>   they were quaking,
> and all the hills moved to and fro. I looked, and lo, there was no man,
> and all the birds of the air had fled. I looked, and lo, the fruitful land was a desert,
> and all its cities were laid in ruins
> before the LORD, before his fierce anger. (Jer. 4:23–26 RSV)

The ultimate goal is the restoration of God's people to their land under a new covenant. But the land must return to a state of *tôhû wābôhû*. Only then can something genuinely new spring up.

Preparation for liberation

The purgation that arises from the dismantling of the cosmos can thus be seen from the positive side as its preparation for liberation. In this sense the groaning of the world is precisely what enables the creation to move on to its glorious destiny; the chrysalis must be broken so that the butterfly can emerge. Note the final sentence in Sergeii Bulgakov's typically penetrating meditation on the meaning of art:

> Things are transfigured and made luminous by beauty; they become the revelation of their own abstract meaning. And this revelation through beauty of the things of the earth is the work of art. The world, as it has been given to us, has remained as it were covered by an outward shell through which art penetrates, as if foreseeing the coming transfiguration of the world.[25]

---

25. Sergeii Bulgakov, quoted in Brian Horne, 'Divine and Human Creativity', in Colin E. Gunton (ed.), *The Doctrine of Creation* (London: Continuum, 2004), p. 142. Cf. Bulgakov's comments on 'Art and Theurgy': 'Art must have hidden in its depths a prayer for the transfiguration of the created order, but it is not itself called to the daring enterprise of sophiurgic experiment. It must, patiently and hopefully, carry the cross of an insatiable yearning in its own passionate hunger, and await its hour' (in Rowan Williams [ed.], *Sergeii Bulgakov: Towards a Russian Political Theology* [London: Continuum, 1999], p. 158).

The image of transfiguration is another way of expressing the meaningful positive relationship between the now world and the new world. Jesus' earthly body is not destroyed on the mount of transfiguration. But it is, however briefly, caught up into another order of existence, one that anticipates the glory of the resurrection to come.

Yet it is fitting to remember that this future glory comes only through the de-creation of the crucifixion. It is here that Jesus paradoxically finishes the work the Father gave him to do (John 19:30); this is the moment of supreme artistry, where he strips away the outward shell that covers the world, and frees it for a new and better life.

9. JÜRGEN MOLTMANN: CREATION AND THE RESTRUCTURING OF TRINITARIAN PANENTHEISM

David Rainey

Introduction

For the English-speaking world, the major publication of Jürgen Moltmann's theology began in 1967 with his *Theology of Hope*.[1] In 1981 he published *The Trinity and the Kingdom of God*, and by then he had developed a fully established pantheistic theology[2] and it was within his particular panentheism that Moltmann articulated his doctrine of creation. John Cooper writes:

> Moltmann has developed the most extensive explicitly panentheistic Christian theology of the late twentieth century. He embraces panentheism because he is convinced that it has the most faithful contemporary model of the God of the Bible and explanation of the Christian faith.[3]

Jürgen Moltmann's panentheism has influenced not only his theology of creation but also his concern for ecology, and it runs like a thread through many

---

1. Jürgen Moltmann, *Theology of Hope*, tr. James W. Leitch (London: SCM, 1967).

2. Jürgen Moltmann, *The Trinity and the Kingdom of God: The Doctrine of God*, tr. Margaret Kohl (London: SCM, 1981).

3. John Cooper, *Panentheism: The Other God of the Philosophers from Plato to the Present* (Nottingham: Apollos, 2007), p. 237.

of his published works. Alan Torrance acknowledges that few books have stimulated the discussion of the theology of creation as has Jürgen Moltmann's *God in Creation* (1985).[4] Moltmann's 1985 doctrine of creation is based on his previous studies *The Church in the Power of the Spirit* (1977) and the collected essays from *The Future of Creation* (1979), and he continued exploring the theme in later works such as *Life in the Spirit* (1992). The doctrine of creation, according to Moltmann, is based on his doctrine of the Holy Spirit; he states, 'By the title *God in Creation* I mean God the Holy Spirit,'[5] and so his constructive approach would become a doctrinal exposition of pneumatology in the light of the Trinity with eschatological implications. Moltmann is less concerned about the minute compartmentalization of creation and, instead, wants to see creation in all its interrelationships in order to understand creation in a new way. From his Christian perspective he would also call this messianic theology done with an ecumenical agenda.[6]

Jürgen Moltmann's messianic doctrine of creation is a specific Christian contribution to ecological discussion. By messianic he means that the doctrine has a Christological focus with a future orientation; for Moltmann, creation can be interpreted only in the light of its future.[7] With his trinitarian focus, pneumatic creation is concerned about the future, with the perfection of creation brought to its fulfilment in the Spirit. The Spirit is not only in creation; the Spirit is the creator of community. This emphasis then, for Moltmann, is part of the fellowship of creation, in which each part of the created order, in its own way, participates. Each part exists not in itself but in relation to all the other parts; it is the Holy Spirit that creates this community of fellowship. The unity of creation, according to Moltmann, is not found within the structure of creation. It is a unity created by the power of the Spirit.

Pneumatological language permeates his work on creation. As one would expect, resurrection is the key to the Christian interpretation of future fulfilment in the power of the Holy Spirit. Resurrection directly relates to creation in the new heavens and the new earth. As Moltmann summarizes it, 'The Holy Spirit

---

4. Alan Torrance, '*Creatio ex Nihilo* and the Spatio-Temporal Dimensions, with Specific Reference to Jürgen Moltmann and D. C. Williams', in Colin E. Gunton (ed.), *The Doctrine of Creation: Essays in Dogmatics, History and Philosophy* (London: T. & T. Clark International, 1997), p. 83.

5. Jürgen Moltmann, *God in Creation: An Ecological Doctrine of Creation* (London: SCM, 1985), p. xii.

6. Ibid., p. xv.

7. Ibid., pp. 4–5.

is the power of the resurrection. The power of the resurrection is the life-giving Spirit. It is *ruach*, the creative power of God, through which God communicates his energies to his creation.'[8]

Moltmann's proposal maintains the transcendence of God as Creator, but transcendence alone leaves the door open for exploitation. To transcendence is added God's immanence or presence in creation through the Holy Spirit. It is the presence of the Spirit that gives value to creation. This becomes important if we are to avoid the continuing ecological disaster of our time. God does not stand against creation; God is present in creation through the Spirit. As one might expect, this, according to Moltmann, opens the door to God's suffering with creation. Since God is prepared to indwell creation, he is prepared to suffer with creation.[9]

Part 1: The theology of creation

The knowledge of creation

Moltmann's theology of creation does not begin in a biblicist exegesis of texts. In the OT the doctrine of creation springs out of God's saving activity for Israel.[10] It is the exodus, the establishment of the covenant and the giving of the Promised Land that create the basis for a doctrine of creation. In the Christian perspective, creation is grounded in the promise of the Father, the creative activity of the Son and the sanctifying work of the Spirit. Moltmann distinguishes between natural theology, with its origin in Stoic philosophy, and revealed theology with its origin in Scripture,[11] But Moltmann is prepared to assert that 'revealed' theology and 'natural' theology are not two separate theologies but, rather, both combine to create one theology of creation.[12]

Trinitarian creation

A few brief comments on the Trinity and Christology will place the doctrine of the Holy Spirit in relation to the Father and the Son. The doctrine of the Trinity is the distinctive Christian contribution to the understanding of creation,

---

8. Ibid., p. 67.

9. Ibid., pp. 13–16.

10. Jürgen Moltmann, *Science and Wisdom*, tr., Margaret Kohl (London: SCM, 2003), p. 36.

11. Moltmann, *God in Creation*, p. 57.

12. Ibid., p. 59.

and so the Christian understanding of the world is shaped by the history of Christ, but this does not negate the OT accounts of creation. Christians have taken the messianic eschatology of the OT and interpreted OT monotheism in a trinitarian manner. From the conviction that salvation includes both humanity and the whole of creation, the implication is asserted by Moltmann that Christ is the ground or foundation of creation. Moltmann then develops what he understands to be *sophia* (wisdom) Christology. Jesus Christ is the Son and the eternal wisdom of the Father, because Jesus Christ, who died and was raised from the dead, continues to sustain creation and in this event demonstrates God's wisdom, Moltmann continues by stating:

> The trinitarian doctrine is determined by the revelation of Christ: because Jesus was revealed as the Son of the eternal Father, the Wisdom and creative Word which are identified with the Son also take on a personal and hypostatic character which they lack in the Old Testament testimonies . . .[13]

The Spirit as creator

In the NT the future experience of salvation is made present through the Holy Spirit, and it is the Christian community that begins to experience the new creation. This is the meaning of the gift of the Spirit as eternal life. The Spirit is the experience of the indwelling God in creation. Now since we are the temple of the Holy Spirit both personally and corporately, the church is the place to proclaim that the Spirit preserves creation against the 'annihilating Nothingness'.[14] Since creation experiences annihilation through continuing ecological disasters, Moltmann understands that God, 'through the Spirit . . . suffers with the sufferings of his creatures'.[15] Moltmann can then affirm that 'the Holy Spirit is God himself',[16] but he makes a unique contribution to our understanding of the trinitarian fellowship. The One who gives life to the world and allows it to participate in God's eternal life is the creative Energy – the Spirit. In this sense the Father is the creating origin of creation, the Son is the shaping origin and the Spirit is the life-giving origin.[17] If we emphasize only the transcendence of God, we are led to deism; if we emphasize only the immanence or presence of God, we are led to pantheism. But Moltmann discovers in

---

13. Ibid., p. 95; see also Moltmann, *Trinity and the Kingdom*, pp. 103, 114–118.

14. Moltmann, *God in Creation*, p. 96.

15. Ibid., p. 97.

16. Ibid.

17. Ibid., p. 98.

panentheism a third way: 'In the panentheistic view, God, having created the world, also dwells in it, and conversely the world he has created exists in him. This is a concept which can really be thought and described in trinitarian terms.'[18]

In the history of Western science the world became a mechanistic object to study, understand and control (as it was, e.g., for Isaac Newton). Inevitably this enterprise lost sight of the role of the Holy Spirit in creation. Eventually the mechanistic concept replaced the organic, and this led to the elimination of God from creation. Without the doctrine of the Holy Spirit there can be no effective Christian doctrine of creation, and the concept of a peaceful community between humans and nature will be ignored.[19]

To gain an appropriate understanding of creation from a Christian hermeneutic Moltmann believes it was appropriate to put forward the following:

1. The Spirit is the principle of creativity, the Spirit creates new possibilities, the Spirit is 'the principle of evolution'.[20]
2. The Spirit is the holistic principle of life, that is, the life of cooperation, harmony and community.
3. The Spirit is the principle of individuation.
4. The Spirit is the principle of openness.

In Moltmann's trinitarian formulation the distinction in God between the Word and the Spirit is that the Word became flesh and the Spirit indwells flesh. The Spirit, moreover, is the self-limiting, indwelling God who suffers in order to bring hope. Later we shall discover how important this conception becomes for Moltmann. In any case, Moltmann concludes that this type of trinitarian theology of creation is preferable to a more rigid panentheism. It is important to understand Moltmann at this point. Philosophical panentheism is an inadequate model of the God of creation because of its inability to differentiate God's immanence in creation from God's transcendence. Moltmann's conviction is that trinitarian theology can maintain that important distinction.[21]

Creation as an open system

We have begun to see hints of Moltmann's intention to include natural science alongside his Christian trinitarian theology. Moltmann opposes what he calls

---

18. Ibid.
19. Ibid.
20. Ibid., p. 100.
21. Ibid., pp. 102–103.

the closed system of creation. In this system, creation is thought to be originally perfect but subsequently corrupted by sin; redemption thus represents the return of creation to its original state. Since creation originally had been perfect, it had been self-sufficient. Moltmann points out that this closed-system model for creation leads to all sorts of problems for how we understand the future or 'glory'. The term 'glory', which is continually referred to in his study, is a reference to the goal of creation, its eschatological fulfilment.[22] Moltmann argues that rather than awaiting the recovery of a perfect and complete past, creation is aligned towards the future. Moltmann objects to the traditional 'subdue the earth' language,[23] which implies that creation is a closed system. What is needed instead, Moltmann argues, is the joining of creation and eschatology so that creation is seen as open, still in the process of becoming. This would be asserted in his later work *Science and Wisdom*: 'If theology wants to give a summary account of God's creative activity, it must then view creation as the still open, creative process of reality.'[24]

Moltmann continually refers to creation as an 'open system' and emphasizes that creation does not find its unity within itself; rather, it is found in its Creator, the Triune God.[25] An important statement in line with this has implications for ecology: 'The creating God makes the world an *ec-static* reality. It has its foundation, not in itself, but outside itself – in him. It has its unity, not in itself, but outside itself – in him. In this sense it is an "open system".'[26] Moltmann also strongly reacts against any monarchical or hierarchical structure in God that could become the foundation for interpreting creation. For Moltmann, such hierarchical structures legitimate exploitation. Earlier in his writings Moltmann asserts that there is a necessary reciprocity between God and creation, a perspective that supports his particular emphasis on panentheism. He states, 'Just as God goes out of himself through what he does, giving his world his own impress, so His world puts its impress on God too, through its reactions, its aberrations and its own initiatives.'[27] As Richard Bauckham interprets Moltmann, 'Trinitarian theology requires us to think, not of a simple dichotomy

22. Ibid., p. 55.

23. Ibid., p. 119.

24. Moltmann, *Science and Wisdom*, p. 38. Moltmann would also insist, 'Time's structure is a-symmetrical. It is open for a future which does not have to be the return of what was at the beginning' (ibid., p. 37).

25. Moltmann, *God in Creation*, p. 159.

26. Ibid., p. 161.

27. Moltmann, *Trinity and the Kingdom*, p. 99.

between God and the world, but of a tension within God himself, who is both transcendent beyond the world and pervasively immanent within it.'[28]

Meaning in the creation model

Creation is established out of God's love, and so the meaning and purpose of creation is determined from God. Its beginning is a statement about its consummation as an open system. Both creation and humanity are created with potentiality, and humanity has fallen short of its potential. This failure to reach one's potential thus becomes for Moltmann another way of defining sin.[29] Sin, in this sense, is the antithesis to eschatology that gives meaning to creation.

The concept of creation *ex nihilo* is very important for Moltmann,[30] but as we shall see it takes a particular turn in Moltmann's theology. The question asked by Moltmann is 'what does it mean for God to be the Creator of a world which is different from him, and yet is designed to correspond to him?'[31] In response, Moltmann first observes that, in the Genesis creation account, 'God "created" the world indicates God's self-distinction from that world ... This means that the world is not in itself divine; nor is it an emanation from God's eternal being ... Creation is something absolutely new.'[32] Secondly, Moltmann asserts that the creation narrative reveals that God has a purpose for creation (as was already discussed above). Finally, Moltmann states that our understanding of God 'makes all things clear'. For Moltmann, the Genesis account reveals that 'the world was created neither out of pre-existent matter, nor of the divine Being itself'.[33] The later theological interpretation of creation as *creatio ex nihilo* is therefore unquestionably an apt paraphrase of what the Bible means.

Moltmann distinguishes God's free will from God's being. Creation is from God's free will but not from his being. God's free will is understood as coinciding with his love.[34] This leads Moltmann to assert God's priority over creation and creation's contingency in God. He would insist, '*Creatio ex nihilo* ... is an expression intended to convey the liberty of the Creator and the contingency of all being – both its initial contingency and the contingency that is permanent and

---

28. Richard Bauckham, *The Theology of Jürgen Moltmann* (Edinburgh: T. & T. Clark, 1995), p. 186.

29. This is developed in *Science and Wisdom*, p. 41.

30. Ibid., p. 120.

31. Ibid., p. 72.

32. Moltmann, *God in Creation*, pp. 72–73.

33. Ibid., p. 75.

34. Ibid., pp. 75, 79–80.

fundamental.'[35] So it is important to note that from the beginning God created out of his free will and love; and this eventually helps explain what it means for humanity to be created in his image. It is not the soul that is distinctive to humanity; it is the 'image of God': 'as image, men and women correspond to the Creator in their very essence'.[36]

Moltmann's particular conception of *creatio ex nihilo*, God's free will and God's love lead him to raise concerns about A. N. Whitehead's process philosophy and its stepchild, process theology. He clearly states:

> If the idea of the *creatio ex nihilo* is excluded, or reduced to the formation of a not-yet-actualized primordial matter 'no-thing', then the world process must be just as eternal and without beginning like God himself . . . the process must itself be one of God's natures. And in this case we have to talk about 'the divinization of the world'.[37]

Moltmann concludes that process philosophy has no convincing doctrine of creation due to its perceived essential limitation on God. Process philosophy is able to deal only with the preservation of creation and the ordering of creation out of chaos.[38] It is important to recognize, therefore, that Moltmann distinguishes his trinitarian panentheism from philosophical panentheism and clearly considers the former to be the preferred model for articulating an ecological concern for creation.[39]

The concept of zimsum

This brings us to one of the more intriguing concepts in Moltmann's trinitarian theology of creation, *zimsum*, which he explains in *God in Creation*. Moltmann works with the *zimsum* of the Jewish mystical tradition (Kabbalism) based on Isaac Luria. *Zimsum* conceives that there is 'space' within God. Moltmann locates this 'space' in the self-limitation of God; it is not, for Moltmann, an essential limitation of God's being but rather a kenotic limitation, the result of God's self-emptying of himself. As Moltmann puts it, 'the omnipotent and omniscient God withdraws his presence and restricts his power'.[40] For Moltmann this creates God-forsakenness, and, by extension, it provides a model for sin and

---

35. Ibid., p. 38.

36. Moltmann, *God in Creation*, p. 77.

37. Ibid., p. 78.

38. Ibid., pp. 78–79.

39. Moltmann, *Trinity and the Kingdom*, p. 106.

40. Moltmann, *God in Creation*, p. 87; see also *Trinity and the Kingdom*, pp. 109–111.

godlessness. Another way to express this according to Moltmann is, 'Nothingness contradicts not merely creation but God';[41] the self-limitation of God made creation possible; and this led to the self-limitation of God's omnipotence. Moltmann roots this conception in Philippians 2:7, which he interprets as a reference to God's internally withdrawing himself. In his later work Moltmann expands on this idea. He compares *zimsum* to birth pangs and suggests, 'Where God withdraws himself he can create something whose essence is not divine, can let it coexist with himself, give it space, and redeem it.'[42] This understanding is foundational to Moltmann's doctrine of salvation, but there are further important implications for how he conceives of God's relationship to his creatures: 'Because of the restriction of his omniscience he cannot foresee how those he has created will decide and how they will develop . . . He learns from them.'[43]

According to Moltmann, then, God is still, in the present time, self-limited; yet, eventually, God will be all in all (1 Cor. 15:28). Central to Moltmann's eschatology is therefore the expectation that the nothingness where God is not (*zimsum*), the result of God's self-limitation, will eventually be overcome. 'The *eschatological creation* of the kingdom of glory finally proceeds from the vanquishing of sin and death, that is to say, the annihilating of Nothingness.'[44] For Moltmann the kingdom of glory 'is the inner motivation of the divine history of the covenant'.[45] Thus '*Creatio ex nihilo* in the beginning is the preparation and promise of the redeeming *annihilatio nihili*, from which the eternal being of creation proceeds.'[46] Interestingly, it appears that God requires some form of redemption to overcome *zimsum*, but Moltmann is not prepared to reach this conclusion. He states:

> In Christian theology one would not go so far as to declare God 'in need of redemption' together with his people Israel; but nevertheless, God has laid the sanctification of his Name and the doing of his will in the hands of human beings, and thus also, in its way, the coming of his kingdom.[47]

---

41. Moltmann, *God in Creation*, p. 88.

42. Moltmann, *Science and Wisdom*, p. 119.

43. Ibid., p. 120.

44. Moltmann, *God in Creation*, p. 90 (his italics).

45. Moltmann, *Science and Wisdom*, p. 38.

46. Moltmann, *God in Creation*, p. 40.

47. Jürgen Moltmann, 'God's Kenosis in the Creation and Consummation of the World', in John Polkinghorne (ed.), *The Work of Love* (London: SPCK, 2001), p. 148.

Salvation, in this sense, is God's taking up Nothingness into himself, the God-forsakenness experienced in the death of the Son in this primordial space, and he overcomes it in the death and resurrection of the Son, Jesus Christ. God then becomes omnipresent. The cross is now the promise of the future. Clearly, this requires the resurrection of Christ, which is the promise of the future. As John Cooper has explained this, 'It is God's self-negation that both separates and binds the Father and the Son on the cross so that reconciliation and redemption result. In the end, the negative dynamic in God's creativity is transformed into his eternal kingdom.'[48] He adds, 'There is no "dark side" to God – no side where he could be conceived of as the destroyer of his own creation and of his own being as Creator.'[49]

Moltmann further elaborates his thoughts on *zimsum* ten years later in the publication *Chaos and Complexity: Scientific Perspectives on Divine Action*, where he calls his contribution a 'thought experiment'.[50] Again he rejects classical theism, deism and process philosophy, and he further describes panentheism in relation to *zimsum,* now spelled *tzimtsum*, as the preferred model for divine action. *Tzimtsum* is defined as follows: 'God as eternal and omnipotent restrains Godself to allow creation to be, thereby giving it time and providing it with a habitat of its own. God's omniscience is limited by God to such an extent that the future is open and experimental to God.'[51] Interestingly – and consistent with his position – he concludes that 'we can no longer think of God's being as the highest reality (*ens realissimum*) for all realized potentialities, but rather as the highest possibility and as the enabling of all potential realities'.[52]

A few critical responses
John Polkinghorne expresses a great appreciation for the doctrine of creation and eschatology of Jürgen Moltmann. Polkinghorne approvingly makes use of Moltmann's Kabbalistic *zimsum*. Unfortunately, Polkinghorne makes no attempt to analyse *zimsum*. But he does suggest an interesting revision of Moltmann's

48. Cooper, *Panentheism*, pp. 252–253.

49. Ibid., p. 257.

50. Jürgen Moltmann, 'Reflections on Chaos and God's Interaction with the World from a Trinitarian Perspective', in Robert John Russell, Nancey Murphy and Arthur R. Peacock (eds.), *Chaos and Complexity: Scientific Perspectives on Divine Action* (Vatican City State: Vatican Observatory / Berkley: Center for Theology and the Natural World, 1995), p. 205.

51. Ibid., p. 207.

52. Ibid., p. 209.

panentheism: 'I do not accept panentheism . . . as a theological reality for the present world, but I do believe in it as the form of eschatological destiny for the world to come.'[53]

Colin Gunton also criticizes Moltmann's panentheism, observing that 'it is possible to conceive a created world that is external to God and which does not yet exclude interrelationship and omnipresence'.[54] Gunton adds that there is little biblical support for creation from the absence of God. He continues:

> If God as creator is the one who gives reality to the other, must he do it by making space within rather than without himself? Space, like time, is a function of the created world. Similarly there is no suggestion in the Bible that the act of creation is anything but a joyful giving of reality to the other . . . This suggests that the metaphor of kenosis has been displaced from soteriology, where it belongs, to the doctrine of creation, where it does not . . .[55]

Gunton considers Moltmann's emphasis on kenotic creation to be misleading, and he also rejects Robert Jenson's related notion of 'roominess' in God.[56] According to Gunton, 'If the creation is to be truly creaturely, it requires its own time and space which is given by God but not continuous with his reality.'[57]

Alan Torrance accepts that Moltmann works from the conviction that God created out of nothing – neither the being of God nor pre-existent material – but he criticizes the panentheistic ontology that Moltmann employs in his attempt to work through the tensions created by these two negations and to reconstruct the doctrine of creation *ex nihilo*.[58] While creation is out of the free will of God and, secondly, out of God's unconditional love, Torrance perceives a 'before–after' structure in Moltmann's notion of God's free will. This requires,

---

53. John Polkinghorne, *The God of Hope and the End of the World* (London: SPCK, 2002), p. 114–115; this view was previously expressed in John Polkinghorne, *Science and Christian Belief: Theological Reflections of a Bottom-up Thinker* (London: SPCK, 1994), p. 64.

54. Colin E. Gunton, *The Triune Creator: A Historical and Systematic Study* (Edinburgh: Edinburgh University Press, 1998), p. 141.

55. Ibid.

56. Robert Jenson's precise statement was as follows: 'If creation is God's making room in himself, then God must be *roomy*' (Robert Jenson, 'Aspects of a Doctrine of Creation', in Gunton, *Doctrine of Creation*, p. 24 [Jenson's italics]).

57. Gunton, *Triune Creator*, p. 142.

58. Torrance, '*Creatio ex Nihilo*', pp. 83–84.

according to Torrance, an understanding of what influences God's 'before–after' decisions. According to Torrance, we end up with anthropomorphisms being projected onto God and make God a part of an infinite process. Still, Moltmann does not move in the normally recognized process philosophical or theological tradition, and Moltmann himself admits that this type of theology 'has no doctrine of Creation'.[59]

Torrance labels Moltmann's concept of *zimsum* (God's self-limitation) a kenotic protology.[60] Before God acted outwardly, God acted inwardly to limit himself. Or, as Moltmann explains, 'In order to create a world "outside" himself, the infinite God must have made room beforehand for a finite in himself.'[61] What has happened is that there is space within God, which God vacated – and so we now have a new panentheism. Interestingly, Torrance claims that this notion is reminiscent of the Newtonian container model of the universe.[62] Torrance also seems to suggest that Moltmann has a concept of time that might be called 'pre-creation', observing that 'Moltmann identifies *creatio ex nihilo* with a temporally original creation of an initial state of affairs and set conditions – an event which follows earlier events in God.'[63] The *zimsum* idea creates other dilemmas for theology. Moltmann's multivaried understanding of evil is problematic. Since if there is space within God where God is not, does this not lead to additional problems concerning evil? God then has within the Godself perversion of the good. But this becomes a problem only if where God is not is the foundation of evil; this is Godforsakenness. Moltmann defines sin or evil as 'the perversion of good, the annihilation of what exists, the negation of the affirmation of life'.[64] If creation is created for the potential to become good, as Moltmann argues, and history is the process that leads to its eventual glory, then some form of evil is in the very creative act at the beginning. It seems that Moltmann does recognize this, but he leaves it unresolved within God until the final glorification.

---

59. Ibid., pp. 86–87.

60. Ibid., p. 88.

61. Moltmann, *God in Creation*, pp. 86–87.

62. Torrance, '*Creatio ex Nihilo*', pp. 90–91.

63. Ibid., p. 92.

64. Moltmann, *God in Creation*, p. 168. Interestingly, in Bauckham, *Theology of Jürgen Moltmann*, ch. 9, 'Creation and Evolution', there is no reference to *zimsum*, and, in Geiko Müller-Fahrenholz, *The Kingdom and the Power: The Theology of Jürgen Moltmann* (London: SCM, 2000), ch. 9, 'Creation: The Wonder of Existence', the discussion on *zimsum* is so brief as to be virtually ineffective.

It is clear that Colin Gunton and Alan Torrance give no credence to panentheism nor Moltmann's restructuring of panentheism. It is perhaps worth observing that a more extensive analysis of an appropriate theism that is able to account for divine action in creation has been presented by Nancey Murphy. Murphy's extensive and technical article on theology, philosophy and natural science begins with the controversy over the behaviour of quantum-level creation; she then moves to the macro-level creation. A lengthy quote from her work will help understand her proposal:

> In brief, the following is my position. In addition to creation and sustenance, God has two modes of action within the created order: one at the quantum level (or whatever turns out to be the most basic level of reality) and the other through human intelligence and action. The apparently random events at the quantum level all involve (but are not exhausted by) specific, intentional acts of God. God's action at this level is limited by two factors. First, God respects the integrity of the entities with which he cooperates – there are some things that God can do with an electron, for instance, and many other things he cannot (eg., make it have the rest-mass of a proton, or a positive charge). Second, within the wider range of effects allowed by God's action in and through sub-atomic entities, God restricts his action in order to produce a world that *for all we can tell* is orderly and law-like in its operation. The exact possibilities within higher reaches of the natural order by means of cooperation with and governance of sub-atomic entities are highly debatable and will be considered below. But I hope to show that by taking quantum events as the primary locus of divine action it will be possible to meet many of the theological needs placed upon such a theory without running into insuperable theological or scientific objections.[65]

Nancey Murphy does not see panentheism or a restructured panentheism as necessary to explain divine action within the created order. 'What God creates has a measure of independent existence relative to God,' Murphy writes, and 'this created entity, however small and ephemeral, has an existence independent of God'.[66] Murphy is therefore not hesitant to affirm a particular form of theism that supports cooperation with the divine without requiring domination.

---

65. Nancey Murphy, 'Divine Action in the Natural Order', in Russell, Murphy and Peacock, *Chaos and Complexity*, pp. 339–340 (her italics).

66. Ibid., pp. 340–341; see also p. 355, where she rejects panentheism.

Part 2: Ecology

Creation and eschatology

Interestingly, in Moltmann's 1975 publication *The Future of Creation* he insists that if creation is to survive the constant destruction of nature by humanity, then Christianity must work with science.[67] A more critical version of this argument appears in his 1985 *God in Creation*, and it is reaffirmed again in *Science and Wisdom*.[68] But to advance his more critical view, it was necessary for Moltmann to place eschatology and creation in closest relation. As he states, 'Not only will eschatology continue to be understood in the light of creation, but creation will be understood in the light of eschatology.'[69] Sin is the closing of the creation system; that is, creation is not able to achieve its potential. Salvation is then the opening of the closed system; hence the importance of eschatology and redemption. In Christian theology, creation can achieve its potential only through grace, and, through grace the eschatological vision for the future of creation is one of fulfilment.[70] This is God's indwelling the new creation, and this is universal. A more negative version of this is contained in the text from 1 Corinthians 15:24–26, but it ends in full restoration after sin and death are destroyed.

Moltmann's proposal works against the subject–object dichotomy of the closed system, a dichotomy that he claims is entailed by the view that the original creation was 'closed'. This view, Moltmann argues, is now discredited and fails in any case to provide an effective model for ecology. Moltmann's own eschatological approach requires a symbiosis of humanity and nature. The misappropriation of 'subduing' creation has led to the exploitation and destruction of creation. Moltmann therefore expresses the restoration model in Christological terms:

> he came not to be served – not to rule – 'but to serve'. And he served in order to make us free for fellowship with God and for openness for one another. In the light of Christ's mission, Gen. 1:28 will have to be interpreted in an entirely new way: not 'subdue the earth' but 'free the earth' through fellowship with it.[71]

---

67. Jürgen Moltmann, *The Future of Creation* (London: SCM, 1975), p. 115.

68. Moltmann, *Science and Wisdom*, p. 33: 'The ecological crisis caused by the progressive destruction of nature has been brought about by Christianity and science jointly.'

69. Moltmann, *Future of Creation*, p. 116. This is repeated in Moltmann, *Science and Wisdom*, p. 34.

70. Moltmann, *Future of Creation*, pp. 122–125.

71. Ibid., p. 129. Again this is repeated in Moltmann, *Science and Wisdom*, p. 50.

This appears to be anti-Nietzschean and the 'will to power'; instead, it is the language of service and fellowship and reconciliation. It is important to point out that Moltmann asserts that the ecological solution can be discovered if culture finds its bearing by understanding the biblical world view rather than the Cartesian mind–body dualism world view that allowed humans to dominate creation.[72]

Science and technology

The ecological crisis is grounded in the industrialized nations that, Moltmann believes, established their foundations on misinterpreted Christian principles. The ecological crisis in these countries has resulted, according to Moltmann, from misinterpretation and misapplication of the biblical injunction to 'subdue the earth'. This problem is founded on the promise of the human ability to dominate nature and rule over it. Moltmann considers this to be a product of European and American Christianity. A new doctrine of ecological concern is required to address the current disaster.

Moltmann tackles the problem from what he claims is a holistic perspective. The ecological crisis is a product of misinterpreted theology and misappropriated science, and has caused a social crisis that in turn has led to a personal crisis. A reshaping of society's economic structure is required, although people and society are not prepared to face the challenge.[73] One of the problems is that science and technology have orchestrated the ecological crisis;[74] yet it is assumed that the problem can be resolved by the use of science and technology. But underlying this are the 'structures of power'. So we must deal with the politics of science.[75] Human complicity in the ecological crisis is now related to the overly optimistic confidence placed on the authority of science and technology.

In Moltmann's analysis, civilizations are established on the values of development, expansion and conquest. It is the acquisition of power and the pursuit of happiness that defines modern civilizations. The Jewish-Christian tradition has been held to account for this 'will to power', but according to Moltmann the development did not suddenly appear in modern times. It can be traced back to the Renaissance.[76] Ever since the Renaissance, power was more important than truth and goodness.

---

72. Moltmann, *Future of Creation*, pp. 147–149.

73. Moltmann, *God in Creation*, pp. 20–25.

74. Moltmann, *Science and Wisdom*, p. 48: 'It is a pattern of domination and exploitation.'

75. Moltmann, *God in Creation*, pp. 25–26.

76. Ibid., p. 26.

If knowledge is power, then science and technology are accountable. Science and technology enabled humanity to be masters and possessors of nature, but Moltmann paints this as a somewhat terrifying picture, observing, 'For the victim nature, scientific and technological civilization is undoubtedly the most terrible monster ever to appear on earth.'[77] This is why science is no longer an automatic positive partner to the environmentally conscious theology; and this is true both of capitalist and Marxist countries. It can be added here that relationship brings responsibility and leads to accountability.

In line with this, Moltmann is critical of the overemphasis on the history of creation, or 'belief in creation', when the 'concept of creation' has not received enough attention. The concept of creation as designed for the 'praise of God's glory' would create a response to 'the ecological crisis of scientific and technological civilization'.[78]

Moltmann expresses deep concerns about the 'objectification' of nature which assumes that it is there to be used by human ingenuity. Humanity was the subject; nature was the object. Moltmann argues that for a proper ecological environment to occur, nature or creation would have to be in line with humanity.[79] At this point Moltmann points out that Karl Marx missed the significance of creation and saw nature at the disposal of humanity. The Marxist philosopher of history Ernst Bloch, in recognizing Marx's weakness here, was also rejected by the Marxist ideologues.

Perhaps here we can note that this picture of creation in balance, beauty and regeneration was developed already in Anselm's *Cur Deus Homo*. As Stephen Holmes helpfully writes concerning salvation, sin and creation, 'This, for Anselm, is the final demonstration of how serious sin is: not the infinite guilt of the sinner, but the disordering of the beauty of God's creation.'[80] Importantly, for Anselm the context was the hierarchical model of medieval feudalism, and so God's honour is offended. For Moltmann, the context is trinitarian panentheism, and so it is God's being that is damaged. Yet both theological models are concerned about the recovery of creation's integrity or beauty.

---

77. Ibid., p. 28.

78. Ibid., pp. 31–32.

79. Ibid., pp. 40–45.

80. Stephen Holmes, *Listening to the Past: The Place of Tradition in Theology* (Carlisle: Paternoster, 2002), p. 43.

Conclusion

Jürgen Moltmann presents real challenges for interpreters in his doctrine of creation. His ecological concerns are genuine and, interestingly, he advocates a return to a biblical world view as the preferred option for theology today. Along with his well-known trinitarian relational theology, he proposes a new way of seeing creation and living in creation. His most controversial contribution will continue to be his thoroughly developed panentheism along with the incorporation of the medieval understanding of *zimsum* as a resolution for understanding God's relation to creation – and as the crucial reason for the church's care for creation. In his model, to destroy creation has a direct bearing on the being of God. Not all will agree that this is the preferred way to see God and creation, but perhaps Alan Torrance was correct when he stated a number of years ago[81] that no theologian has stimulated the discussion on God and creation as has Jürgen Moltmann.

© David Rainey, 2014

---

81. See n. 4 above.

10. ON BEING GREEN WITHOUT PLAYING GOD: COLIN GUNTON'S ENVIRONMENTAL ETHIC

Graham J. Watts

Introduction

The 2012 Tyndale Fellowship Conference followed closely on the most recent world summit, called in an attempt to 'save the planet'. News reports from before and after the event offer rather cryptic comment:

> High above Rio de Janeiro, on the precipitous peak of Corcovado, the giant statue of Christ the Redeemer is being picked out in green light at night. The way things are going, He is likely to be the only leader turning more verdant as a result of the more figurative summit opening today 2,300 feet below. For as more than 100 presidents and prime ministers fly into the 'marvellous city' for the first Earth Summit in two decades, an unprecedentedly weak set of conclusions is being prepared.[1]

> After more than a year of negotiations and a 10-day mega-conference involving 45,000 people, the wide-ranging outcome document – The Future We Want – was lambasted by environmentalists and anti-poverty campaigners for lacking the

---

1. *Daily Telegraph*, 19 June 2012, available at http://www.telegraph.co.uk/earth/environment/9341645/The-Rio-Earth-Summit-is-it-destined-to-fail-the-world.html (accessed 28 June 2012).

detail and ambition needed to address the challenges posed by a deteriorating environment, worsening inequality and a global population expected to rise from 7bn to 9bn by 2050.[2]

However one views the so-called environmental crisis of our age, presumably the Christian response is to say that it is the height of arrogance to state what future we want. This world and its future belong to God and Christ is Redeemer and Judge. The future is God's. But how does our faith in God, how do our doctrines of God and creation, impact the way we understand environmental issues? Does trinitarian theology have anything to say to the current debate? I believe it does, and it is here that the theology of Colin Gunton may provide some clues.

Gunton has been justifiably described as one of the most significant British theologians of the late twentieth century. While he would have preferred to avoid the label 'evangelical' because of what he considered unhelpful connotations, he was in the forefront of the fight against the prevailing liberalism in many academic circles. During his tenure as Professor at King's College London, he not only established Systematic Theology as a vibrant and vital discipline, but attracted a wide range of students, some from theologically conservative churches, anxious to learn from a theologian committed to the local church as much as to theological orthodoxy.

The purpose of this chapter is to offer a brief, preliminary assessment of Gunton's approach to environmental ethics. This is not in order to jump on the bandwagon of popular environmentalism – such a move would have been the complete antipathy of all that Gunton stood for. Rather, it is in recognition that Gunton has bequeathed to following generations a distinctive doctrine of creation, which carries implications for contemporary ethical concerns. Much of what will follow is deeply appreciative of Gunton's contribution; to him I believe we owe an enormous debt in the way in which he sought to place the relationship between God and creation at the heart of theology. My concern is simple: where Gunton does deal with ethical implications, he suggests important theological underpinnings but he is yet rather quixotic and eclectic when it comes to practical consequences. In the concluding chapter of *The Triune Creator* he makes reference to the rearing of chickens in battery farms and the use of the motor car, but one has the feeling that these are inserted somewhat at random merely for the sake of saying something of

---

2. *Guardian*, 23 June 2012, available at http://www.guardian.co.uk/environment/2012/jun/23/rio-20-earth-summit-document (accessed 28 June 2012).

practical import.[3] He even expresses his own reluctance to make explicit application: 'my concern is not to provide answers, but to suggest that a theology of creation does provide essential material for thought about the way we treat our world'.[4] For a theologian so deeply indebted to Barth, who consistently saw ethics as integral to doctrine, this is surprising. Of course, this may be because he did not live to complete his theological programme; but my suspicion is that this is more a consequence of certain theological decisions at the heart of his doctrine of creation.

Mapping Gunton on the theological landscape: Trinity and creation

A brief summary of key influences and the general shape of Gunton's theology will be helpful in setting the scene. This will lead to an outline of his trinitarian doctrine of creation before we look at his understanding of human responsibility within creation. This could be tackled in a number of ways, but I shall focus on his conception of the *imago Dei*. The concluding discussion will focus on his notion of ethics as best approached from the perspective of human createdness that emphasizes the place of humanity within creation. Gunton believes that this would avoid the idolatrous belief that we can 'save the planet'. It is only when we recognize our place in relation to God, as creatures, that we can properly begin to live ethically.

If one locus governs Gunton's theology, it is the doctrine of the Trinity. His early theology was heavily influenced by Karl Barth; his doctoral work, supervised by Robert Jenson, was a comparison of Barth and Hartshorne's doctrine of God.[5] Here his critique of process theology and respect for Barth's achievements are clear. Yet over the course of his career his own understanding of the Trinity changed significantly, such that he came to repudiate much of Barth's work. Stephen Holmes has helpfully charted this development and traces much of the change to Gunton's engagement with the work of John Zizioulas.[6] Gunton develops an ontology of persons in relation that is

3. Colin E. Gunton, *The Triune Creator: A Historical and Systematic Study* (Edinburgh: Edinburgh University Press, 1998).

4. Ibid., p. 231.

5. Colin E. Gunton, *Becoming and Being: The Doctrine of God in Charles Hartshorne and Karl Barth*, 2nd ed. (London: SCM, 2001).

6. Stephen Holmes, 'Towards the Analogiae Personae et Relationis', in L. Harvey (ed.), *The Theology of Colin Gunton* (London: T. & T. Clark, 2010), pp. 32–48.

heavily indebted to Cappadocian trinitarianism. He has in his sights a critique of Western theism, which he sees as offering a monistic doctrine of God, as well as much modern trinitarian theology, which he regards as tying God too closely to creation. He is as equally suspicious of Moltmann's panentheism as he is of process theology. God is distinct from creation, yet intimately related to creation. This can only be so on the basis that God is a being in communion; hence the language of otherness in relation comes to the fore in his writing. Gunton seeks to explain the relation between God and creation in such a way as to exclude modern immanentist theologies, as well as mechanistic, deistic models that effectively evacuate God from the world. In order to do this he returns to the early church fathers, notably Irenaeus and the Cappadocians.

Another aspect of Gunton's thought that is well known is his use of the doctrine of the Trinity to critique the culture of modernity. It was during the writing of the Bampton lectures, later published as *The One, the Three and the Many*, that Gunton launched a parallel attack on Cartesian metaphysics and Western theism.[7] As the Enlightenment raised human individualistic rationality to be the arbiter of all that is true, good and beautiful, so Western theism's abandonment of the Trinity contributed to what he refers to as the transcendence of the one over the many. Newtonian physics and theological reductionism come together effectively to exclude God from creation. As is well known, Gunton lays much of the blame for the failure of Western theology at the feet of Augustine. In his earlier work it is Aquinas who receives the greatest criticism, but later Augustine assumes something of the status of a theological ogre. He stands accused of subsuming the three under the one and of a misguided doctrine of divine simplicity. Gunton is also deeply critical of Augustine's doctrine of creation, which he sees as reintroducing a modified version of the Platonic theory of forms. In his article on creation in *The Cambridge Companion to Christian Doctrine*, Gunton highlights two catastrophic consequences for Western theology.[8] First, when God is conceived monistically, in terms of absolute willing, it is no surprise that the question of predestination comes to the ascendancy. Consequently, redemption is severed from creation and the cosmic dimension of final restoration is lost.

---

7. Colin E. Gunton, *The One, the Three and the Many: God, Creation and the Culture of Modernity* (Cambridge: Cambridge University Press, 1993).

8. Colin E. Gunton, 'The Doctrine of Creation', in Colin E. Gunton (ed.), *The Cambridge Companion to Christian Doctrine* (Cambridge: Cambridge University Press, 1997), pp. 141–157.

Secondly, creation comes to be viewed as an arbitrary act rather than an expression of love. Consequently, within the Western tradition creation becomes separated from Christology and Pneumatology. 'Without attention to the incarnational dimensions of the divine agency in creation, and the part played by the Creator Spirit, the doctrine of creation comes to appear arbitrary and irrelevant.'[9] His argument is that an essentially non-trinitarian theology shackled any attempt to conceive adequately of God's relationship with creation. It is this that Gunton sees, in part, as lying at the heart of the fateful division between theology and science:

> the doctrine of the superior status of the heavens and the inferiority of the material world were contaminations of the doctrine of creation which had been adopted into the tradition. They derived from its 'Babylonian captivity' to a non-Trinitarian theology in which God the Son and God the Spirit were crowded out by a pagan ontology. . . . the platonic forms effectively displaced the eternal and incarnate Son as the means by which God the Father was related to the world. The outcome was that God was conceived to be related to the world by an immaterial structure rather than by the one who became flesh. The effective exclusion of the doctrine of the Trinity from the structuring of the Christian doctrine of creation is therefore at the root of its Babylonian captivity and of the apparent mutual exclusion of theology and science.[10]

While it is not my current purpose to analyse Gunton's critique of Augustine, it should be noted that his entirely negative reading has been criticized by the likes of Lewis Ayres, one among several offering revised readings of Augustine.[11]

So the parameters of Gunton's thought are consistent. If the Trinity is, to use Coleridge's phrase, 'the idea of ideas', how do we adequately conceive of the triune God's relationship to creation? What does that mean for human personhood and human responsibility?

Gunton's response is to construct a theology of trinitarian mediation. God's presence is mediated through his two hands – the Son and the Spirit. Borrowing from Irenaeus, this is Gunton's preferred way of describing God's relation to creation. For Irenaeus this was, of course, a way of countering Gnosticism, whereby goodness is confined to that which is spiritual, thus effectively denying the incarnation. Gunton identifies this metaphor as a key way to express the

---

9. Gunton, *One, the Three*, p. 205.

10. Gunton, *Triune Creator*, p. 116.

11. Lewis Ayres, *Augustine and the Trinity* (Cambridge: Cambridge University Press, 2010).

God–creation relationship in such a way that God is not collapsed into creation, and neither is God's presence evacuated from creation. Ontologically this is an example of otherness in relation. God is other than his creation, but that otherness is constituted by relation in a way that is analogous to the relationship between Father, Son and Holy Spirit.

Gunton makes further use of Irenaeus in his understanding of the distinctive work of God's 'two hands'. For Gunton, Christ is the principle of unity in creation: 'in Him all things hold together'. In Christ creation will come to fulfilment, and again Gunton borrows Irenaeus' language of recapitulation. God is at work in creation to bring all things to fulfilment in the new heaven and the new earth. The role of the Spirit is twofold – to particularize and to work within creation eschatologically. Gunton sees this twofold work of the Spirit exemplified in the incarnation:

> the particularity of persons does not imply their homogeneity . . . the distinctive humanity of Jesus was constituted by his relation to the Father mediated by the Spirit. In his life, death, resurrection and ascension is to be discerned the eschatological action of God the Spirit.[12]

Gunton maintains that one of the failures of Western theology is a failure of particularity. It is the Spirit who constitutes the particularity of the human Jesus in space and time; it is the same Spirit who constitutes the particularity of all that is distinct within creation and who is the eschatological driving force that brings all things to fulfilment – recapitulation in Christ. This process Gunton refers to as God's project. Creation was not perfect, from which it fell, only to be restored finally through Christ. Rather, creation was good, with potential to grow and develop towards fulfilment. Humanity was created and placed within a garden that was to be tended and worked. For Irenaeus, humanity had a part to play in God's intention to bring all things to completion in Christ. On this account the fall was not so much a loss of something inherent within humanity, but a loss of the potential to develop in the way intended by God. It is a loss of something that we did not actually possess. It is a failure to take our proper part in God's intention for creation. Questions arise: What is the human contribution to God's project under this pattern? How are we called to tend the garden created by God? And what is the consequence of the fall? One way of elucidating this is to look at Gunton's understanding of the image of God. What does it mean to be fully human, created in God's image?

---

12. Gunton, *One, the Three*, p. 205.

The image of God

In a recent paper Paraskevè Tibbs correctly highlights two key themes in Gunton's understanding of the *imago Dei*.[13] First, any account of what it is to be human must be a matter of humanity in relation to God – his is a relational anthropology. Secondly, because creation and redemption are in and through Christ, anthropology must be derived from Christology. As expressed in Colossians 1:15, it is the human Jesus Christ who is the perfect image of God – he alone is the archetypal bearer of the image. He is the agent of creation, the firstborn of all creation, and also the goal, the one in whom all creation finds eschatological fulfilment. The image of God is thus not primarily physical resemblance, although Gunton does sometimes refer to this, neither is it human rationality; it is relationship with God. This is mirrored in the Genesis account of humanity created in God's image as male and female – a relational category. Thus the vertical relationship between God and humanity is reflected in the horizontal relationship with 'the other' that is between male and female and between humanity and creation. Echoing his emphasis on trinitarian relations, Gunton argues that we are only authentically human when we are in 'mutually constitutive relations to one another'.[14] When it comes to non-human creation, Gunton sees no final ontological distinction between us and the rest of the created order; humanity and the rest of creation are bound together in that human beings have a task to care for and nurture creation.

It is immediately apparent that Gunton envisages a very close relationship between the otherness in relation that characterizes the being of God and the otherness in relation that is constitutive of the horizontal relationships between humanity and creation. This begs the question 'In what way can we legitimately draw parallels between the ontology of God's being and created reality?' Traditional theology often takes recourse to analogy in some form or another. Gunton's primary way of approaching this is through what he terms 'open transcendentals' – those things that all beings hold in common.[15] He identifies three: particularity, relationality and perichoresis. Particularity, or substantiality, is simply what distinguishes one thing from another; it is why one thing is not another; it is why I am not you and you are not me. Relationality balances particularity; we are what we are because our particular being is determined by

---

13. P. Tibbs, 'Created for Action: Colin Gunton's Relational Anthropology', in Harvey, *Theology of Colin Gunton*, pp. 116–129.

14. Gunton, *Triune Creator*, p. 208.

15. See especially the discussion in Gunton, *One, the Three*, pp. 141–145.

our relationship to the other. Nausnera has argued that Gunton takes this from Zizioulas: God has no ontological being apart from his being in communion.[16] Similarly, to be a person is to be in constitutive relation with another or others. The third open transcendental is perichoresis, which defines the manner of the relation and unites the particulars. By the use of these 'open transcendentals' Gunton seeks to apply concepts such as person and relation both to God and humanity in conceptually similar ways while nonetheless avoiding foundationalism.

Some questions are pertinent. First, is such a univocal conception of the ontological categories of person, relation and communion really tenable? There is to be sure a sense in which we have become aware of the interconnectedness of creation. We are aware of the intimate nature of our relationship with creation and how various bio-systems interweave one another. Otherness in relation seems a logical category by which to explore the nature of creation from a theological standpoint. I am less clear how perichoresis can be understood within creation: In what way is this a fundamental attribute of created being? Gunton does admit the challenge here, and recognizes that to speak of perichoresis with regard to humanity and creation is to speak analogically, but I am not finally convinced by this approach. It rests on the idea that human personhood is constituted by interpersonal relations in a way that is analogous to the Trinity. This may be useful in countering an overemphasis on individualism, but I would suggest that human persons are not only beings in relation. The doctrine of analogy is being asked to bear considerable weight if we are to think of human personhood as analogous to mutual indwelling. Secondly, Gunton has been criticized for misinterpreting the theology of the Cappadocians, perhaps because he reads them through the lens of Zizioulas. Thus Nausnera argues that the Cappadocians did not simply reduce ousia to communion.[17] They sought to hold them in tension; yet in Gunton there is a sense that the language of hypostasis is prioritized over ousia, with the result that it becomes difficult to understand precisely what personal concreteness really means.

There is a third point that deserves fuller treatment. By depending heavily on Irenaeus, Gunton's portrayal of the fall may be prone to the same shortcomings sometimes identified in Irenaeus. There are some who accuse Irenaeus of having no doctrine of the fall, but this would be to overstate the case. What

16. Bernhard Nausnera, 'The Failure of a Laudable Project: Gunton, The Trinity and Human Self-Understanding', *SJT* 62.4 (2009), pp. 403–420.

17. Ibid., pp. 413–414.

is envisaged is a turning away from God with the consequent failure to fulfil the true human vocation with regard to God's project. It is a loss of potential rather than a loss of something already actualized. An analogy drawn over fifty years ago – and now doing the rounds on one or two blogs – is a helpful illustration. A healthy newborn baby is unable to talk – but carries the potential to do so. However, an injury may well prevent that potential being realized. Such is the state of Adam. He is a child, created in God's image, but as a result of the fall he will not grow into the future intended by God and as such his relation to the rest of creation is not fulfilled in the way intended by God. As with many illustrations, this breaks down if pursued in detail, but the general point is made.

Thus the fall in Gunton is understood as a break in proper relationship within creation. This does not completely negate the fact of our being in the image of God; we are less Christlike, but the image remains, albeit in a limited form. Whether this is an adequate doctrine of the fall is open to question. There is a lurking suspicion that the full consequences of human sin may not be adequately accounted for. This becomes clear when we ask about the ongoing rupture of creation. For example, Gunton regularly – almost obsessively – blames Enlightenment rationalism and Western theology for the rise of Western individualism. Is the failure of Western theism really so much a constitutive reason for this? Or is it more the case that the rise of individualism is itself a symptom of human sin? The Genesis narrative refers to a serious rupture in relationship with God and consequently in our relationship with the rest of creation. Might it be that Gunton's reluctance to spell out practical human action is, in part, a reflection of a deficiency in the doctrine of sin, which, in turn, comes from his reading of Irenaeus?

Gunton's approach to ethics

Celia Deane-Drummond argues that the specific task of environmental ethics is to develop principles that aid practical human action; it is not just about describing the place of humanity in creation.[18] To be sure, Gunton does offer some practical suggestions, but, as noted earlier, these are rather piecemeal. Yet a truly Christian response that is grounded in a serious doctrine of creation is a pressing need. It is surely an urgent task for Christian theology to engage

---

18. Celia Deane-Drummond, *A Handbook in Theology and Ecology* (London: SCM, 1996), p. 5.

seriously with environmental concerns on the basis of a genuinely Christian construction of the world as God's creation.

Gunton's approach in *The Triune Creator* focuses on eschatology and the place of humanity in the created order. The eschatological emphasis is consistent with the Irenaean conception of creation as a process towards which God is bringing all things to recapitulation in Christ, through the Spirit. One result of this approach, however, is that ethics can become passive – let God be God. If God is working all things to the appointed end, then human action might be seen as secondary at best. This seems to me to be compounded by Gunton's use of Christoph Schwöbel's term 'an ethic of createdness'. Gunton quotes extensively from Schwöbel, arguing that since the task of preserving creation is God's work, creation is 'not in the same sense a field of human action as, for instance, to speak of politics, science or business'.[19] This argument is intended to counter any merely anthropocentric approach to ethics. Again, a quotation from Schwöbel: 'the same absolutism of human action which has characterized the human exploitation of creation is now returning in the guise of rescuing it'.[20] It is argued that a theologically more responsible approach is to develop not a creation ethic, but an ethic of createdness. This serves to emphasize our place within the created order, while avoiding misguided attempts to offer an entirely human-centred approach to environmental problems.

Much of this is helpful. Modern environmentalism does seem to carry an almost messianic fervour, that unless we all behave in a certain way then we shall not be able to save the planet. Theologically we can never save the planet; that is the height of idolatry, putting ourselves in the place of Christ. Yet surely more needs to be said. Left at this, the resultant ethic is passive. I do not think this is Gunton's intention, but I am not sure that he avoids the charge.

Schwöbel's ethic, adopted enthusiastically by Gunton, is arguably one of *restraint*.[21] To claim that the work of creation, including sustaining and preserving it, is a divine and not a human task, is an inadequate response to key biblical texts, notably Psalm 8. If by emphasizing an ethic of createdness Gunton implies a general passivity in anticipation of divine intervention, then perhaps he has, albeit inadvertently, succeeded only in opening the door to defending comfortable Western apathy. In what follows I suggest two ways in which

---

19. Gunton, *Triune Creator*, p. 228.

20. Quoted in ibid., p. 229.

21. I am grateful to one of our doctoral students and research fellows at Spurgeon's College, Rev. Roland Sokolowski, for his observations here in the light of Gunton's use of Irenaeus.

Gunton's approach to ethics might be developed in a more active direction. One relates to a kingdom ethic; the other to virtue ethics.

The question of human action might be addressed by a return to Irenaeus, in particular his doctrine of the Spirit in relation to the coming of the kingdom of God. For Irenaeus, the work of the Spirit is incrementally at work in the believer. We should note that this is in line with his view of redemption as deification – theosis. But the Spirit effects a change in attitude – a radical newness of life that Irenaeus links closely with the coming of the kingdom of God. Again I note in passing that for Irenaeus this meant a literal millennial understanding, but we can put that to one side – the key point is unaffected. For Irenaeus there is a close link between the work of the Spirit and human cooperation in the coming of the kingdom of God. This implies a vigorous ethical commitment to the kingdom, through the indwelling Spirit. Yet the link between Spirit and kingdom in the here and now, so strong in Irenaeus, is not fully carried through in Gunton. The language of the kingdom has both present and future eschatological reference: now, and not yet. But by constructing his ethics primarily in the context of future eschatology, there is a tendency for Gunton to underplay the kingdom imperative to act now. When added to his emphasis on human createdness, which foregrounds our creaturely limitations, Gunton's project risks leading to an essential passivity that may be unable to answer the question 'What then shall we do?'

A second proposal again stems from initial moves made by Gunton but which, in my view, could be extended. Gunton tends to find a focus for what he terms 'creation ethics' in the worship life of the church, in particular the sacraments. The word of God remains central for Gunton; his theology of the sacraments is thoroughly Reformed in the sense that their efficacy rests on the word of promise. Yet in baptism and communion the material world is brought to centre stage in the liturgical life of the church. The stuff of creation, water, bread and wine, through the promise of God and action of the Spirit become representative of the life, death and resurrection of Jesus Christ. Gunton sees a close link between the liturgical life of the church and the broader relationship of creation, church and Creator. He makes this link through Romans 12:1–2. We are to present our bodies as living sacrifices . . . and our bodies are related to the rest of the creation as part of the whole. Bear in mind that for Gunton we are what we are in relation to the other. Through our bodies we interact with other human beings, tend the earth and offer praise to God. If worship is about the whole of life, then our sacrifice of worship involves our relationship with that part of creation we immediately indwell. Of course, not all human action is positive. We can either tend the garden or pollute it; we can cooperate with the perfecting Spirit in offering our lives sacrificially to the Father, or we may not. So how do we align our actions with those of the Spirit? By being transformed, as Romans 12:2 states, by the renewing of our minds. Gunton argues that the conceptual link is sacrifice. Just as the sacrifice of Jesus Christ on the cross is the source of life for us, so, it is the paradigm for our calling within the world. The divine act of redemption was sacrificial; so too was the divine act of creation. Gunton does not mean to imply any theology of kenosis, self-emptying, or some way in which God opens space within himself, as in Moltmann. God's act of creation was free, not necessary to his being – an act of grace, love and freedom. The pain, he says, comes from creation's refusal to be God's creation, from the desire to assert rights over the Creator. The pain comes from the rejection of the gift; thus it is that the once for all sacrifice of Christ is the true source of redemption, through which all creation will come to praise its maker.

So the primary human response to the sacrifice of Christ is praise and worship; Romans 12 teaches that the renewed mind will be able to test and approve the will of God, and thus live in step with the Spirit. This is as far as Gunton seems prepared to go. But why stop there? If Christ is the proto-typical image of God, and transformation is about our being more conformed to the likeness of Christ, could we understand our role within creation in terms of sacrifice and priesthood? This might be a logical extension of Gunton's work, and Tibbs makes the link.[22] Is this part of what it means to be a royal priesthood, a people belonging to God? Adam is called by God to name, tend, reap and consume the fruits of the garden. His call to be the steward of God's creation involves both vertical and horizontal relations. Of course, Adam sought the one fruit not given to him by the Creator, resulting in the fall, as a result of which we come to see creation as an end in itself rather than in relationship with God. Tibbs argues that this is a failure of priesthood. The fulfilment of all priestly promise is found in Christ, our High Priest. In him we are called to be a holy nation, a royal priesthood, a people belonging to God. Biblically, part of our calling is to offer creation back to God as a sacrifice of praise. The implications of this calling, as spelled out in 1 Peter, include living in proper relationship with one another in the church, in society, in marriage and, by extension, our proper use of the material world. In this way we shall bear testimony to the world. God is perfecting creation; perhaps our part in that can be understood not simply in terms of stewardship, but priesthood, understood in the terms of 1 Peter – relationally. This might counter the rampant indi-vidualism of our age as well as recognizing that the earth really is the Lord's

---

22. Tibbs, 'Created for Action'.

and everything in it; both of these themes were, of course, crucial for Gunton. Tibbs goes even further: 'envisioning the image of God in terms of a unique relationality of priesthood works to correct the destructive division that has taken place in the West between the religious and the secular'.[23]

I confess, nonetheless, to being uncomfortable with this use of the language of priesthood. Richard Bauckham has explicitly rejected such use of priestly language on the grounds that it easily slips into a form of hierarchy whereby humanity mediates between God and creation.[24] He locates this tendency within Eastern Orthodox theology, notably John Zizioulas, but also notes how this has become influential among Western writers.[25] In response he argues convincingly that there is no biblical warrant for suggesting that creation needs humanity to offer its praise to God. By contrast, human responsibility for creation is held alongside an affirmation that creation itself offers praise to God. In Bauckham's view, a view of human stewardship as priestly in nature 'deprives the creatures of their own God-given ways of being themselves to the glory of God'.[26]

Given this critique, it would be preferable to retain the language of stewardship and hold in balance both the responsibility we have for creation and the recognition that creation itself is able to bring glory to God. By poor stewardship we both lessen our own standing within the created order and diminish the ability of creation to sing God's praises. Perhaps one way forward would be to view stewardship as one particular aspect of virtue ethics. The central point in the recent emphasis on virtue is that good ethical decisions are made by good people. On this view ethics is first about character and only secondly about making good decisions. It is when our character is shaped by the Spirit of Christ that we shall act in ways that reflect our calling within the created order. Character is shaped relationally. We are moulded by the gospel narrative, by the community to which we belong and by the indwelling Spirit, who is moving creation towards

---

23. Ibid., p. 126.

24. R. Bauckham, *Living with Other Creatures: Green Exegesis and Theology* (Milton Keynes: Paternoster, 2012), pp. 151–153. I am grateful to R. J. Berry for alerting me to Bauckham's rejection of the use of priesthood in this context.

25. Given that Zizioulas was a significant influence on Gunton, not least in relation to the concept of personhood, it may be possible to see a link here. That influence may also lie behind Gunton's reference to the sacraments in relation to creation. Tibbs is arguably following Gunton's inclination in developing the idea of human priesthood in relation to creation care.

26. Bauckham, *Living with Other Creatures*, p. 153.

the eschaton. This is the import of Romans 12: it is only as we allow ourselves to be shaped by Christ, rather than the world, only as we are prepared to offer our bodies as living sacrifices, that we are able to understand God's purposes in any given circumstance.[27] This avoids being overly prescriptive on detail in the mistaken view that we can 'save the planet', and it meshes well with an ethic of createdness, yet potentially gives scope for a more active ethical commitment. It also means that, as Christians, we do have something unique to say on matters of the environment, but we also recognize that the Spirit of God is not limited to the church. We can make common cause with those who seek the good of creation. We are not among those who seek to save the planet. But we are called to partake in God's purpose to bring creation to final fulfilment and offer ourselves and creation itself back to him as a sacrifice of praise.

Conclusion

Despite reservations, I remain deeply appreciative of Gunton's theological agenda. Nausnera suggests that Gunton's trinitarian theology does not finally lead to the radical consequences for human life that he proposed. The title of Nausnera's article, 'The Failure of a Laudable Project', is, I suggest, mistaken. It is not that Gunton's project has failed; rather, it begs questions. The tentative suggestion of this chapter is that, while Gunton's ethics remain passive for understandable reasons, we might benefit from expanding the horizon of this thought by linking the work of the Spirit to a kingdom ethic, and combining his ethic of createdness with an understanding of our calling towards creation as good stewards, with the emphasis from virtue ethics on 'good'. The statue of Christ the Redeemer over Rio may be bathed in green light. But it is the ascended and returning Christ who will bring all things to completion. Our calling is to be responsible stewards: green but not naive idolaters.

© Graham J. Watts, 2014

---

27. Tom Wright's recent work on virtue ethics attempts to bring together eschatological and kingdom perspectives while retaining the central focus on character formation as an aspect of discipleship. It is interesting that he also seeks to incorporate the language of priesthood, yet avoids the hierarchical and sacramental approach identified as problematic by Bauckham. See N. T. Wright, *Virtue Reborn* (London: SPCK, 2010).

11. DOES DISPUTING EVOLUTION DISCOURAGE CREATION CARE?

R. J. Berry

'In the beginning God created the heavens and the earth' (Gen. 1:1).[1] Until the end of the sixteenth century or thereabouts, this statement raised no difficulties. But as knowledge of the world and causative mechanisms grew, questions began to arise. To what extent does God work through natural processes? Assuming he does, is the room for his operations diminished and his sovereignty challenged? The simplest answer has always been to ignore or deny the findings of science or the integrity of scientists. But this cannot be a real answer. As Augustine pointed out sixteen centuries ago:

> It is a disgraceful and dangerous thing for an infidel to hear a Christian, presumably giving the meaning of Holy Scripture, talking nonsense on these topics [the natural world] . . . To defend their utterly foolish and obviously untrue statements, they will try to call upon Holy Scripture for proof and even recite from memory many passages which they think support their position, although they understand neither what they say not the things about which they make assertions.[2]

---

1. Bible quotations in this chapter are from the RSV.
2. Augustine, *The Literal Meaning of Genesis*, tr. J. H. Taylor (New York: Paulist, 1982), pp. 42–43.

A rather more sophisticated solution has been to import the appearance of divine action by repositioning God as an architect or engineer, as most notoriously expounded by William Paley, particularly in his *Natural Theology or Evidences of the Existence and Attributes of the Deity Collected from the Appearances of Nature* (1802). God is involved, but relegated to a deist operator, not the 'hands-on' Sustainer of the Bible.

However, the *Evidences* are not even particularly Christian. Paley based his notions of right and wrong on purely natural reasoning, 'confident that all men could be brought to agree'.[3] There were efforts as early as 1830 to remove Paley's books from the compulsory reading list at Cambridge University because of 'his emphasis on Bentham's utilitarian principles'.[4] But the recognition of so-called 'deep time' and 'deep space' made Paley's approach intellectually impossible as well as theologically questionable. Even as he wrote, it was becoming apparent that the Earth was hundreds of thousands, if not millions of years old. This stretching of time was an Achilles heel for traditional natural theology. A creator could presumably design an organism perfectly adapted to a particular environment, but this perfection would disappear if the environment was not constant. Adaptation to climate, to the physical structure of the Earth's surface, or to predators or competitors is possible only if organisms themselves can change. At the same time, better knowledge of the distribution of animals and plants was leading to the suggestion that there might have been separate acts of creation in different places.

All this stirred considerable theological ferment in the first half of the nineteenthth century. Traditional natural theology was under threat. It received a near-fatal hammer blow in 1844 with the publication of the *Vestiges of the Natural History of Creation* by Robert Chambers, effectively a tract against Paley's deism.[5] Chambers wrote that when there is a choice between special creation and the operation of general laws instituted by the Creator, 'I would say that the latter

---

3. O. Chadwick, *The Victorian Church*, vol. 1 (London: A. & C. Black, 1970), p. 577.

4. Ibid.

5. J. Secord, *Victorian Sensation* (Chicago: University of Chicago Press, 2000). Ernst Mayr, *The Growth of Biological Thought* (Cambridge, Mass.: Harvard University Press, 1982), p. 515, attributed the final death knell of natural theology to Charles Darwin fifteen years later. Mayr declared that 'explaining the perfection of adaptation by materialistic forces (selection) removed God, so to speak, from his creation. It eliminated the principal arguments of natural theology, and it has been rightly said that natural theology as a viable concept died on November 24, 1859 [the date of publication of *On the Origin of Species*].'

is generally preferable as it implies a far grander view of the divine power than the other.'[6]

Charles Darwin had already formulated his evolutionary ideas when the *Vestiges* appeared. He welcomed the book on the grounds that 'it has done excellent service in calling in this country attention to the subject and in removing prejudices', although 'the geology strikes me as bad and his zoology far worse'.[7] But significantly, the geologist Karl Vogt (1817–95), who translated the *Vestiges* into German, used it as a vehicle to attack religion for opposing scientific advances. Together with his contemporary Ludwig Büchner (1824–99), author of *Kraft und Stoff* (1857; English ed. 1864, as *Force and Matter*) he is regarded as a significant catalyst in splitting science from religion and for the consequent assumption that there is nothing outside the material world. Paley, Vogt and Büchner all contributed – in different ways – to the notion of a dualism between Creator and creation.

Fifteen years after the *Vestiges* came *On the Origin of Species*, presenting evidence of evolutionary change that made sense of a mass of facts in comparative anatomy, biogeography, classification and fossils, and providing an easily understood way of how the world could come into being without supernatural agency. Is Charles Darwin the Antichrist? Or did Oxford theologian Aubrey Moore get it right when he wrote, a generation after the *Origin*, that Darwin did the work of a friend under the guise of a foe?[8] For Moore, Darwinism was

> infinitely more Christian than the theory of 'special creation' for it implies the immanence of God in nature, and the omnipresence of His creative power . . . Deism, even when it struggled to be orthodox, constantly spoke of God as we might speak of an absentee landlord, who cares nothing for his property so long as he gets his rent. Yet nothing more opposed to the language of the Bible and the Fathers can hardly be imagined.[9]

The fact of evolutionary change was rapidly accepted.[10] Owen Chadwick judged that 'the compatibility of evolution and Christian doctrine was

---

6. R. Chambers, *Vestiges of the Natural History of Creation* (London: John Churchill, 1844, p. 116).

7. Letter from Charles Darwin to J. D. Hooker, 7 Jan. 1845.

8. A. Moore, 'The Christian Doctrine of God', in C. Gore (ed.), *Lux Mundi* (London: John Murray, 1889), pp. 57– 109 (99).

9. A. Moore, *Science and the Faith* (London: Kegan Paul, Trench, Trübner, 1892), pp. 184–185.

10. J. R. Moore, *The Post-Darwinian Controversies* (Cambridge: Cambridge University Press, 1979).

increasingly acknowledged "among more educated Christians" between 1860 and 1885; after 1876, acceptance of evolution was both permissible and respectable'.[11] Ironically in the light of future events, Darwin's ideas were readily assimilated by conservative theologians because of their strong doctrine of providence.[12] Many of the authors of the *Fundamentals*, produced between 1910 and 1915 to expound the 'fundamental beliefs' of Protestant theology and that have led to the word 'fundamentalism' entering the language, were sympathetic to evolution. One of the contributors (G. F. Wright) wrote, 'If only the evolutionists would incorporate into their system the sweetness of the Calvinisitic doctrine of Divine Sovereignty, the church would make no objection to their speculations.'[13] Princeton theologian B. B. Warfield, a passionate advocate of the inerrancy of the Bible, declared, 'I do not think that there is any statement in the Bible or any part of the account of creation, either as given in Genesis 1 and 2 or elsewhere alluded too, that needs to be opposed to evolution.'[14]

Difficulties

Darwinian evolution has become scientific orthodoxy, but it raises theological questions – and these are repeatedly used in attempts to discredit the whole of evolutionary science.

The evolutionary process involves death, disease, stress and an enormous amount of apparent waste. It troubled Darwin. He wrote to his American Christian friend Asa Gray:

> I had no intention of writing atheistically [in the *Origin*] . . . There seems so much misery in the world. I cannot persuade myself that a beneficent and omnipotent God would have designedly created the Ichneumonidae [parasitic wasps] with the express

11. Chadwick, *Victorian Church*, pp. 23–28. It is said that in 1880 only two 'working naturalists' in the United States were not evolutionists: R. Numbers, *The Creationists: The Evolution of Scientific Creationism* (New York: Knopf, 1992), p. 7.

12. D. N. Livingstone, *Darwin's Forgotten Defenders: The Encounter Between Evangelical Theology and Evolutionary Thought* (Grand Rapids: Eerdmans, 1987).

13. Cited by C. A. Russell, *Cross-Currents* (Leicester: Inter-Varsity Press, 1985), p. 163.

14. See M. A. Noll and D. N. Livingstone (eds.), *B. B. Warfield: Evolution, Science and Scripture* (Grand Rapids: Baker, 2000), p. 130.

intention of their feeding within the living bodies of caterpillars, or that a cat should play with a mouse.[15]

Theologians and moralists have never stopped wrestling with this dilemma.[16] Leading geneticist and former Jesuit Francisco Ayala urges, 'As floods and droughts were a necessary consequence of the fabric of the physical world, predators and parasites, dysfunctions and diseases were a consequence of the evolution of life.'[17]

A second and specifically scientific problem is that natural selection – the most important agent of evolutionary change – depends on inherited variation, which originates in random changes in the chemistry of genes (i.e. in DNA). However, adaptation results from the selection of advantageous variants in breeding individuals, and this is a deterministic process. Darwinian evolution is not the result of chance.

More important and perhaps underlying much of the theological debate is concern that evolutionary processes can be described without necessarily invoking any metaphysical agent. This has led many authors to try to find room for God somewhere in the evolutionary mechanism, most commonly in somehow directing the nature of the mutational events. But behind this is an even bigger worry: Is God necessary? Has the demise of Paley's Watchmaker meant that God is irrelevant in and therefore excluded from the evolutionary process? This is, of course, the argument of the 'new atheists', but it is also influentially embraced by some distinguished philosophers, largely by defining 'methodological naturalism' (the assumption that the laws of nature determine natural events) in an arbitrarily limited way (i.e. that any supernatural agent does not exist).[18] Michael Ruse has discussed evolutionary naturalism at length and confirms that the problem is largely due to an over-restrictive definition of naturalism.[19]

---

15. Darwin Correspondence Database, available at http://www.darwinproject.ac.uk/entry-2814 (accessed 21 June 2012).

16. C. Southgate, *The Groaning of Creation* (Louisville: Westminster John Knox, 2008); R. J. Berry and T. A. Noble (eds.), *Darwin, Creation and the Fall* (Nottingham: Apollos, 2009).

17. F. J. Ayala, *Darwin's Gift to Science and Religion* (Washington: Joseph Henry, 2007).

18. E.g. Alvin Plantinga, *Where the Conflict Really Lies* (New York: Oxford University Press, 2011). Plantinga defines naturalism as meaning 'there is no God'.

19. Michael Ruse, *Evolutionary Naturalism* (London: Routledge, 1995); *Can a Darwinian Be a Christian?* (Cambridge: Cambridge University Press, 2001), pp. 94–111.

The debate about naturalism has much less substance than its proponents claim.[20]

Darwin's demolition of any need for a Watchmaker in the Paleyan sense effectively eliminated 'purpose' from the vocabulary of biologists.[21] This did not stop attempts to find signs of non-randomness in the evolutionary record that might indicate some sort of external control. A number of influential churchmen (among whom Charles Raven was a leader)[22] tried to reconcile Christianity with post-Darwinian biology by claiming that evolutionary change was driven by some sort of internal *élan vital*. They were encouraged by (mistaken) claims in the early post-Darwinian years that the fossil record and comparisons between apparently related forms seemed to show some sort of directionality and also by the way that the first generation of geneticists savaged the importance and effectiveness of natural selection. They joined in a torrent of speculation in the early 1900s that there was some form of inner progressionist urge along the lines propounded in Henri Bergson's *L'Evolution Créatrice* (1907), Berg's *Nomogenesis* (1922), Willis's *Age and Area* (1917), Smuts's *Holism* (1926), Driesch's entelechy, Osborn's aristogenesis and orthogenesis.

The attempt to 'modernize' theology by forcing it to fit into scientific ideas was short-lived. Peter Bowler has chronicled its fate in detail, and concluded, 'Neo-orthodoxy transformed the churches in the late 1930s and 1940s ... [Unfortunately] neo-orthodoxy didn't want an alternative view of creation or a return to the argument from design – it just wasn't interested in science.'[23] Ironically, Simon Conway Morris's analysis of data unavailable to Raven's Modernists suggests that their fears of randomness and non-directionality were unfounded: 'The idea that evolution is open-ended, without predictabilities and indeterminate in terms of outcomes is negated by the ubiquity of evolutionary

---

20. E. Sober, *Did Darwin Write the Origin Backwards?* (New York: Prometheus, 2011).

21. The idea of purpose in biology lingers on, despite receiving its effective death knell with the *Origin*; see e.g. M. Ruse, *Darwin and Design* (Cambridge, Mass.: Harvard University Press, 2003); D. R. Alexander and R. Numbers (eds.), *Biology and Ideology from Descartes to Dawkins* (Chicago: University of Chicago Press, 2010).

22. Perhaps the most notorious of the Modernists was Bishop Ernest Barnes of Birmingham, who as an undergraduate had been a pupil of R. A. Fisher, a key author of the neo-Darwinian synthesis; see e.g. P. J. Bowler, 'Evolution and the Eucharist: Bishop E. W. Barnes on Science and Religion in the 1920s and 1930s', *BJHS* 31 (1998), pp. 453–467.

23. P. J. Bowler, *Monkey Trials and Gorilla Sermons* (Cambridge, Mass.: Harvard University Press, 2007), p. 187.

convergence . . . The evidence now strongly suggests humans to be an evolutionary inevitability.'[24]

The enthusiasm of a past generation of liberal theologians for 'progress' still recurs, although its connection to evolution is now little more than a footnote to history.[25] However, the association of evolution with a particular version of theology has left a residue of suspicion in many theological circles, especially among evangelicals, and may well contribute to a theological reluctance to engage seriously with evolutionary science.[26]

Varieties of 'creationism'

Religious confusions about evolution continue to be stirred by various manifestations of 'creationism', outside both science and orthodox theology. Modern 'creationism' began, effectively, with the extreme literalism of Seventh-day Adventism, focused by George McCready Price and his cry, 'No Adam, no Fall; no Fall, no Atonement; no Atonement, no Saviour.'[27] This understanding attained worldwide notoriety in 1925 in the notorious 'Monkey Trial' of John Scopes in Dayton, Tennessee.

The Scopes trial was a disaster for anti-evolutionists,[28] and organized 'creationism' lapsed into relative quiescence until 1961 and the appearance of

---

24. Simon Conway Morris, 'How Evolution Discovers the Song of Creation', *SCB* 18 (2006), pp. 5–22 (13).

25. Evolutionary progressionism still lives on in theology through the influence of 'process theology' and in particular the writings of Teilhard de Chardin; see e.g. D. A. S. Fergusson, *The Cosmos and the Creator* (London: SPCK, 1998); R. J. Berry, 'The Lions Seek Their Prey from God', *SCB* 17 (2005), pp. 41–56.

26. This unwillingness is not universal. See e.g. M. S. Northcott and R. J. Berry (eds.), *Theology After Darwin* (Milton Keynes: Paternoster, 2009); Berry and Noble, *Darwin, Creation and the Fall*; S. C. Barton and D. Wilkinson (eds.), *Reading Genesis After Darwin* (Oxford: Oxford University Press, 2009); C. Cunningham, *Darwin's Pious Idea* (Grand Rapids: Eerdmans, 2010); M. Tinker, *Reclaiming Genesis* (Oxford: Monarch, 2010); G. J. O'Brien and T. J. Harris, 'What on *Earth* Is God Doing? Reading Theology and Science Through Biblical Theology', *PSCF* 64 (2012), pp. 147–156.

27. R. L. Numbers, *The Creationists: The Evolution of Scientific Creationism* (New York: Knopf, 1992), p. 373, n. 32.

28. E. Larson, *Summer for the Gods* (Cambridge, Mass.: Harvard University Press, 1998).

The Genesis Flood, written by John Whitcomb, a Bible teacher, and Henry Morris, a hydraulic engineer.[29] The authors rejected the conclusions of geology, palaeontology and archaeology on the grounds that the world had been so ravaged by a worldwide flood that (they claimed) orthodox stratigraphy cannot be applied. They argued that there was no reason to doubt that the world was older than a few thousand years.

A more nuanced approach is 'Intelligent Design' (ID). Although vehemently denied by its advocates, ID is effectively an attempted revival of the Divine Watchmaker thesis. ID first came to general awareness in a book written by a Californian lawyer, Phillip Johnson.[30] This was a reaction against the naturalism of Richard Dawkins and some rather sophisticated criticisms of elements of conventional evolutionary theory by palaeontologist Colin Patterson and biochemist Michael Denton.[31] The main complaint of Johnson and his followers was not evolution as such, but their assumption that belief in evolution leads inevitably and inexorably to atheism. A scientific case for ID has been claimed by a biochemist, Michael Behe, on the grounds that some biological mechanisms and processes are 'irreducibly complex' and incapable of evolution by natural selection.[32] Behe's examples have received short shrift from reviewers;[33] and some argue they are in fact nothing more than the assumption that God can be found in the gaps in knowledge – an assumption that is open to contradiction by further discoveries.[34] An objection to the teaching of ID in biology classes

---

29. J. C. Whitcomb and H. M. Morris, *The Genesis Flood* (Grand Rapids: Baker, 1961).

30. Phillip E. Johnson, *Darwin on Trial* (Downer's Grove: InterVarsity Press, 1991).

31. D. A. Yerxa, 'Phillip Johnson and the Origins of the Intelligent Design Movement, 1977–1991', *PSCF 54* (2002), pp. 47–52. See also P. E. Johnson and D. O. Lamoureux, *Darwinism Defeated?* (Vancouver, B.C.: Regent College Publishing, 1999).

32. Michael Behe, *Darwin's Black Box* (New York: Free Press, 1996); *The Edge of Evolution* (New York: Free Press, 2007).

33. N. Hanks, *God, the Devil and Darwin* (New York: Oxford University Press, 2004); P. Kitcher, *Living with Darwin* (New York: Oxford University Press, 2007); D. R. Alexander, 'After Darwin: Is Intelligent Design Intelligent?', in Northcott and Berry, *Theology After Darwin*, pp. 22–40.

34. The notion of the 'God of the gaps' is said to have originated with Henry Drummond, *The Ascent of Man* (Glasgow: Hodder & Stoughton, 1904), who chastised those Christians who point to things that science could not yet explain – 'gaps which they will fill up with God' (p. 333); he urged them to embrace all nature as the work of 'an immanent God, which is the God of Evolution, [a concept]

was upheld in an American court on the ground that ID 'is not science and cannot uncouple itself from its creationist and thus religious antecedents'.[35]

A God who is not too small

ID has a much wider acceptance in Christian circles than it warrants.[36] The reason for this probably lies in its seductiveness in apparently finding a place for a 'hands-on' God, one who is a Designer as well as a Creator and Redeemer. This is an understandable and laudable ambition, but it portrays a God who is far too small; one who cannot really be understood as Sustainer as well as Creator (Ps. 104:28–30; Col. 1:17; Heb. 1:13). As Donald MacKay wrote:

> The God in whom the Bible invites belief is no 'Cosmic Mechanic'. Rather is he
> the Cosmic Artist, the creative Upholder, without whose constant activity there

---

infinitely grander than the occasional wonder-worker, who is the God of an old theology' (ibid.). Francis Collins, *The Language of God* (New York: Free Press, 2006), pp. 93, 193, 195, warns, 'faith that places God in the gaps of current understanding about the natural world may be headed for crisis if advances in science subsequently fill those gaps. Faced with incomplete understanding of the natural world, believers should be cautious about invoking the divine in areas of current mystery, lest they build an unnecessary theological argument that is doomed to later destruction . . . ID is a "God of the gaps" theory, inserting a supposition of the need for supernatural intervention in places that its proponents claim science cannot explain . . . The warm embrace of ID by believers, particularly by evangelical Christians, is completely understandable, given the way in which Darwin's theory has been portrayed by some outspoken evolutionists as demanding atheism. But this ship is not headed to the promised land; it is headed to the bottom of the ocean.' ID advocates resist the view that it is a version of 'God of the gaps'.

35. E. C. Scott, 'Creation Science Lite: "Intelligent Design" as the New Anti-Evolutionism', in A. J. Petto and L. R. Godfrey (eds.), *Scientists Confront Intelligent Design and Creationism* (New York: Norton, 2007), pp. 59–109. ID advocates have argued that the court decision was government-imposed censorship, stifling legitimate debate; see e.g. William Dembski and Jonathan Witt, *Intelligent Design Uncensored* (Downers Grove: InterVarsity Press, 2010), pp. 148–152.

36. A popular book by Lee Strobel, *The Case for a Creator* (Grand Rapids: Zondervan, 2004), which purports to be a well-balanced investigation into evolution and biblical faith, is fatally marred by the selection of the 'witnesses' interviewed by Strobel.

would be not even chaos, but just nothing . . . To invoke 'natural processes' is not to escape from divine activity, but only to make hypotheses about its regularity . . .[37]

Acceptance of God as an active creator does not require an understanding of how he works. As Michael Polanyi pointed out, all machines (including life itself) operate by principles made possible and limited by physical and chemical laws, but they are not defined by them and may be controlled by another set of laws, which harness the lower-level physico-chemical laws for a purpose outside those laws.[38] This is not dissimilar to the idea that an event may have more than one explanation – an idea at least as old as Aristotle who distinguished material and efficient causes (which answer the question 'How?') from formal and final causes (which answer the question 'Why?'). There is a logical fallacy in assuming that we know everything about an event when all we are doing is answering the question 'How?' Probably the most satisfying model of divine activity in the natural world is complementarity, building on ideas developed by Niels Bohr to bring together the wave and particle concepts of the electron.

Complementarity has suffered because it has sometimes been used improperly to link (or explain away) contrasting explanations, but it is undoubtedly a powerful and satisfying way to bring together scientific and religious explanations. Its value in science–religion debates is due in particular to Donald MacKay. He pointed out that a painting can be described both in terms of the distribution of chemicals on a two-dimensional surface and also as the physical expression of a design in the mind of an artist. In other words, the same material object can have two or more 'causes', which do not contradict or overlap, but are undeniably complementary. MacKay then extended the idea into a dynamic form, using the analogy of a television programme that can be 'explained' in terms of electronics and the physiology of vision, but also as the intention of the programme producer who is telling the story – and who can change (or suspend) the images at will.[39] In the context of evolution, it is entirely logical to believe in God as Creator and Sustainer and simultaneously accept a conventional scientific account. Naturalism is not a valid

---

37. D. M. MacKay, *Science and Christian Faith Today* (London: Falcon, 1960), pp. 10, 15.

38. M. Polanyi, *Knowing and Being* (London: Routledge & Kegan Paul, 1969), p. 232.

39. MacKay, *Science and Christian Faith*, pp. 9–10. See also C. M. Rios, 'Claiming Complementarity: Twentieth-Century Evangelical Applications of an Idea', *PSCF* 63 (2011), pp. 75–84.

argument against divine action – unless, as we have seen, it is arbitrarily defined to exclude God.[40]

A theology of nature

Where does all this leave belief in the biblical God who is active and sovereign in his creation?[41] The sort of natural theology espoused by the authors of *The Genesis Flood* and their followers or by the adherents of ID with their emphasis on irreducible complexity is not really tenable.[42] Notwithstanding, the Bible is clear that God can be seen as controlling events in the natural world (Acts 14:17; Rom. 1:19, 20) and his work inferred therein (Ps. 104; Matt. 6:26–30). This recognition is important. Religious debates over evolution are significant for students or seekers (as Augustine realized), but they have had a much more influential and dangerous aspect in distracting from discussion of a theology of nature, which properly relates the God revealed in Scripture to his creation.[43]

One important aspect of an inadequate theology of nature has been to distract attention from creation care. The very first command in Scripture directed to humankind is 'Be fruitful and multiply, and fill the earth and subdue it; and have dominion over the fish of the sea and over the birds of the air and over every living thing that moves upon the earth' (Gen. 1:28). The command to 'be fruitful and multiply' is given to all animals (Gen. 1:22); but only humans are told to 'subdue' and 'have dominion'. This has too often been interpreted to sanction unlimited exploitation of the natural world, but to argue this is to

---

40. 'It is impossible for a scientific discovery given by God to contradict a Word given by God. If therefore a scientific discovery, as distinct from a scientific speculation, contradicts what we have believed to be implied by the Bible, it is not a question of error in God's Word, but of error in our way of interpreting it' (D. M. MacKay, 'Science and the Bible', in M. Tinker [ed.], *The Open Mind* [Leicester: Inter-Varsity Press, 1988], pp. 150–154 [150]).

41. O'Brien and Harris, 'What on *Earth*?'

42. R. Rice, 'Creationist Ecology?', *Bulletin of the Ecological Society of America* 67.1 (1986), pp. 8–10; Petto and Godfrey, *Scientists Confront*, esp. pp. 244–247.

43. Karl Barth's rejection of natural theology has been widely examined and criticized: e.g. T. F. Torrance, 'The Problem of Natural Theology in the Thought of Karl Barth', *RelS* 6 (1970), pp. 121–135; J. Barr, *Biblical Faith and Natural Theology* (Oxford: Clarendon, 1993). The debate surrounding Barth's views are outside the remit of this chapter.

ignore the context of the verse. The command is given in the context of humankind 'made in God's image'. This is a phrase much debated,[44] though C. F. D. Moule concludes that it is most satisfyingly understood as 'that which sees it as basically responsibility'.[45] It underlines our relationship with the Creator: 'The uniqueness of human beings consists in their being God's counterparts. The relationship to God is not something which is added to human existence; humans are created in such a way that their very existence is intended to be their relationship to God.'[46] It is further emphasized by the ideal of rule for ancient Israel, which was servanthood, not despotism (Ps. 72). We are God's vicegerents on earth. The common description is that we are his stewards. Some see stewardship as implying an absent landlord, a hierarchy or a vassal,[47] but we should not be distracted by terminology.[48] Possible alternative words are agent, manager, factor, trustee or simply creation carer. The key is that we have a responsibility towards our world as a consequence of being in God's image; we are not merely animals with an interest in protecting our kin and resources.

The tradition of stewardship was clearly manifest in the behaviour and farming successes of Benedictine monasteries.[49] In his commentary on Genesis 2:15, Calvin wrote, 'The earth was given to man, with this condition, that he should occupy himself in its cultivation . . . Let everyone regard himself as the

---

44. J. R. Middleton, *The Liberating Image* (Grand Rapids: Brazos, 2005).

45. C. F. D. Moule, *Man and Nature in the New Testament* (London: Athlone, 1964), p. 5.

46. C. Westermann, *Genesis 1–11* (London: SPCK, 1984), p. 158.

47. C. Palmer, 'Stewardship: A Case Study in Environmental Ethics', in I. Ball, M. Goodall, C. Palmer and J. Reader (eds.), *The Earth Beneath* (London: SPCK, 1992), pp. 67–86; P. Santmire, 'Partnership with Nature According to the Scripture: Beyond the Theology of Stewardship', *CSR* 32 (2003), pp. 381–412; R. J. Berry (ed.), *Environmental Stewardship* (London: T. & T. Clark, 2006).

48. James Lovelock relates it to an etymology of 'swineherd' or 'pig-keeper' ('The Greening of Science', in Tom Wakeford and Martin Walters [eds.], *Science for the Earth* [Chichester: Wiley, 1995], p. 61).

49. Lynn White, 'The Historical Roots of Our Ecologic Crisis', *Science* 155 (1967), pp. 1203–1207, ended his inquiry by proposing Francis of Assisi as the patron saint of ecology. René Dubos has suggested that Benedict would be a better choice since 'reverence [for the natural world] is not enough, because man has never been a passive witness of nature' (René Dubos, *A God Within* [London: Angus & Robertson, 1993], p. 173).

steward of God in all things he possesses.'[50] A century after Calvin, Sir Matthew Hale, a distinguished seventeenth-century Chief Justice of England, expanded the idea in a book *The Primitive Origination of Mankind*, published in 1677:

> If we observe the special and peculiar accommodation and adaptation of Man to the regiment and ordering of this lower World, we shall have reason, even without Revelation, to conclude that this was one End of the Creation of Man, namely, to be the Vice-gerent of Almighty God, in the subordinate Regiment especially of the Animal and Vegetable Provinces.[51]

Hale's conclusion was damaged by the rationalization of his contemporary John Locke, that a person's labour belongs to them. Since individuals own their own labour, society is not involved and property rights carry no social obligation. It was an argument that degraded stewardship responsibilities and effectively opened the way to the Industrial Revolution. People changed from responsible stewards and God's image-bearers to being 'human resources'.

Notwithstanding, the stewardship tradition has remained strong. But it needs careful handling. Richard Bauckham argues the problem is that

> stewardship remains, like most interpretations of the Genesis 'dominion', an image that depicts the human relationship to creation in an entirely 'vertical' way. It sets humans above the rest of creation, sharply differentiated from it, in God-given charge of it.[52]

Although the stewardship model 'has had an enormous influence for good in giving Christians a framework within which to approach ecological issues with concern and responsibility, it also has distinct limitations that consist more in what it does not say than what it does'.[53] Bauckham's main criticism is that stewardship carries the implication that humans are set over creation, not within it. A major theme for Bauckham is that our creatureliness is more fundamental than our distinctiveness. 'We need the humility to know ourselves as creatures

50. J. Calvin, *Genesis*, tr. J. King (Edinburgh: Banner of Truth Trust, 1847), p. 125.

51. Matthew Hale, *The Primitive Origination of Mankind, Considered and Imagined According to the Light of Nature* (London: William Godbid, 1677), p. 370.

52. Richard Bauckham, *Living with Other Creatures* (Waco: Baylor University Press, 2011), p. 62.

53. Richard Bauckham, *Bible and Ecology* (London: Darton, Longman & Todd, 2010), p. 2 (publication of Bauckham's Sarum Lectures of 2006, titled 'Beyond Stewardship: The Bible and the Community of Creation').

within creation, not Gods over creation, the humility of knowing that only God is God,[54] a point made unequivocally in Job 38 – 41.

> so often, in the Christian tradition, we have thought of the non-human creation merely as a stage on which the drama of the history of God is being played out – and a temporary stage at that, due to be dismantled and removed when the story reaches its final climax.[55]

Despite the apparently clear inference of stewardship in Scripture, there is a persistent assumption that God has given us the Earth to do with it whatever we want; the concept of 'creation carer' remains stubbornly peripheral in mainstream Christian thinking. A major encouragement to this misinterpretation has been a much-reproduced article by American historian Lynn White, that

> Christianity is the most anthropocentric religion that the world has ever seen . . . Christianity, in absolute contrast to ancient paganism and Asia's religions (except, perhaps, Zoroastrianism), not only established a dualism of man and nature, but also insisted that it is God's will that man exploit nature for his proper ends. . . . Despite Darwin, we are *not*, in our hearts, part of the natural process. We are superior to it, contemptuous of it, willing to use it for our slightest whim.[56]

White's argument has been widely criticized by both historians and theologians, but there is uncomfortable truth in his diagnosis. There is also a danger that in reacting against it and identifying more closely with the non-human environment, we risk aligning ourselves with somewhat marginal theologies (or heresies), such as feminism, Gaia, Teilhardism, or even pantheism or animism. This may well be a factor in the fact that conservative evangelicals – particularly in the United States – have tended to shy away from active environmentalism.[57] The tragedy of this equivocation is that it has led Christians away from the divine mandate of creation care.

---

54. Ibid.

55. Bauckham, *Living with Other Creatures*, p. 46, n. 46.

56. White, 'Historical Roots', p. 1206 (his italics). White's analysis impressed Francis Schaeffer, who reproduced the *Science* article in his pioneering *Pollution and the Death of Man* (London: Hodder & Stoughton, 1970).

57. A significant exception to this generalization in the US was the 'Evangelical Declaration on the Care of Creation', for which see R. J. Berry, (ed.), *The Care of Creation* (Leicester: Inter-Varsity Press, 2000).

God's world

How we relate to the natural world depends on whether we regard it as provided for our use or whether we value it and act as true stewards of God. Since the 1970s[58] there has been an ever-increasing awareness of environmental problems – climate change, pollution, biodiversity loss, population increases, and so on. More and more people are concerned about these effects – and their implications for justice, because, tragically, the highest number of people impacted by them are the poor, unable to mitigate the impacts of environmental assaults.[59]

---

58. Often dated to the recognition of a finite 'Spaceship Earth', first seen in images taken by the Apollo 17 astronauts in 1972.

59. The first major secular initiative to describe and act on the situation was the United Nations Conference on the Human Environment in Stockholm in 1972. It had the unfortunate effect of separating efforts towards development (and the alleviation of poverty) from environmental concern. This provoked a World Conservation Strategy (1980) emphasizing the interdependence of development and environment and identifying the key need for sustainability in resource use. This spawned the Brundtland Report (*Our Common Future*) in 1987 and thence a revised Conservation Strategy (*Caring for the Earth*) in 1991. *Caring for the Earth* introduced ethics as an essential element of conservation and development practice and was a source document for the UN Conference on Environment and Development in Rio de Janeiro in 1992 (the 'Earth Summit'). This has been followed by the World Summit on Sustainable Development ('Rio+10') in 2002 and the UN Conference on Sustainable Development ('Rio+20') in 2012. The momentum from these led to a set of Millennium Development Goals (2002) which have a large environmental component; a Millennium Ecosystem Assessment (2001–5) which concluded that 'human actions are depleting Earth's natural capital, putting such strain on the environment that the ability of the planet's ecosystems to sustain future generations can no longer be taken for granted' (*Ecosystems and Human Well-Being: Synthesis Report* [Washington, D.C.: Island, 2005], p. 1); and an Earth Charter – 'a declaration of fundamental ethical principles for building a just, sustainable and peaceful global society in the 21st century', available at http://www.earthcharterinaction.org (accessed 27 Aug. 2013). The Ecosystem Assessment and the targets in the Millennium Development Goals are part of an increasing global perception that we are living off natural capital. They represent important – probably vital – elements for providing a sustainable future for humankind. But they have been driven entirely without acknowledgment of a creator or any underpinning theology.

Religious involvement in environmental matters has been considerable, but certainly not as an instigator or important driver of opinion. Only after the first UN Conference on the environment and the publication of the World Conservation Strategy did the first religious milestone appear: Jürgen Moltmann's convincing the 1983 Assembly of the World Council of Churches (WCC) that the traditional Christian call for 'peace with justice' was futile unless it took place within a *whole* creation, a creation with 'integrity'. Moltmann's advocacy led to the replacement of the concept of a 'Just, Participatory and Sustainable Society', which had dominated WCC policy in the 1970s, with a more inclusive 'Justice, Peace and the Integrity of Creation' (JPIC) Programme. It was welcomed by developing countries, which had (rightly or wrongly) associated 'sustainability' with the maintenance of colonial injustice. For them, JPIC implied the rejection of a global hegemony in favour of regional associations. It was also important that environmental concern should be seen as integral to 'justice' and 'peace'; the concept of the 'integrity of creation' was intended to convey the dependence of creation on its Creator and the worth and dignity of creation in its own right.

The JPIC process culminated in a global consultation in Seoul in 1990, which revealed more discord than harmony; sectional and marginal interests dominated the reports and blunted the conclusions. In response, the World Evangelical Fellowship Unit on Ethics and Society set up an Evangelical Environmental Network and drafted an 'Evangelical Declaration on the Care of Creation'.[60]

Other Christian initiatives include successive Lambeth Conference Declarations calling for action on the environment. The Church of England General Synod has commissioned and received fairly substantial reports on three occasions.[61] The Second European Ecumenical Assembly (in Graz, 1997) led to the setting up of EcoCongregation, a programme of involvement and commitment for local churches, and a European Christian Environmental Network that sponsors a 'time for creation' every autumn. Two Crosslinks missionaries in Portugal established 'A Rocha', dedicated to creation care and now working in 18 countries.[62] In 2010 the Cape Town Commitment of the Lausanne Movement

---

60. 'Evangelicals and the Environment', *ERT* 17.2 (1993), pp. 117–286; R. C. J. Carling and M. A. Carling (eds.), *A Christian Approach to the Environment* (Cheltenham: John Ray Initiative, 1955); Berry, *Care of Creation*.

61. *Man in His Living Environment* (London: Church House, 1970); *Our Responsibility for the Living Environment* (London: Church House, 1986); *Sharing God's World* (London: Church House, 2005).

62. P. Harris, *Kingfisher's Fire* (Oxford: Monarch, 2008).

declared, 'we cannot claim to love God while abusing what belongs to Christ by right of creation, redemption and inheritance; we care for the earth and responsibly use its abundant resources, not according to the rationale of the secular world, but for the Lord's sake'.[63]

Notwithstanding, most Christian-motivated concern for the environment remains pragmatic, responding to anthropocentric damage rather than being driven by theological conviction. It is very uncommon to find groups including creation care in their evangelism, despite the widely accepted Fifth Mark of Mission 'to strive to safeguard the integrity of creation and sustain and renew the life of the earth'.[64] There have been prophets, but few of them. A recent prophet is Chris Wright, who has detailed the crucial place of creation care in mission:[65]

1. A good creation can only be the work of a good God (Job 12:7–9; Pss 19; 29; 50:6; 65; 104; 148; Acts 14:17; 17:27; Rom. 1:20).
2. This means the creation has intrinsic value. 'We need to be careful to locate an ecological dimension in mission not primarily in the need-supplying value of the earth to us, but in the glory-giving value of the earth to God.'[66]
3. The OT constantly treats creation in relation to God. There is a sacredness about the non-human created order we are called on to honour – but not to worship, which would be to exchange the Creator for the created.[67]
4. The goal of creation is God's glory, an aim not confined to humankind, but one we share with the rest of creation, and which is linked to the fullness of the earth ('the magnificently diverse abundance of the whole biosphere'[68]) (Pss 24:1; 50:12; 104:24; Mic. 1:2).

Wright's analysis supports and amplifies the often quoted *reductio ad absurdum* comment of Charles Cranfield on Romans 8:20:

---

63. Lausanne Library didaskofile, p. 19.

64. *Mission in a Broken World: Report of ACC-8 Wales 1990* (Church House Publishing for the Anglican Consultative Council, 1990), p. 101.

65. C. J. H. Wright, *The Mission of God* (Nottingham: Inter-Varsity Press, 2006), pp. 397–420.

66. Ibid., p. 399, n. 56.

67. W. Brueggemann, *The Land* (Philadelphia: Fortress, 1977).

68. Wright, *Mission of God*, p. 405, n. 56.

What sense can there be in saying that the 'sub-human creation – the Jungfrau, for example, or the Matterhorn, or the planet Venus – suffers frustration by being prevented from properly fulfilling the purpose of its existence?' The answer must surely be that the whole magnificent theatre of the universe, together with all its splendid properties and all its life, created for God's glory, is cheated of its true fulfilment so long as man, the chief actor in the great drama of God's praise fails to contribute his rational part. The Jungfrau and the Matterhorn and the planet Venus and all living things too, man alone excepted, do indeed glorify God in their own ways; but since their praise is destined to be not a collection of individual offerings but part of a magnificent whole, the united praise of the whole creation, they are prevented from being fully that which they were created to be, so long as man's part is missing, just as all the other players in a concerto would be frustrated of their purpose if the soloist were to fail to play his part.[69]

The Romans 8 passage underlines the fact that our calling is not simply to ourselves and our current neighbours, or even to our children and grandchildren, but to the whole future of creation. In Francis Bridger's words:

We are called to be stewards of the earth by virtue not simply of our orientation to the Edenic command of the Creator but also because of our orientation to the future. In acting to preserve and enhance the created order, we are pointing to the coming rule of God in Christ . . . The knowledge that it is God's world, that our efforts are not directed toward the creation of an ideal utopia but that we are, under God, building bridgeheads of the kingdom serves to humble us and to bring us to the place of ethical obedience.[70]

In similar vein, Tom Wright concludes, 'Jesus is coming – plant a tree.'[71] David Fergusson puts it, 'Creation can only be understood from the perspective of redemption. There is too much wastage, pain and untimely death to make this view possible apart from a particular conviction about the meaning of Christ's

69. C. E. B. Cranfield, 'Some Observations on Romans 8:19–21', in Robert J. Banks (ed.), *Reconciliation and Hope: New Testament Essays on Atonement and Eschatology Presented to L. L. Morris on his 60th Birthday* (Grand Rapids: Eerdmans; Exeter: Paternoster, 1974), pp. 224–230 (227).

70. Francis Bridger, 'Ecology and Eschatology: A Neglected Dimension', *TynB* 41.2 (1990), pp. 290–301 (301).

71. N. T. Wright, 'Jesus Is Coming – Plant a Tree', in *The Green Bible* (London: Collins, 2008), pp. I172–I185.

death and resurrection';[72] for Oliver O'Donovan, 'The redemption of the world, and of mankind, does not serve only to put us back in the Garden of Eden where we began. It leads us on to that further destiny to which, even in the Garden of Eden, we were already directed';[73] Richard Bauckham insists, 'Salvation is not the replacement but the renewal of creation. God's purpose in history and in the eschatological future does not abstract humans from nature, but heals the human relationship with nature.'[74] Henri Blocher argues, 'If man obeys God, he would be the means of blessing the earth, but in his insatiable greed . . . and in his short-sighted selfishness, he pollutes the earth and destroys it. He turns a garden into a desert (cf. Rev 11: 18). That is the main thrust of the curse of Genesis 3.'[75]

The implication from Scripture appears unequivocal: creation care is not an optional extra for enthusiasts, but is inseparable from our calling as Christians. A theology of nature is integral to the whole of God's working – in creating, sustaining and redeeming.[76] As Christians we have a certain hope and sure future. Our reasons for failing in creation care are doubtless as wide as any other causes of failure – greed, self-interest, short-sightedness, and so on. But for too many of us, and underlying other reasons for failure, is a defective understanding of God's world and our responsibility to God for it. Failure to care for creation is a failure of obedience; it is sin.

Recalcitrant dualism

The link between creation care and evolution disputing now becomes clear. How we treat creation depends on how we view and value it. As 'environment' it nurtures, supports and surrounds us. We damage it at our peril.[77] Government

72. David Fergusson, *The Cosmos and the Creator* (London: SPCK, 1998), p. 87.

73. Oliver O'Donovan, *Resurrection and Moral Order* (Leicester: Inter-Varsity Press, 1986), p. 55.

74. Bauckham, *Bible and Ecology*, p. 150.

75. Henry Blocher, *In the Beginning* (Leicester: Inter-Varsity Press, 1984), p. 184.

76. N. J. Toly and D. I. Block (eds.), *Keeping God's Earth* (Downers Grove: InterVarsity Press; Leicester: Apollos, 2010).

77. R. Carson, *Silent Spring* (Boston: Houghton Mifflin, 1962); D. H. Meadows, D. L. Meadows and J. Randers, *The Limits to Growth* (New York: Universe, 1972); M. Lynas, *Six Degrees* (London: Fourth Estate, 2007); R. S. White (ed.), *Creation in Crisis* (London: SPCK, 2009); B. McGuire, *Waking the Giant* (Oxford: Oxford University Press, 2012).

Chief Scientist John Beddington has described the 'perfect storm' coming to humankind, faced (as we are) with the need to produce 50 per cent more food and energy and have available 30 per cent more fresh water by 2030, while coping with climate change and population growth.[78] If the earth is little more than the stage for God's salvific purposes, it becomes a mere object; it is degraded from that which is the delight of the Creator as set forth in Scripture and although it can be legitimately treated as useful and necessary, it is still a 'thing'. This implies a dualism between the material and the spiritual that seems very close to the theorizing of Plato and Descartes, reinforcing the outlook implanted by the eighteenth-century 'Enlightenment'. Aubrey Moore saw the possibility of Darwinian thought as a way of uniting God's transcendence and immanence,[79] but the subsequent history of evolutionary disputes throughout the twentieth century have destroyed this for many Christians. The situation has been made even worse by the distracting stridency of the 'new atheists'.

The insidiousness of persistent dualism is challenged by the drumbeat message in Scripture of God's covenant. In the Noahic covenant (Gen. 9:8–17) God explicitly includes 'all creatures' alongside Noah and his family. Indeed, it can be argued that there is a covenant with the whole created order implicit within the act of creation itself – and that would suggest a relationship between God and creation before the appearance of human beings.[80] (Jer. 33:25 – 'These are the words of the Lord: If there were no covenant for days and night, and if I had not established a fixed order in heaven and earth, then I could spurn the descendants of Jacob and of my servant David.') God renewed his covenant repeatedly throughout history – with Abraham, Jacob, Moses, David, culminating with Jesus the Christ. The God of Creation and the God of Redemption are one and the same (Rev. 4:6–11).

Robert Murray challenges, 'Have theologians betrayed the Bible's message?' He is clear that

---

78. John Beddington, 'Food, Energy, Water and the Climate: A Perfect Storm of Global Events?', available at http://www.bis.gov.uk/assets/goscience/docs/p/ perfect-storm-paper (accessed 15 June 2012).

79. See n. 8 above.

80. See e.g. Robin Routledge, *Old Testament Theology: A Thematic Approach* (Nottingham: Apollos, 2008; Downers Grove: IVP Academic, 2009), pp. 164, 321; 'Mission and Covenant in the Old Testament', in Rollin G. Grams, I. Howard Marshall, Peter F. Penner and Robin Routledge (eds.), *Bible and Mission: A Conversation Between Biblical Studies and Missiology* (Schwarzenfeld: Neufeld, 2008), pp. 8–41 (16–17, 32–33, nn. 37–39).

the Bible teaches us that neither sin nor salvation are affairs merely between us as individuals and God; sin entails alienation from our nature which relates us to God's other creatures, while salvation entails our re-integration in a vaster order of harmony which embraces the whole cosmos, as we may interpret Paul's tersely-expressed vision in Romans 8.[81]

Tom Wright describes Romans 8:18–28, as

one of the most central statements in the New Testament about what God intends to do with the whole cosmos. [T]he matter is set out quite clearly. [But] the passage is regularly marginalized in mainstream Protestant interpretations . . . Paul's whole argument is that the renewal of God's covenant results in the renewal of God's creation.[82]

David Atkinson argues that a 'fully biblical theology of covenant and creation commits us to respond urgently to the questions posed by climate change, and that such a response is centrally part of the Gospel of a God who "so loved the world"'.[83]

A practical way forward in all this was proposed five centuries ago by Francis Bacon and apparently endorsed by Charles Darwin when he reprinted Bacon's words on the title page of the *Origin*: 'Let no man out of a weak conceit of sobriety or an ill-applied moderation, think or maintain that a man can search too far or be too well studied in the book of God's words or in the book of God's works; divinity or philosophy; but rather let men endeavour an endless progress or proficiency in both.' Psalm 19 clearly states the characteristics of these two books of God.

If we acknowledge God as author of both the Bible and the book of works, it seems obvious that we shall understand his purposes fully only when we read both books. Anything that hinders us in this discipline must surely be falling short of the divine command. The study of evolution may be seen as the study of creation, and hence part of the study of God's Book of Works. It should be probed for what it is, namely a scientific enterprise, not an exegetical problem. It is unnecessary to contrive to keep God involved in the evolutionary machinery.

---

81. Robert Murray, *The Cosmic Covenant* (London: Sheed & Ward, 1992), p. 165.

82. N. T. Wright, *New Heavens, New Earth: The Biblical Picture of the Christian Hope*, Grove Biblical Series B11 (Cambridge: Grove, 1999), p. 11.

83. David Atkinson, *Renewing the Face of the Earth* (Norwich: Canterbury Press, 2008), p. 2.

He is integral to it. God's Book of Words makes it abundantly clear that we are part of his creation and that we are called to care for it – humans (neighbours) and 'nature' alike.

> Great are the works of the LORD;
>> studied [or pondered] by all who have pleasure in them.
> (Ps. 111:2)[84]

© R. J. Berry, 2014

---

84. R. J. Berry, 'The Research Scientist's Psalm', *SCB* 20 (2008), pp. 147–161.

AFTERWORD: ETHICAL DECISION-MAKING

I. Howard Marshall

This service is the practical and religious culmination of our conference, though not its conclusion. It raises down-to-earth questions of Christian ethics that it is essential for all of us to take back to our institutions and congregations and to our own personal reflection times. In this setting my present task is to help us all to set an agenda and to encourage us all to pick it up and take it further.[1]

At conferences and other occasions like this one I find that often I get fired by the topic, fill a page of my notebook with ideas and suggestions for further progress and action, and then I depart, filled with enthusiasm to take them further. Forty-eight hours later, or less, the demands of ordinary daily routine and life have dimmed the enthusiasm. Time has been filled by other concerns, some of them very immediate and pressing; I'm back on my own and I lack the stimulation of the friends whom I have met here. In consequence little or nothing gets done, unless perhaps I am a conference speaker, and receive an

---

[1]. This is a lightly revised version of the sermon given at the closing service of the 2012 Tyndale Fellowship Triennial Conference, where most of the chapters that appear in this volume were first presented, and I have retained the oral style. I am no expert on issues of creation and environment, and consequently the illustrations and applications are very general in character.

email with the suggestion 'Perhaps we can get a book out of all this, so would you care to revise your paper?' What do we need to do after this conference, and where do we get the energy and motivation to ensure that we do not lose interest before we reach the M1 on the way home?

A side entrance

Let me begin at a side door to the issue. The name of Rowan Williams should be known to most of us in the UK and especially in the Anglican communion. Certainly I shall never forget the morning service in a church near Leicester at which a member of the congregation led the intercessions shortly after the announcement of his nomination and asked for God's blessing on 'our new Archbishop of Canterbury, Rowan Atkinson'. Rowan *Williams* (not Mr Bean) raised an important question in one of his more accessible essays that formed an introduction to *The Cambridge Companion to Christian Ethics*. In a discussion entitled 'Making Moral Decisions' he raises the question of how you live harmoniously in a congregation or denomination or other group in which the members hold different views on ethical practices.[2]

Williams makes the point that our individual choices regarding moral decisions show or need to show

> the character of the God who called me and the character of the community I belong to; my God is a God whose concern for all is equal; my community is one in which all individual actions are measured by how securely they build up a pattern of selfless engagement with the interest of the other – which in itself . . . is a manifestation of the completely costly directedness to the other that is shown in God's act in Christ.[3]

Our actions are to give to the community 'in such a way that what results is glory – the radiating, the visibility of God's beauty in the world'.[4] This statement is one that could equally well have been made by John Piper or James Hamilton with their relentless emphasis on our duty to glorify God in all that we say and

---

2. Robin Gill (ed.), The *Cambridge Companion to Christian Ethics* (Cambridge: Cambridge University Press, 2001), pp. 3–15.

3. Ibid., p. 7.

4. Ibid.

do, not only to please him but also to show his beauty in such a way that other people will be moved to glorify him.[5]

But before we think that we have arrived in a paradise where this admirable aim is achieved, Williams then raises the question of what we are to do within this community of faith when other people's moral decisions differ from ours. These people are those

> who are happy to make themselves accountable, in prayer and discussion and spiritual direction. Yet their decisions may be regarded by others as impossible to receive as a gift that speaks of Christ – by others who seek no less rigorously to become aware of who they are in Christ and who are equally concerned to be accountable for their Christian options.[6]

Williams himself may have had partly in mind the different cultural attitudes to homosexual practices between liberal Western churches and traditionalist African Christian churches. In the chapter, however, his explicit example is the tension between sincere Christians who tolerate and even defend the use of weapons of mass destruction and those like himself, to whom acceptance of such weapons is anathema. How can people with such different views meet in harmony at the Lord's table? How far do we go in fellowship within the same church or Christian group that tries to find room for attitudes we find intolerable? The question is there for both liberals and evangelicals, granted that both camps are concerned for their moral integrity and for the honour and glory of God. And part of the cost, says Williams, is that the existence of both groups in the one Christian communion leads both sides to admit that they may to some extent be wrong in the position that they hold and that they think is the tradition of their church. For Williams, particularly in his archiepiscopal role, holding the church together despite such tensions is the priority, even if there will be limit-situations when it becomes impossible, as with the exodus of the confessing church in Nazi Germany.

---

5. John Piper's quote available at http://www.goodreads.com/author/quotes/25423. John_Piper (accessed 5 Dec. 2012); James M. Hamilton, Jr., *God's Glory in Salvation Through Judgment: A Biblical Theology* (Wheaton: Crossway, 2010).

6. Gill, *Cambridge Companion*, p. 8.

The problems to be tackled: complexity and technicality

Problems of this kind with multiple answers certainly arise in the area of creation and the environment that is the concern of this conference. How do we use without abusing the world, nay the universe, that we understand theologically as God's creation? Let us remember that people have come near to blows over the siting of the Manchester airport runway or the destruction of a nature reserve just outside Aberdeen. The discussion groups that are concerned with our conference topics are very much the sorts of mixed constituencies that Rowan Williams had in mind. This is not surprising and is probably inevitable given the nature of the questions that occupy us. Some of the difficulties that arise and lead to what may be almost diametrically opposed practices are such as the following.

1. Factually complex issues. Many, if not most, of the differences in outlook and performance that arise are not so much moral and spiritual matters but are factual and practical. They arise from the extraordinary complicatedness of so many issues, whether economic (Does Fair Trade actually work?), or scientific (What are the causes and consequences of global warming?) or medical and dietary (Is genetically modified produce safe?). These are so tricky that many solutions can only be tentative and there are deep divisions over the diagnoses and the healing policies. All this can cause varying degrees of paralysis instead of action.

2. Labouring in vain. Many feel that all the labour of Christians and other people of goodwill is but a pinprick in the side of an enormous set of problems that will never go away in whole or in greater part. The task is too great as a whole for the people of God as a whole. Or is it? Even if we in the rich nations inverted tithing, living on one tenth of our income and giving away the remaining 90 per cent, we should still not be doing enough. And it may be better to hang on to our capital as an ongoing base for dealing with future problems than do a once-for-all C. T. Studd style download of the lot.

3. Establishing priorities. Given that resources are limited, there is the problem of establishing priorities. For example, do you give more to those who may need it more but who show little or no initiative of their own? The difficulty of answering such questions decisively may hinder us from actually doing anything.

4. Give up all that you have. We as individuals are confronted by so many pressing and overwhelming demands upon our generosity that we begin to wonder to what extent it is right for us to spend any money upon ourselves except for bare necessities or even less.

5. Sinful blindness and unwillingness. We dare not ignore the factor of human sinfulness that leads to biased practices such as the unjust and selfish allocation and consumption of resources by both the rich and the poor. And I have to remember that *I am one of these sinners*, liable to committing those secret sins of whose sinful character I am not aware.

These five types of issues form a set of situations where people will behave differently from one another for various reasons. Not all will solve the factual issues in the same kinds of ways, not all will be as generous and selfless as others, because of the different degrees of sinfulness that they suffer from, not all will feel the same pressures to thrift because of the different commitments they have to the care of their children or their elderly parents. And one might add that the different degrees of ordinary human competence, energy and zeal that we possess lead us to work and produce at different rates and with different levels of efficiency. How, then, shall we live, and how do we cope with these situations?

Get the biblical basis right

For a starting point let me ask whether we have agreement on the fundamental Christian ethical principles that form the context for our discussion. (Here is the nearest that I shall get to direct exposition of Scripture in this address.) The basic summary of Christian behavioural principles in the NT is surely to be found in 1 Corinthians 10:31 – 11:1, where Paul sums up his teaching:

> Whether you eat or drink or whatever you do, do it all for the glory of God. Do not cause anyone to stumble, whether Jews, Greeks or the church of God – even as I try to please everyone in every way. For I am not seeking my own good but the good of many, so that they may be saved. Follow my example, as I follow the example of Christ. (NIV)

This text can be dissected to produce some four criteria for judging behaviour, whether prospectively or retrospectively.

First, different believers had different attitudes to the eating of food that had been offered in sacrifice to other gods; for some the consumption was tantamount to partaking in idolatry and worshipping a false god; for others the same food was religiously neutral, no matter what other people made of it, and they could partake of it without any problems for themselves. For all believers the crucial question was whether they *glorified God*, the true God, by participation.

Secondly, did they live in such a way as *not to lead or tempt other people into sin?* 'Stumble' does not mean that the other people get annoyed with me and condemn me as a sinner, but that they are led by my example to do things that are sinful for them, although they are not necessarily sinful for me. (It is not sinful for me to eat food sacrificed to an idol because I do not believe idols really exist, but if I am pressurized to eat food sacrificed to an idol that I believe has some kind of existence, then I am disobeying a clear divine commandment.[7])

Thirdly, were their actions *determined primarily* by what was 'enjoyable' for themselves or even their own good and their own spiritual growth? Or were such motives secondary to the more important criterion of whether their actions would be rather for the good of others? Did they behave in ways that would help other people to be saved?

Fourthly, did they aim to live in such ways that people who imitated them would be *imitating* somebody who behaved as *Christ* would have done?

It would be a profitable exercise to go through these four Pauline principles and in each case ask some four practical questions.

1. Do I make these aims my aims in determining my behaviour? If I say 'Amen' to them at approximately 11.50 am on Sunday, will I be found actually doing them, or at least trying hard to do so, at 12.15 pm and subsequently?

2. Do I find that these aims are relevant to behaviour, such that they make a difference to how I actually behave? Are they too general, or too ambiguous to constitute a challenge to me?

3. Do they lead me to practical ethics that necessarily differ (though not necessarily all the time) from the aims and principles of non-believers? And would it matter if they do not make any difference? Should Christians expect to come up with different attitudes and different solutions to the problems of the environment from those offered by non-Christians? Should there simply be greater motivation and commitment to avoid sinful practices and to encourage better practices from Christians?

4. To come back to our starting question: Do different Christians and Christian groups differ in their understanding of these principles and their practical implications, and if so does it matter? Are our problems and differences due to holding different sets of basic ethical principles or to different deductions and applications of agreed principles?

I focus briefly on one practical problem: every week, if not sometimes almost daily, I get glossy magazines and appeal letters from various charities, both Christian and non-religious, and the majority of them are thrown straight into the WPB ('waste paper bin'), often without even opening the envelopes. The reasons why I give to some of these appeals and ignore others are frankly pretty arbitrary. And there is this guilty feeling that kept coming back to me while

---

7. I say 'clear' but recognize that there will be borderline cases that are complex and have to be teased out.

preparing these remarks, that the needs of others, both for the gospel and for humanitarian aid, are so great that I should be prepared to forgo pretty well all my income beyond what is required for mere subsistence and resources to serve the Lord, and not go on a cruise or buy items that do nothing more than give me personally some pleasure.

Here we may be reminded that in the Gospels we have examples of people being called by Jesus to be the kinds of disciples who leave everything to be with him and to share in his mission. Are we all called to do that? Certainly, the story of the early Christian mission assumed that some were called to go and give up everything, yet at the same time there were the many (doubtless the majority) who did not do so, although they recognized the obligation that lay upon them to provide hospitality, resources and support for those who went out trusting in the Lord to provide for their needs. And there are all the changes in situation between the social and economic structures that shaped the lives of early Christians and those that shape our lives today. Can we apply or reapply the teaching of the NT to ourselves today?

So two problems arise:

1. How do I choose between the competing demands on my purse and on my time? I could give all I have and bankrupt myself without much difficulty, but that is surely foolish. What is spiritually 'reasonable' (Rom. 12:1, AV)?
2. How much of my time and how many of my goods is it right to use and spend on myself and my commitments, such as my wife and children, or my own congregation as opposed to the mission to Bawku or Ouagadougou?

These are practical questions and I have no obvious scriptural answers. The old answer 'You must follow your conscience' is very unhelpful because it is so vague and leaves us at the mercy of subjective considerations. Suppose Scripture had said pay 20 per cent of income rather than 10 per cent or it had said 1 per cent for world development, would we have found reasons for saying, 'That doesn't sound right'? Let me try to suggest some points that may be relevant.[8]

---

8. I have made a few tentative steps in this direction in 'Gospel and Ethics in Paul's Letter to the Roman Church: Developing a Social Ethic for Today', in Lung-kwong Lo, Andrew P. C. Kwong, Peter S. C. Chang and Oi-sze Cheung (eds.), *Bible and Life* (Festschrift for Ronald Fung) (Hong Kong: Divinity School of Chung Chi College, 2007), pp. 10–31.

Two distinctions

1. Mandatory and recommended. I think it may be helpful to pick up an old distinction that distinguished counsels of perfection for those who wished to go further (and, say, attain to a respected and powerful seat), and generally applicable instructions for all believers. One type of Christian ethics used to distinguish between what might be called ordinary commandments and counsels of perfection, with the implication that not everybody was called to, or was capable of, perfection, but some believers might feel called to the latter. This kind of two-stream or two levels of disciples is rightly rejected as not scriptural. However, it is not to be dismissed altogether, and it is a faulty development of something that is actually there in Scripture. We can recognize a distinction between what may be regarded as scriptural categorical imperatives that are binding on all believers and what may be regarded as recommendations, in that they summon us to good actions that are not necessarily required actions (or prohibitions) for all believers. This distinction was well known in Judaism, which distinguished works of the law and the works of love. The former were prescribed and binding on the people. The latter went beyond the call of duty and presumably qualified the doer for a greater reward. If we bring in the general NT teaching about the place of rewards, we shall recognize the danger of doing good out of a desire for a better reward rather than out of pity and grace to the needy or the desire to bring glory to God. The impulse to do good may arise from a desire to be virtuous and worthy of reward that can be selfish unless this desire is transmuted into a desire to live a life that will cause other people to thank God for you.

The practical question then becomes finding out what particular package of works of love God requires from us, recognizing that this may be widely different from person to person and from one situation to another.

2. Clear and dubious. Alongside this classification there is another helpful distinction between commandments that are basically unambiguous in what they demand of us and those whose content and grounding are not so clear. Thus in OT times there was a temple tax with a fixed rate set, namely a tithe; admittedly there could be different formulations of what items had to be tithed. So too in the NT adultery is clearly wrong. Other commandments may be less clear and give room for difference in opinions and practice. It is notoriously debatable whether and in what circumstances divorce and remarriage are permissible. Despite what some advocates of baptism by immersion may say, a waterproof case for baptism being valid only if there is sufficient depth of liquid to totally immerse the candidate is not to be found in Scripture.[9] In this latter kind of case obviously believers on different sides of the debate will claim freedom to live by what they believe Scripture teaches. The same is true of attempts to live environmentally friendly lives.

There may be some correlation between these two types of distinction: that is to say, it is hard to make universal binding commands out of teaching that is not wholly clear and unambiguous, although some people try to do so. The result is that some situations may result in different groups of believers behaving in different ways. A case in point may be the attitude to meat sacrificed to idols in 1 Corinthians and Romans, where some believers felt it was permissible to eat such meat, testifying thereby to God's goodness in providing it and overcoming the superstitions that former non-Christians carried over from their past, while others felt that they should not do so, lest by their attitude of apparent disobedience to God's laws they enticed others into what they felt to be disobedience that led to having a bad conscience over it. Paul's attitude seems to be that the two parties should be prepared to tolerate one another.

But there can be situations where this may be difficult if not impossible. Thus I agree that Scripture condemns in the strongest terms what were then regarded as homosexual activities, and it did so on the basis of its deep understanding of heterosexual relationships being God's will. But some people today would argue that there is at least some uncertainty: whether homosexual orientations are innate or acquired; whether what is forbidden in Scripture is something rather different from the loving relationships of some mature people today; whether it is sensible to encourage or demand chastity from people who do not have the power of the Holy Spirit in their lives.

And indeed here is another distinction between what Christians may wish to see as the ethic of a secular or non-Christian society in which they live and their own ethic as members of the church; we have to be content with some broad general principles in the former because nothing higher is practically possible. Difficulties then arise when some may want the church to live at this lower ethical level. Consider how difficult it was some years ago to get Christians to repeat the '1% for world development' appeal for a second year, even though many of us might feel that Christian believers should be generous to a higher level than that.

---

9. I. Howard Marshall, 'The Meaning of the Verb "Baptize"', in S. E. Porter and A. R. Cross (eds.), *Dimensions of Baptism: Biblical and Theological Studies* (London: Sheffield Academic Press, 2002), pp. 8–24. (Revision of article in *EvQ* 45 [1973], pp. 130–140.)

Instead of a conclusion

So what emerges out of this ramble? Essentially the end result is the challenge to us to go on thinking, discussing and acting in this area of Christian living, to settle what are the priorities, and to get on with doing the best we can here and now without waiting for complete solutions.

Care of creation and the environment does confront us with issues like the use of nuclear fuels, the deprivation of rural peoples' livelihoods by chopping down forests, the forbidding of couples to have children and the encouraging of abortions that some people might want to classify as examples of murder of members of God's creation, as when some Australian ethicists have been advocating what they called 'post-natal abortion'. There will be the ongoing agony of striving to deal with such things in the wider context of secular government and politics and international relations.

But there is also the question of debates within the Christian church. Suppose that believers who profess to follow biblical teaching end up by upholding ethical positions that are mutually incompatible, contradictory, even intolerable? How do we live with them and they with us? What do we do in a church where some campaign for the citizen's right to own and carry a gun and others insist on no private ownership of such weapons? Where was it that I saw a notice in the entrance to a small country church that said, 'Gentlemen, please leave your weapons at the door'?[10] Well, at least that was a reasonable compromise for a start.

I was once in a situation where I was in a group to discuss sexuality and advise the church on the matter. The group included people with all shades of opinion, and it was laid down as basic that we accepted one another as sincere Christians and brothers and sisters in Christ. As people told their life stories I felt that there was no way that I could regard some of them as believing Christians and not as agents of Satan masquerading as angels of light. Somehow I managed to avoid having to say openly that this was how I felt, but if I had been a more courageous person I would have had to say, 'I cannot proceed on this basis.' But that would have meant leaving the group and abandoning any hope of influencing its deliberations for good. What should I have done?

So we are back to the agony felt by Rowan Williams. I have not answered his dilemma. I do not know whether it can be answered. I suspect that part of the cost of discipleship is not just sorrow over those who lose their allegiance to Christ but also sorrow over those who want to keep the name of disciple but

---

10. Sorry, no prizes.

without fulfilling its demands. Both types of people are found in the Gospels. And part of the commitment of disciples is rigorous self-examination lest I should have the name but not the quality of life expected of a disciple, lest I should preach to others but not to myself, lest I should show the form of godliness but lack the power of the Spirit. May God give us the willingness to examine our own hearts and lives and to extend to our fellow believers the same kind of love as we need to be shown to us.

© I. Howard Marshall, 2014

INDEX OF SCRIPTURE REFRENCES